Nonna's Italian Kitchen

Delicious Home-Style Vegan Cuisine

Bryanna Clark Grogan

Book Publishing Company
Summertown, Tennessee

Cover and interior art: Kim Trainer
Cover design: Jeanne Kahan

Published in the United States by
Book Publishing Company
P.O. Box 99
Summertown, TN 38483
888-260-8458
http://bpc.thefarm.org

02 01 00 99 98 1 2 3 4 5 6

1-57067-055-2

Grogan, Bryanna Clark
     Nonna's Italian kitchen : delicious homestyle vegan cuisine /
Bryanna Clark Grogan.
        p.   cm.
     Includes index.
     ISBN 1-57067-055-2 (alk. paper)
     1. Vegan cookery. 2. Cookery, Italian. I. Title.
TX837.G6766   1998
641.5'636--dc21   98-29142
                                                   CIP

Calculations for the nutritional analyses in this book are based on the average number of servings listed with the recipes and the average amount of an ingredient, if a range is called for. Calculations are rounded up to the nearest gram. If two options for an ingredients are listed, the first one is used. Not included are optional ingredients, serving suggestions, or fat used for frying, unless the amount of fat is specified in the recipe.

Table of Contents

Dedication

To the memories of my grandmother, "Abuelita," Clotilde Roncagliolo de Urbina (with whom I shared a birthday), and my beloved father, Alejandro Jaime Urbina de Roncagliolo. I miss you so much, Daddy, and I wish you could have tasted everything in this book and given me the benefit of both your palate and knowledge of wines.

And to the next generation, my grandchildren, here are your Nonna's recipes.

Grandmother Clotilde Roncagliolo at the time of her marriage in 1911

My father Alejandro Urbina at Cresta Blanca Winery in the 1950s

Tutto il mondo è paese. (All the world is kin.)

Acknowledgements

Many thanks to my wonderful, loving husband and best friend, Brian Grogan, and to my mother, Eve Urbina, who both try everything and put up with me.

Thank you, maker and guardian of my oven under the trees, always my support and supporter.

Thank you Jenica, Holly, Pat, Fireweed, Mirjam, and Paula, for being my friends. Thank you Bronwyn for the belly dancing classes, which balanced my life while writing this book, and to all my fellow Denman belly dancers for inspiration and enthusiasm.

Thanks to my vegetarian friends who encouraged me, promoted me, gave us bedding plants and organic vegetables, obtained hard-to-get ingredients for me, tried recipes, came to dinner, and who invited *me* to meals.

Special thanks to Jennie Collura and everyone at NAVS (North American Vegetarian Society) for broadening my horizons; and to my long-distance vegan cooking and writing buddies, Fran Costigan (New York's vegan pastry chef extraordinaire) and Joanne Stepaniak in Pennsylvania, for their encouragement.

Introduction

You may wonder why someone with a name like Grogan is writing an Italian cookbook. Grogan is my married name. My paternal grandmother, Clotilde Guerrini Roncagliolo, was a first-generation Peruvian of Italian parentage. Her parents were born in small towns (Moneglia and Chiavari, near Rapallo) on the Italian Riviera di Levante, just south of Genoa. Several generations later, my own grandchildren refer to me as Nonna (or Nonni) instead of Gramma.

I have lived in many out-of-the-way places since I married and left my native California for Canada, and I now live on a small island off the east coast of Vancouver Island. But my father's fond memories of his Italian mother's and aunt's cooking stayed with me.

My own childhood food memories have never left me and have certainly influenced my cooking style and preferences—the winery where my father was employed as a host and wine taster, very much a part of the California Italian winemaking fraternity; my mother's Italian-influenced cooking with fresh California produce and local wines; the Italian chef who cooked for parties at the winery; my teenage years in San Francisco's Marina and North Beach districts, where the corner grocery was always Italian, our favorite restaurants were Italian, and most of our friends and classmates were Italian. My high school was named for Galileo and was just up the street from the Ghirardelli chocolate factory, which wafted tempting fumes over us as we plodded around the field during P.E. class! My young married years were spent in the Commercial Drive district of Vancouver, B.C., which was a virtual "Little Italy" in those days.

These experiences, memories, and tastes have given me a life-long appreciation for the importance of fresh vegetables and herbs, good wines and olive oil as ingredients, and crusty homemade bread. When I became a vegetarian, I turned first to familiar Italian foods which needed little or no adaptation to make them meatless. Good pasta with homemade marinara (tomato) sauce; green salads with my mother's lemon juice, garlic, and olive oil dressing; intensely flavored olives and sun-dried tomatoes; grilled eggplant and zucchini on crusty bread; artichokes, fresh or marinated; polenta with wild mushrooms—how could I feel deprived with such wonderful food?

My natural cooking curiosity has led me to sample and study the cuisines of many countries, but my favorite remains Italian, followed by Chinese and Indian They are the three greatest cuisines in the world, in my opinion, in terms of variety and scope. (This is not to in any way denigrate the delightful cuisines of other nations—I am also very partial to all kinds of Mediterranean cooking, and find something to love about almost every other cuisine!)

One could study any one of these three great cuisines for a lifetime and barely scratch the surface, so I certainly don't consider myself to be an "expert" on Italian cuisine. But, as an ethical vegetarian who tries to follow a vegan lifestyle, I have studied Italian cuisine intensely in an effort to create an egg- and dairy-free Italian vegetarian cooking style which stays true to the soul of "la cucina Italiana."

This book is a very personal collection of recipes—it would take several volumes to cover all of the regional cuisines and to do true justice to the enormous scope of Italian cuisine, even with the "restrictions" of the vegan diet. Here you will find my versions of some very traditional recipes, and some more modern ones (like the popular tiramisú dessert); some very familiar and well-loved dishes, and some that are not so well known in North America, but deserve to be. It is my hope that, as you read and try the recipes, you will be able to adapt some of your own Italian favorites or family heirloom recipes in the vegan style.

Please join me in Nonna's Italian Kitchen.

Bryanna Grogan

I

Italian Cuisine

"The relationship between them [Italians], their food and their land has not yet been ruined by industrial revolution. They enjoy, appreciate and respect good food and they conserve with pride the regional differences in their cooking. . ."

—Elizabeth Romer
Italian Pizzas and Hearth Breads
(New York: Clarkson N. Potter Inc., 1987)

While it is true that Italian cooking is essentially vegetable-based, stemming from the cucina paesana (peasant cuisine) or cucina di povera (cooking of the poor), most Italians cannot imagine why you would not eat meat or fish (particularly a bit of prosciutto [unsmoked ham], anchovies, or chicken broth as flavoring), and to do without cheese and eggs seems to them beyond reason. Even though Italians have traditionally eaten very little meat, the Italian meat industry, like our own, is spending vast amounts of money to convince Italians that meat is indispensable and that anyone who shuns it faces dire health consequences.

I consider myself an "appassionata di cucina," but I am also equally passionate about not eating my fellow creatures or necessitating their agricultural imprisonment and torture by consuming egg and dairy products.

There are many Italians who feel this way too: members of the Movimento Vegan, Associezione Vegetariana Italiana (AVI) and Associezione Culturale Vegitariana (ACV), and publishers and readers of the magazine *Etica e Animale*. I would like to join them in creating a "nuova cucina di magro" (new meatless cuisine)—one that, unlike the old cucina di magro (the Lenten dishes of the past), does not include seafood, eggs, and dairy products, and one that, unlike many of the so-called "vegetarian" Italian recipes of modern times, does not include chicken or meat broth, bits of prosciutto and pancetta (unsmoked ham and bacon), anchovies, lard, or butter.

I took Italian cooking expert Giuliano Bugialli's advice to familiarize myself with the traditional cuisine, and I use the best and freshest (preferably organically and locally grown) ingredients that are available to me and that I can afford. These two components—knowledge of the cuisine and quality ingredients—are the most important in creating good Italian food.

I have tried to address the major food allergies (such as wheat and soy), offering some ideas and variations for using my recipes whenever possible. (Those with dairy or egg allergies have no worries with these recipes!) I have made non-soy versions of most of the meat and dairy substitutes used in this book.

Celiacs and those with wheat or gluten allergies have a much wider choice of excellent Italian-style rice flour pastas available to them these days and can find help in making high-quality wheat-free breads, homemade pastas, cakes, pastries, and even pizza crust in *The Gluten-Free Gourmet Cooks Fast and Healthy* by Bette Hagman (New York: Henry Holt, 1996).

But this is not an allergy cookbook, and I follow no particular "school" of vegetarian cooking. Italian food would be sorry indeed without the tomato/potato/pepper (nightshade) family, onions and garlic, yeasted wheat breads, aromatic vinegars, and wines and liqueurs in cooking. (See page 247 for notes on vegan wines.) Judicious use of salt, sugar, and pepper brings out aroma and taste in simple foods. I use all of these foods with pleasure and without apology.

I don't follow any food combining regime. I do use some refined products, such as high-protein durum semolina pasta (which contains about half as much fiber as whole wheat pasta), but I balance them out with whole grains and other high-fiber plant foods.

If you prefer to use only 100% whole grain products like bread, pasta, and rice, by all means do. I personally find 100% whole grain pizza crust and crusty breads too heavy, so I make them with some unbleached white flour and some whole wheat flour or bran. I've tried brown rice risotto and found it tasted "muddy"—I use brown rice in other ways.

There are some good brands of whole durum semolina wheat pasta that don't feel and taste heavy and pasty, but they are much more expensive than good refined pasta and don't come in as many shapes. I use them sometimes, particularly the macaroni and lasagne noodles, but we usually eat regular pasta, along with a good portion of vegetables and/or beans. You can add some wheat bran and/or ground flaxseed or nuts to bread crumb and/or soy Parmesan toppings for extra fiber too.

I believe that Mediterranean populations remain healthy despite the refined grains they use by virtue of the very large amount of fiber-rich vegetables, fruits, and dried legumes they eat. Dr. Ancel Keys, who pioneered research into the Mediterranean diet, believes that the healthiest people in the world are those in southern Italy, around the Mediterranean, because their diet is mainly vegetarian, the fat they use is olive oil, and everyone eats prodigious amounts of vegetables. He finds the amount of vegetables most Americans eat "shockingly small." In their '90s, Keyes and his wife Margaret continue working and living the good life in southern Italy—living proof, along with their elderly neighbors, of the healthfulness of the rural Italian diet. (See *Eating Well* VII [March/April 1997]: 40-49)

This is not a "diet" or "low-fat" cookbook, either, although most of the recipes are far lower in fat and calories than traditional versions. Not using butter, eggs, meats and meat fats, and cheeses cannot help but make vegan cuisine leaner. (With regular exercise, I actually lost weight while testing recipes for this book!)

I have used extra-virgin olive oil as an ingredient in its own right, to add flavor as well as richness (and sometimes a nondairy butter substitute where appropriate), but if you are on a very fat-restricted diet, you can easily adapt many of the recipes in this book. Avoid the ones containing nuts (or check the fat and calorie counts per serving). Check the recipes for fat-saving tips, such as using chick-pea broth for some or all of the oil in salad dressings and pesto, or using a jelled reduced broth (page 118) to add flavor and glisten to a fat-free vegetable pasta mixture. In many of the recipes, the only fat comes from the olive oil that the vegetables are sautéed in. Although you might lose some flavor, you can steam-fry with no oil by using a nonstick pan and stirring the vegetables over high heat, adding a couple of tablespoons of water, broth, or dry white wine every so often just to keep from the food from sticking. (See the sidebar on page 40.)

Delicious food that is free of animal products is my primary focus. There are so many healthful vegan foods that taste wonderful, why eat something unpleasant just because it is good for you?

I believe that we should relax and enjoy our food the way Italians do—prepare it, serve it, and eat it with love and gratitude. And there is so much more love when no living creature has been sacrificed for our pleasure.

The Evolving Italian Cuisine

Every cuisine is a work in progress.

When I had questions about approaching Italian cuisine from a vegan perspective, it cheered me to read what Robert Helstrom, Executive Chef of Kuleto's Italian Restaurant in San Francisco, wrote in his book *Contemporary Italian* (Harlow & Ratner, Emeryville, CA, 1993): "Whenever you depart from tradition, you risk stepping on some toes." Cecilia Chung, one of the modern exponents of another great cuisine, and owner of San Francisco's China House Bistro, was quoted in the February 1994 issue of *Gourmet* as arguing that any distinctive cuisine evolves with time, and that it's silly to insist that dishes be served exactly as they were a hundred years ago.

In reality, there has really been no such thing as "Italian cooking." There was Sicilian cooking, Genovese, Florentine, etc., and each region, each city, and each town was extremely chauvinistic about its own style of cooking. This extraordinary diversity within such a small country was a legacy of Italy's past of warring city-states, kingdoms, duchies, and papal states, each of which had its own laws and institutions. There were also foreign influences—the French in Piedmont, the Austrians in the north, Yugoslavs in Venezia Giulia, Spaniards in the south, Arabs in Sicily. When Italy was united over a hundred years ago, local patriotism (called "campanalisimo," meaning fanatic loyalty to one's parish bell tower) did not disappear. The citizens of each region felt strongly that their cooking was the best in Italy.

Italy changed dramatically after World War II, and continues to change rapidly. Although there was some industry in the north, before the war Italy was an agricultural country, farmed by peasant sharecroppers under a system called the "mezzadria." In the 1950s and '60s Italy was transformed into a modern industrial consumer society. Peasants moved to the cities or abroad, and southerners moved to the north to find work. Women worked outside the home. It was inevitable that one of the results of "il boom" would be a change in the eating and cooking habits of the majority of Italians.

Culinary borders have now blurred to some extent. No longer can the regions be divided according to cooking fats (butter in the north, lard in the middle, and olive oil in the south), or grains (polenta, egg pasta, and rice in the north, pizza and dry pasta in the south). The southern predilection for cooking with tomatoes has migrated steadily north with the years and the immigrants looking for work. Mass production and the influence of television has brought standardization of many food products.

Despite this rapid change, regional cooking survived. Nostalgia and the quest for a sense of identity have brought about a revival of traditional cooking and, fortunately, a new respect for quality fresh produce and traditional ingredients, such as olive oil.

In industrialized societies the world over, people hanker for the "good old days" and traditional foods that they may only have heard about. Though few would choose to go back to the days of ten-children families and back-breaking hard labor, Italians are relishing the old dishes of the "cucina paesana" or "cucina povera," the polenta with wild mushroom stew, the bean soups, the rough breads. There are still nonnas who can remember and teach the old traditional recipes, and many families and chefs in Italy treasure handwritten recipe books and old cookbooks, even reprints from the Renaissance. Instead of following food fashions and fads from other countries (such as making risotto with kiwis or strawberries, heaven help us!), chefs are now concentrating on seasonal foods and locally grown produce. What many of us think of as traditional Italian peasant dishes from the past, however (such as lasagne bursting with several kinds of meats and cheeses or spaghetti with meatballs), may be part of a "food myth," according to food columnist Barbara Kafka. In her column, "An Opinionated Palate" in the June 1990 issue of *Gourmet*, she wrote that these rich meat- and cheese-laden dishes are actually modern-day adaptations or rare feast-day versions of the simple grain-, legume-, and vegetable-based dishes that sustained our ancestors. Fantasies about a past filled with meat, sugar, and cream have distorted our view of eating in centuries past. The heart and soul of any great cuisine, including that of Italy, are the principal grain and the locally grown legumes, fruits, and vegetables, flavored with the regionally preferred herbs and spices, condiments, and oils.

Italian cooks have always known how to adapt, long being used to scarcity and uncertainty of supply. They adapted their recipes when new foods—tomatoes, beans, and peppers—from the Americas appeared. It stands to reason that Italian cuisine will be able to adapt to whatever the 21st century brings with characteristic verve and good taste.

Combining traditional Italian vegetarian foods with some of the important vegetarian foods of Asia (soyfoods and sea vegetables, for instance), results in the "Asian/Mediterranean model" that nutritionists recommend for health and longevity, *and* allows cooks to "veganize" some of the hearty, traditionally meat- or dairy-based dishes that many people would sorely miss. (More about this on page 15.)

Adding soyfoods to Italian dishes is not so far-fetched. Some of the most important research on soyfoods has been done at the University of Milan. In fact, the National Health Service of Italy provides textured soy protein free of charge to people who suffer from certain cardiovascular diseases as a dietary treatment.

As the food of Italy has changed, so has the style of eating. The main meal of the day was traditionally taken between noon and 3 P.M.— long and leisurely, with the large extended family gathered around the table, which might be placed outside during warm weather. There would be four, perhaps even five courses, ending with fruit, nuts, and cheese, and a digestivo or grappa—a liqueur. (Coffee with milk is never consumed at the end of a meal in Italy— it is taken at breakfast.) The evening meal would then be fairly light—usually pasta en brodo (soup with pasta), or eggs.

Most families try to keep this tradition as often as they can, usually on weekends or holidays, but many families have two working parents, so this simply isn't possible. Breakfast (usually pastry or biscotti and coffee) and lunches (often pizza or panini—sandwiches on crusty rolls) are usually consumed at stand-up food bars, and now the main meal of the day is in the evening. It may simply be a light antipasto dish followed by a small primo or secondo (see page 10), and a salad. Prepared antipasti, contorni (vegetable dishes), and salads are often purchased from delis on the way home (usually of excellent quality and variety, but very expensive—Italians are willing to spend far more on food than we are).

Traditionally, two more small meals were taken, one at midmorning, and one at midafternoon, called merende (or spuntini, a more modern term). This was a country custom and a necessity for laborers, but it makes sense even today, since the Italian breakfast is light, and the evening meal may be eaten quite late. Simple dishes, on the order of antipasti or almost anything with a bit of bread, are suitable for merende.

Italians are not nearly as preoccupied with weight and "health foods" as we are, perhaps because they just assume their food to be healthful. But they are as concerned as we are about looking and feeling good. Since the average Italian does not work nearly as hard physically as past generations, Italian food is getting "lighter," which generally means using smaller amounts of oil and butter. (This is called "la cucina sana.") Lynn Rosetti Kasper, author of *The Splendid Table* (New York: William Morrow and Co., 1992) and proponent of the rich cooking of Emiglia-Romagna, writes that olive oil and reduced stocks are replacing much of the butter and lard used in old-fashioned cooking.

Despite these changes, the kitchen remains the heart and soul of the Italian home and the Italian culture. The production, preparation, anticipation, discussion, and consumption of food have been, and always will be, beloved preoccupations of all Italians.

Yes, changes in the foods we eat are necessary, for the welfare of animals, for the survival of our planet and ourselves, and because of differences in caloric expenditure between our ancestors and ourselves, but I wish that we could all have the love affair with food that Italians have.

Order of Service in a Traditional Italian Midday Meal (*Pranzo*)

In the traditional style, each course is served on its own.

*Antipasto (this means "before the meal")—similar to what we call "appetizers," usually very simple, but can be a small serving of contorno or vegetable secondo (see below);

Primo Piatto (First Course)—small serving of pasta, polenta, gnocchi (dumplings), risotto, or soup;;

Secondo Piatto (Second Course)—traditionally the meat, fish, or poultry course, but many restaurants offer a "secondo piatto vegetariano," which is often just a larger version of an antipasto;

Contorni (literally "that which rounds up")—vegetable side dishes and salads, usually more than one;

Fruit, nuts (and traditionally, cheese);

Dolce (sweet course—pastry, pudding, cake, etc.)—this is optional and would probably be dispensed with in the summer.

*Note: It's basically the size of a dish which determines whether it is an antipasto, merenda, contorno, or secondo—most vegetable dishes can be used as any one of these courses.

For a simple, more modern meal, either mid-day or in the evening, Italians often have only contorni and a larger serving of what would have been the antipasto, primo, or secondo—for instance, a salad, a vegetable dish, and a pasta dish, risotto, or stew. Or, if eating in a restaurant, they might simply have two or three vegetable selections from the antipasti table.

Actually, preparing a succession of small courses in the traditional style is not necessarily very time-consuming or arduous, and it is a wonderful way to sample the variety that Italian food has to offer. You also eat more slowly and feel very satisfied because of the diversity of flavors and textures, rather than the quantity. Some nutrition experts feel that this variety of small portions is one reason that the French and Italians are generally healthier than North Americans. I think the larger quantity of vegetables and bread they eat also has something to do with it.

I have prepared four-course meals for myself and my husband in 30 to 45 minutes. The antipasto can be as simple as a piece of bruschetta (grilled bread) with sautéed mushrooms or greens, or chopped fresh tomatoes and basil. The primo can be leftover soup, a small portion of 8-minute pressure-cooked risotto, or a simple dish of pasta with a quick, light vegetable sauce. The secondo and contorni can be cooking while you serve the first two courses—perhaps an eggless vegetable frittata or tortino, or a stew and a small salad. Fresh fruit is the perfect dessert, or a gelato or sorbetto, if you have some in the freezer. Bread (without butter or margarine) and wine or mineral water are served throughout the meal.

One of the things I love about Italian and Mediterranean cooking is that you don't need any complicated rules about yin and yang and the four elements, or even much detailed nutrition information, to compose a delicious, balanced, and healthful meal. Any Italian will tell you—let the vegetables of the season determine your menu choices; avoid repeating the same type of sauce or other major ingredient or flavoring within a meal; balance a rich dish in one course with a light dish in the next; and attempt to achieve a harmony of flavors and textures in your menu. Mangia bene!

The Regional Cooking of Italy

Piedmont and the Valla d'Aosta region lies in the northwest corner of Italy, near the French and Swiss Alps. The cuisine is strongly influenced by that of France. Turin is the elegant capital, home of the thin breadsticks called *grissini*. Rice and polenta rule here, and from this region comes the hot vegetable dip bagna cauda. The Piedmontese are justly proud of their white truffles and are fond of chocolate desserts.

Lombardy is often called "the garden of Italy," but it is the most industrialized area, as well. The cooking of Lombardy is very rich and diverse (somewhat influenced by Austrian and French cooking), and each of the many ancient cities had its own style. In Milan, the capital, more rice is eaten than pasta, and saffron is used heavily, tomatoes sparingly. Some of the dishes from this region which are represented in this book are layered polenta with sauce, risotto alla Milanese, tortelli di zucca, minestrone alla Milanese, and the sweet bread panettone.

Trentino and the Alto Adige is a region which boasts high mountains and fertile valleys in which rye, wheat, corn, oats, barley, grapes, raspberries, and fruit trees are cultivated. The cuisine is heavily influenced by German and

Austro-Hungarian cooking, with cabbage, potatoes, turnips, and kohlrabi being popular. Buckwheat flour is often used, and dumplings in soup are a favorite. Residents are fond of pastries and sweets which resemble the strudels, filled pancakes, and fritters of Austria.

The Veneto has one of the most elegant cuisines of Italy, a legacy of the wealth of the city of Venice, which was the most affluent city in Europe in the Middle Ages. Sugar, pepper, nutmeg, cloves, ginger, and coffee came first to Venice to be shipped to the rest of Europe. Rice is served with the tremendous variety of vegetables grown in the region—artichokes, peas, cabbages, zucchini, pumpkins, asparagus, tomatoes, onions, and mushrooms. The town of Treviso is famous for its radicchio rosso or red chicory, which is now so popular in North America.

Besides the many risotto dishes that the Veneto is famous for, favorite regional dishes include polenta with beans, bigoli (special whole wheat noodles) in walnut or onion sauce, gnocchi (dumplings) made with potatoes and buckwheat flour, and columba di pasqua, a special dove-shaped Easter bread.

Fruili and Venezia Giulia border the former Yugoslavia and Austria in the northeast of Italy. Bread and vegetables are the mainstay of this cuisine, and vegetable and herb frittate (omelets) are very popular here. You will find many varieties of vegetable risotto dishes similar to those of the Veneto here. This mountainous region is conducive to grape-growing, and many wines are produced here.

Liguria is the narrow coastal region around the Gulf of Genoa, stretching from the French border in the west to La Spezia and the border of Tuscany in the east. The seacoast is the Italian Riviera, with many famous resort towns; the rest of the region is largely mountainous.

The capital city, Genoa, gave the world pesto, the famous basil sauce which is used on pasta, ravioli, and in soups. The whole region is famous for its vegetable cookery and the use of fresh herbs. Vegetable tarts (such as torta pasqualina and polpettone de fagliolini), gratins, and stuffed vegetables are treasured Ligurian dishes. Focaccia is also a specialty.

Tuscany is to many Italians the "heart of Italy," being almost in the center and one of the largest regions. Some of Italy's most beautiful cities are located here: Florence, Siena, Lucca, and Pisa, for example. The language that we call Italian is actually the Tuscan dialect.

Tuscan cooking is simple and refined, utilizing some of the best olive oil in the world, that which comes from Lucca. Tuscans love beans and are often referred to by other Italians as "mangiafagioli," or "bean-eaters." Tuscans

have many fabulous soups and vegetable dishes, including the spinach dumplings called strozzapreti.

Emilia-Romagna is on a rich, fertile plain that contains some ancient towns—Parma, Bolog-na, Ferrara, Modena (home of balsamic vinegar), and Ravenna. Many consider Bologna the gastronomic capital of Italy. It is named La Grassa, "the fat one," because of its very rich cuisine. However, cooks are now using more olive oil than butter and less fat than in earlier times.

Since this is wheat country, Emilia-Romagna is famous for its pasta, and lasagne is reputed to have been invented here. There are many, many recipes for stuffed pastas, including pumpkin ravioli. Fruits and vegetables abound here, and the region is famous for several good liqueurs and fruit-flavored brandies.

Umbria is the only region in Italy besides Lombardy with no coastline, but it has many lakes, rolling hills, and ancient hillside towns. Assisi, the birthplace of St. Francis, is located in Umbria. Wheat, vegetables, olives, plums, figs, and many varieties of mushrooms are grown here, and the region is famous for black truffles. The city of Perugia is known for its chocolates and pastries. Many simple, but delicious, pasta dishes are served here—spaghetti with garlic, olive oil, and hot pepper; long noodles dressed with olive oil, garlic, tomato, and mushroom sauce; spaghetti with walnut sauce; and ribbon noodles with herb and garlic tomato sauce, to name but a few.

Le Marche, or the Marches, is not well known to foreign travellers. It is largely agricultural with rolling hills of fruit and olive trees, wine grapes, and fields of vegetables and wheat. Local specialties are pea soup with tomato, garlic, and herbs; spicy bean soup; cheesey ravioli called calcioni; fava beans with an onion sauce; and risotto with mushrooms.

Rome and the Lazio combine the cooking of northern and southern Italy. The markets are full of the abundant produce grown in the region—broccoli, peas, fennel, artichokes, and tomatoes that are used in many of the region's recipes. Vegetables are often dressed with agrodolce sauce, a sweet and sour sauce. Carciofi all Romana, artichokes stewed with olive oil, garlic, and mint (an herb commonly used in Roman cookery), and carciofi all giudea, deep-fried artichokes, are two of the region's most famous dishes. Pasta dishes abound, but semolina dumplings and rice croquettes are also popular. The famous torta di ricotta is a popular dessert.

Abruzzi and the Molise are mountainous areas, stretching from the Adriatic Sea to some of the highest peaks in Italy. The simple, strong cuisine reflects the landscape. Frittate and chick-pea dishes are popular, and hot peppers are used in many dishes. Pepper is even used in a local cookie called pepatelli.

Campania is one of the most beautiful regions in Italy, boasting the Bay of Naples, Mount Vesuvius, the magnificent Amalfi Drive, and the vibrant city of Naples. The area is fertile and vegetables grow here all year round. Consequently, some of the most delicious vegetable dishes in Italy are made here.

Naples is the home of pizza, with a history going back two thousands years. Naples is also well known for its macaroni and rich tomato sauces. "Alla Napoletana" means that a dish contains a rich tomato sauce. Eggplant alla Parmigiana actually originates in this region, as do calzone (stuffed pizzas), pasta alla puttanesca (with a quickly made, spicy olive and tomato sauce), and strangulaprievete or "priest stranglers" (potato dumplings in tomato sauce).

Basilicata, or Lucania, tucked in between Campania and Calabria, is one of the poorest regions of Italy, with an almost totally mountainous terrain. Despite this, wheat, vegetables, citrus fruits, figs, nuts, olives, and wine grapes are grown wherever possible. The cooking is simple and austere, largely based on pasta, vegetables, and beans with garlic, herbs, hot peppers, and capers for flavoring. Some local dishes are a purée of dried beans served with cooked beans and bread; pasta with lentils; macaroni dressed with olive oil, capers, garlic, and hot peppers, sometimes served with chickpeas.

Calabria, once the richest region of Italy, is now plagued by earthquakes and poverty, lack of water, and a mountainous terrain. However, farmers still grow eggplant, peppers, tomatoes, artichokes, olives, figs, almonds, citrus fruits, and grapes. Macaroni with artichokes, fried eggplant with a sweet and sour sauce, ciambatta (or gianfottere in local dialect), a vegetable stew, and tomatoes stuffed with mint- and garlic-flavored pasta are some of the delectable regional dishes featuring local vegetables.

Apulia, the heel of the Italian boot which is surrounded by water, is reminiscent of Greece. Though poor, the region produces potatoes, eggplant, artichokes, fennel, fava beans, asparagus, melons, olives, citrus fruits, wheat, and wine grapes. Bread is an important staple, and the diet is based on pasta and vegetables. Onions are used in quantity, and greens of all kinds stuff pasta and dress pasta dishes. From Apulia comes la capriata, a delicious bean purée drizzled with olive oil and served with cooked greens; a thick green minestrone; pizza rustica, a two-crust pizza; fusilli with arugula and tomato sauce; tiella, a casserole of potatoes, onions, vegetables, and herbs; and stuffed eggplant with garlic, tomatoes, and bread crumbs.

Sicily is an island in the Mediterranean and grows most of the citrus fruits in Italy. It also produces a substantial amount of Italy's wheat, which accounts for a cuisine based on bread and pasta. Artichokes, eggplant, zucchini, tomatoes, broccoli, peppers, fennel, olives, capers, grapes, figs, pomegranates, and other exotic fruits grow here.

Sicilian cooking is flavorful and spicy and often reflects the influence of the Arabs who ruled the island in years past. Sweets, especially, are Arab-influenced, making use of sesame seeds, almonds, pistachio nuts, anise, and honey.

Caponata is a famous Sicilian relish of eggplant and celery in a sweet and sour dressing. Other local specialties include broccoli cooked with olives and wine, chick-pea fritters, and several pasta dishes with eggplant.

Sardinia is another island, mountainous and not very populous. The staple food is a thin bread called carta di musica ("sheets of music") which is preferred over pasta by the locals. Eggplant, zucchini, cauliflower, peas, fennel, fava beans, string beans, artichokes, nuts, and many fruits grow here. Like Sicilians, Sardinians are fond of sweet pastries, especially made with honey, almonds, and dried fruits. There are several delicious soups, including a cauliflower soup and a fava bean soup. Regional dishes include culingiones, a ravioli stuffed with spinach and saffron in tomato sauce; culuriones, potato ravioli in tomato sauce; white beans cooked with olive oil, garlic, tomatoes, and vegetables; and vegetable tortas.

II
Ingredients and Equipment for Italian Cooking

"Taste is produced by the expressive use of the cuisines that have come down to us. One becomes fluent in a cuisine as in a language, steeping oneself in its idioms, getting its accents right. Cooking well is like the telling use of language: Expression must be vigorous, clear, concise. There can be no unnecessary ingredients or unnecessary step. A dish may indeed be complicated, but in terms of taste every component, every procedure must count."
—Marcella Hazan
Marcella's Italian Kitchen
(New York: Alfred A. Knopf, 1986)

Is there a place for animal product substitutes in Italian cooking?

I agonized over the question of whether I should include dishes with any sort of substitutes for animal products, or make it strictly traditional Italian vegetable and bean dishes made with olive oil, vegetable broth, herbs, etc., leaving out any anchovies, cheese, butter, cream, etc., that may have been used in the original version. In the end, I decided that this would be too limiting for most people (myself included), so I have used only good-quality alternatives that result in as mouth-watering and satisfying dishes as the originals, not those used just for the sake of recreating (badly) every familiar Italian dish.

To do this I have borrowed from the Chinese and Japanese Buddhist tradition, which has had thousands of years to develop a very sophisticated and delicious vegetarian (mostly vegan) cuisine which includes mock "meats," "seafood," and "poultry" made primarily with tofu, wheat gluten (seitan), bean curd skin (yuba), and mushrooms and other fungi.

Another aspect of using animal-food alternatives is that we don't have to give up our culinary heritage when we follow a vegan lifestyle. One of the things that often causes family rifts and arguments when one member becomes a vegetarian is that he/she will no longer eat the foods that their families have always held dear, especially on festive occasions. These foods may be one of the last links to a family's ethnic background. Many of these cherished foods are of animal origin because they are feast dishes. If you have a good idea of how to flavor meatless versions of these dishes so that they taste very similar to the original, you can often use dairy and meat alternatives in these dishes and make them so delicious and authentic that your grandmother will be astounded!

I think that Westerners often disdain animal product alternatives because their use has not been a part of Western culture as it has been in Asia, where even non-vegetarians frequent Buddhist vegetarian restaurants for various holidays when animal products are proscribed. And I also believe that alternatives have not been part of the Western culture because dairy products and seafood have usually been allowed when people were "fasting" (except in very strict Eastern Orthodox communities).

In any case, you may choose to avoid meat, fish, and poultry alternatives because you never liked the "real thing" in the first place, but most of us would have a difficult time living without dairy alternatives, so they seem to be more "acceptable" in our society. My style of Italian cooking is certainly not dependent on meat substitutes, or even dairy alternatives, but these recipes may convince reluctant family members that a vegan diet does not mean restriction and suffering! (I have not used any recipe in the book that has not been enjoyed by both omnivores and vegetarians of my acquaintance.)

I have tried, wherever possible, to use Italian (or, at least, European) ingredients, but there are some instances where only Asian ingredients will give a satisfying result. For instance, for a "beefy" flavor, I have used primarily the soaking water from dried boletus mushrooms, and sometimes Marmite, a British yeast extract. But, sometimes a little soy sauce helps the flavor.

Anchovies, which are used far more than most people suppose as a flavoring in Italian cooking (especially so-called "meatless" cooking), have a complex, salty, fermented flavor very much like a light Japanese miso, so miso is what I use in place of anchovies. The proportions are ¾ to 1 teaspoon miso for each anchovy fillet, or use an equal amount of miso if anchovy paste is called for. (You can also use chick-pea miso if you have a soy allergy.) This substitution won't work in sauces which consist primarily of anchovies. For a more pronounced "seafood" flavor, flakes of dulse or nori, two common sea vegetables, can be utilized in sauces, vegetable stews, and soups. Oyster mushrooms or the root vegetable salsify (also known as oyster plant) can be used in place of seafood in some dishes, as well, along with the sea vegetable flakes. Thinly sliced grilled eggplant and zucchini with lemon juice and olive oil can be a delicious alternative to pickled fish.

For the flavor of pancetta (bacon) and prosciutto (ham), unsmoked Italian pork products which are used extensively as flavoring, a little roasted Chinese sesame oil and salt (with freshly ground black pepper, in the case of pancetta) mixed with olive oil gives just the right amount of flavor. You don't necessarily want everything to taste constantly of olive oil, as good as it is.

As I mentioned before, soy products are being experimented with in Italy, because Italian medical researchers have been at the forefront of research into soy and its effect on heart disease. I'm reliably informed that you can buy soy gelati all over Rome! So I have no compunctions about using soy products in place of dairy products, such as in my soy ricotta (made with tofu). In my opinion, homemade soy ricotta is superior to the grainy, watery ricotta available in supermarkets here in North America (and to the sour cottage cheese that many people mistakenly use in lasagne, etc.). In fact, very fresh tofu consumed the day it is made is very reminiscent of ricotta.

Silken tofu and cashews can be also used to make creamy "goat cheese" spreads (miso adds a rich fermented taste) and "mascarpone" (a rich Italian cream cheese), as well as pastry cream, a rich-tasting besciamella (white sauce), gelati, and custards.

Marinated firm or extra-firm tofu also makes a delicious chicken substitute (which I call breast of tofu), and a type of fermented "cheese" that can be used instead of ricotta salata (a salted ricotta that can be sliced or crumbled like feta).

If you have an allergy to soy, I have provided recipes for nondairy ricotta, ricotta salata, mascarpone, gelati, creamy sauces, and desserts using nuts, such as cashews and almonds, and rice milk.

I also use tofu to make delectable vegetable tarts, frittate (omelets), and tortini (savory molded casseroles). In these I use some nutritional yeast flakes, not a typical European ingredient, but one which adds nutrients and an "eggy" flavor.

Another soy product that works well in many Italian recipes is textured soy (or vegetable) protein. The chunks make excellent scaloppine (the word "scaloppine" simply means "small bits") and stews, and the granules make delicious polpettone (meat loaf), polpetti (meatballs), and salsicce (sausages). If you have an allergy to soy products, I have provided recipes for all of these meat alternatives using seitan (flavored, cooked wheat gluten).

The new and delicious, modern commercially made soy, rice, oat, and almond milks can be used in place of milk. (I enrich these with silken tofu, cooked white rice, or raw cashews for "cream.") In fact, almond milk was used frequently in ancient times and is still used as a refreshing beverage in some parts of Italy. We prefer "light" soymilk, so we dilute the full-fat product by half with water and add 1 tablespoon Grade A maple syrup per quart of diluted soymilk. My husband even makes a delicious cappuccino with this diluted version, using one of the new inexpensive, but amazingly efficient, plunger-style milk-frothers.

There are very few prepared commercial vegan products that I depend upon. (We have a more limited choice of vegan products here in Canada.) You may wish to try Tofutti Better Than Cream Cheese, if it is available in your area—it can make a very acceptable substitute for mascarpone (the rich Italian cream cheese). There are some excellent nondairy ice creams and fruit ices that can be used in place of gelati and sorbetti.

I use Soymage's vegan Parmesan cheese substitute which I think is quite delicious. (Don't bother with cheap bulk soy Parmesans containing casein, a milk by-product—they taste like salted chalk.) You can use half as much as the Parmesan called for in a recipe. See page 250 for information on ordering this in bulk, at a great savings. You may wish to simply use some toasted or seasoned bread crumbs (page 32), ground toasted nuts, or a drizzle of good olive oil, as many Italians do. A soy-free alternative to soy Parmesan is homemade Cashew Sprinkle on page 37. Other than the Soymage Parmesan substitute mentioned previously, I have not found an acceptable cheese substitute that does not contain casein (a dairy product). If a creamy texture is needed, I use my vegan bechamel or white sauce, the cream sauce that is used in many Italian (and European) recipes. Americanized versions of lasagne call for copious amounts of cheese; Italian recipes more often use white sauce and a small amount of Parmesan. Many authentic Italian pizzas do not contain cheese at all, so there is really no need for a substitute.

Contrary to popular opinion, many Italian recipes (especially from the north) contain butter. I have cut down as much as possible (but not eliminated) all fats in my recipes, using the best type for the most flavor. I use extra-virgin olive oil, but, in some cases, a good butter substitute is essential. Margarines, with good reason, have received bad press lately. Most are not dairy-free, taste awful, and contain hydrogenated fats (the source of "trans" fats) and chemicals. But, times are changing. When oil just won't do, I use Canoleo brand 100% canola margarine, which contains primarily nonhydrogenated oil, no preservatives or dairy, and, best of all, it tastes great!* Ask your health food store to carry it if you can't find another with good flavor (see page 250 for the manufacturer's address). A new spread with no hydrogenated oil is Spectrum Naturals Spread, but I have not been able to experiment with it here in Canada.

---

*If you are allergic to soy, however, please note it is not soy-free.

For those who crave a substitute for bacon, sausages, and "cold cuts," Yves Veggie Back Bacon or Canadian Bacon is an excellent substitute for North American smoked ham, but not for the unsmoked ham that Italians prefer. You can use it instead of "speck," a smoked Italian ham used in some northern recipes that have German/Austrian influence. Lightlife and Yves also make vegan low-fat "cold cuts" that you might like to try, but they are more like the Americanized versions, so I use them for American-style recipes, not Italian. Lightlife Lean Links makes a mild Italian "sausage" that is quite good, but I also make my own (see pages 177 and 183).

There are many brands of beef and chicken substitutes that are vegan and low-fat—the list grows daily, it seems. Experiment with them (and read labels for hidden animal products, like egg whites) if you don't want to make your own. These products range from the simple (marinated seitan, marinated, baked, and smoked tofu, marinated tempeh, crumbled flavored tofu, dry textured soy protein, and seitan mixes), to the very sophisticated (a myriad of patties, cutlets, and hamburger replacements), many available at your local supermarket. The hamburger replacements and "crumbles" are especially handy in familiar Italian-American recipes such as ragù-type spaghetti sauces and meatballs and are well received by most non-vegetarians. They might be useful in persuading reluctant family members to try vegetarian foods.

Cooking Note: Remember that when you substitute a meat alternative for meat in a favorite recipe, it is not going to give off any juice while cooking—on the contrary, it is going to absorb liquid. So add more liquid (about a cup in a stew for four people), in the form of wine and/or broth, to your recipe. You may also need to add a little more of the "odori" (flavoring agents)—the herbs, onion, garlic, etc.

A very important component of Italian cooking is a light, but very flavorful, vegetarian broth. My first choice is a simple vegetable broth that you can make yourself in large amounts a couple of times a month and freeze, either in containers or as ice cubes for use in small amounts. It can be reduced to make a broth concentrate or a jelled broth (see page 118). I also use the soaking water from dried boletus mushrooms for a "beefy" broth. Porcini are the prime boletus, but I agree with chef and cookbook author Deborah Madison that the South American variety yields an excellent broth—and it's half the price! A little Marmite, the British-made yeast extract also adds a "beefy" flavor (see Mail Order Sources, page 248).

My second choice, and one that I use often because I cook a batch of organic chick-peas every week, is a seasoned chick-pea broth (page 119), which can be strained to a clear, tasty liquid that jells almost like chicken broth.

My third choice is broth made from either Massel vegetarian broth cubes or Morga Soya Cubes. These are both MSG- and preservative-free, and the Massel cubes are also soy-free and kosher. McCormick's Low-Fat All-Vegetable Bouillon Cubes are an MSG-free supermarket brand that are quite tasty. Another brand that I have just recently tried is Superior Touch/Better Than Bouillon Vegetable Base, a vegetarian broth paste made in the U.S., but also available in Canadian supermarkets. I know that these may not be available where you live, so experiment with all of the cubes, pastes, and powders you can find until you find one that contains no animal products, preservatives, or MSG, and that you would not mind drinking on its own as a hot beverage. Italian broth is light, so you dilute commercial broths a bit, unless you want intense flavor in some particular recipe.

Many vegan chefs recommend Vogue Vege Base. Chef Jean-Marc Fullsack recommends Morga Fat-Free Vegetable Broth Mix or Swanson's Clear Vegetable Broth (in cans). *Fine Cooking* magazine recommends Perfect Additions Rich Vegetable Stock, which is available frozen in specialty markets all over the U.S. (see Mail Order Sources, page 248). Other new brands of vegetable stock in cartons are now coming out as I write this. You may have a local "stock shop" which sells homemade vegetable broth, as well.

Try to use your own broth whenever possible, but don't be ashamed to use a good quality broth cube or base—Italian cooks and chefs use them frequently. In the past, European broth cubes have been superior to North American bouillon cubes, but we now have more variety and better quality to choose from. A good broth base can make all the difference in a dish such as vegetarian risotto.

The Pantry

One of the first things I realized when I began doing research for this book was that you don't have to have a pantry full of exotic ingredients in order to cook Italian. I found that I was using a fairly modest list of ingredients over and over again to create an infinite number of dishes.

Italian cooks plan their menus around what vegetables and fruits are in season or available that day and always have the following items on hand:

dry pasta	cornmeal	onions & garlic
extra-virgin olive oil	white kidney (cannellini) beans	celery
good-quality canned tomatoes	romano (or pinto or cranberry) beans	carrots
good-quality vegetarian broth cubes
dried chick-peas		salt & peppercorns
lentils	red wine and balsamic vinegar	
arborio and long-grain rice		herbs & spices
	lemons	wine

With these ingredients, fresh produce, and crusty Italian bread you can be ready for anything. What makes the cuisine complex is the use of fine quality ingredients and the way these ingredients are combined.

Detailed Pantry List

The following list offers detailed information on some of the ingredients listed above, as well as other foods that would be helpful to have in a vegan Italian pantry. If you cannot obtain some of the ingredients listed here (or one of the suggested substitutes), consult the Mail Order Sources on page 248:

neutral-flavored cooking oil, such as canola (see page 22)

wines for cooking—dry red, dry white, also Italian marsala (or use a good dry sherry, madeira, or sauterne), white vermouth; You don't have to use an expensive wine for cooking; moderately priced wines will do just fine. But use one that you wouldn't object to drinking, and don't use salted "cooking wines." *Note:* You can use nonalcoholic wines if desired. (See page 250.)

pure flavor extracts—vanilla, anise, almond, orange, lemon

liquors for baking and cooking (use appropriate extracts if you prefer—see Mail Order Sources)—grappa (or aquavit or vodka); amaretto; Frangelico; rum; brandy (and/or cherry brandy); coffee liqueur; anise liqueur

dry durum semolina pasta (no eggs), see page 76

rice (arborio rice and long-grain), see pages 132-34

flour—unbleached white, whole wheat, and white and whole wheat pastry flours

chick-pea flour

wheat bran

pure gluten powder for making seitan meat alternatives and firming up soy meat alternatives

custard powder (plain, no vanilla; try gourmet shops)

nutritional yeast flakes (Red Star Vegetarian Support Formula from a natural food store or see Mail Order Sources, p. 249)

cornstarch, wheat starch, potato starch, or white rice flour

sugars—white only if you're sure it's beet sugar; otherwise use turbinado sugar, Sucanat (granulated sugar cane juice), or other unbleached sugars; Grade A maple syrup; corn syrup—see pages 214-16

other dried and canned legumes—large lima beans (gigantes), or broad beans or favas; split peas

textured soy (vegetable) protein granules and chunks (see pages 173-75)

dried porcini (cepes) and/or boletus mushrooms; Porcini are much more expensive than South American dried boletus, which are quite tasty, as long as you purchase ones which are still flexible and not shriveled and dusty. Use dried shiitake only if you can't find dried boletus mushrooms

jars of roasted red peppers

jars of marinated artichokes

canned artichoke hearts in water (or use frozen artichoke hearts)

sun-dried tomatoes (plain dried and marinated in oil)

small jars of pickled capers

jars of imported Italian pickled vegetables and relishes

good quality fruit jams, jellies, and preserves, in particular, apricot for baking

EnerG Egg Replacer

aseptically packaged nondairy milks and good-tasting nondairy milk powders

Marmite (preferably) or other yeast extracts, such as Vegemite, Vegex, Sovex, and Savorex.

gravy browner like Kitchen Bouquet

aseptically packaged boxes of extra-firm *silken* tofu

lite soy sauce or tamari

Dutch cocoa powder

instant espresso powder

agar powder or flakes (vegetarian gelatin)

aluminum-free baking powder, baking soda, and cream of tartar

sea vegetable flakes, such as nori and dulse

potatoes (russets and red-skinned)

green onions

parsley (preferably the flat-leafed Italian type, but *not* cilantro!)

fresh mushrooms

leeks

a good-tasting, dairy-free margarine (I prefer Canoleo brand.)

roasted (Chinese) sesame oil

tofu (can be a reduced-fat brand), medium-firm, firm, and extra-firm or pressed

regular baking yeast

Soymage 100% dairy- and casein-free Parmesan substitute, or soy-free alternative, page 37. See page 250 for ordering.

olives of various kinds

light soy or chick-pea miso, a fermented Japanese bean and grain paste, to use as an anchovy substitute; see page 16

French or espresso-roast coffee beans (can be Swiss-water decaf)

nuts and seeds (almonds, raw cashews, hazelnuts or filberts, pine nuts, walnuts, sesame seeds)

unsweetened and semisweet chocolate, dairy-free

full-fat soy flour (for pasta-making)

bread crumbs—plain and seasoned (pages 31-32)

citrus peels (preferably organic, for baking)

Extra-Virgin Olive Oil and Other Cooking Oils

According to some, olive oil is the panacea for all of our degenerative diseases; according to others, olive oil is just another fat that will add calories and endanger your immune system.

As usual, the truth is somewhere in between. Olive oil contains more monounsaturated fat than other oils (77%), and monounsaturated fat, in moderation, does not seem to heighten the risk of heart disease nor does it oxidize rapidly to become carcinogenic. It does less to encourage breast cancer growth than any oil. But a quote from one study cites: "The weight of international epidemiologic studies supports the conclusion that only low levels of fat intake are protective against breast cancer. . . . the lowest recorded levels of breast cancer are found in societies where the intake of fat is far lower than 20 percent of total calories."*

---

*Kradjian, Robert M., M.D., *Save Yourself from Breast Cancer*, (New York: Berkeley Books, 1994). Other information from Weil, Andrew, M.D., *Natural Health, Natural Medicine*, (Boston: Houghton Mifflin, 1990).

For the last few years I have used very little fat of any kind in my cooking and have written three books on very-low-fat vegetarian cooking. I believe that most North Americans eat far too much fat of all kinds, and my research convinces me that a diet of only 20% calories from fat or lower is the most healthful for our immune systems and most likely to be protective against heart disease, stroke, cancer (particularly breast, prostate, and colon), and other degenerative diseases.

Eating no animal products is the first and most important step in a protective diet, in my opinion, but you can very easily eat an otherwise very healthful vegan diet that is quite high in fat. When I first became a vegan, I actually gained weight because I was using a lot of oil, olives, avocados, nuts, and nut milks. It was only when I learned to cook with almost no fats, and to use more soyfoods, legumes, and fat-free vegetables and grains that my weight stabilized. I'm glad that I spent several years cooking with almost no added fats, because it changed my family's taste and tolerance for fats and broke me of the habit of automatically cooking with random amounts of oil.

In my Italian and other Mediterranean cooking, I use olive oil a little more freely, but I am careful to balance this out with low-fat foods. We even occasionally have a fried antipasto dish, but we are so unaccustomed to it now that we can only eat a small portion. With regular exercise, I actually lost weight while testing recipes for this book.

As a result, I still advocate a low-fat diet, with a few high-fat foods, such as olives, olive oil, nuts and seeds, nut milks, etc., used judiciously for flavor and added richness. Sometimes I cook a dish with no added oil and then just drizzle a little good olive oil on top, so that we can really taste it. This way we keep our fat level at about 20% of total calories without complicated figuring. If you have a health problem that indicates that your fat level should go lower, to 15% or 10%, you can use less olive oil and other fats (for instance, "steam-frying" onions, etc., as described on page 40, with no added oil).

Olive oil, of course, is an important ingredient in Italian cuisine, not just a cooking fat. Definitely stick with extra-virgin olive oil, which is from the first pressing;"pure" olive oil is actually a mixture of very refined and virgin oils. Taste many brands from various countries, and see which you prefer. You will probably have several favorites, with different qualities. Some olive oils are very light in both color and body, as well as flavor; others are very green, quite heavy, and/or very olivey-tasting. I like a very fruity, green olive oil, and I like some of the Greek olive oils. If you like a particularly expensive, but tasty, brand, you might want to keep that exclusively for using raw on salads and as a topping on foods. A "peppery" taste is often praised, but don't confuse that with a burning sensation in the back of the mouth, which indicates rancidity!

You can do an olive oil tasting with some friends, perhaps each supplying a different brand. Taste the oils "straight," just eating a little plain bread or a slice of apple in between. According to the experts, a fine olive oil will be tasted on the palate, and a bad one will be tasted in the throat, with a nasty aftertaste and a fatty feeling in the mouth.

A good supermarket brand is Filippo Berio extra-virgin (*not* the "extra light"—"light" olive oil just means light in flavor, not fat!). Aprilia, De Cecco, and Costa d'Oro are also good, fairly inexpensive brands.

If you like, you can also perform an interesting test on your olive oil by pouring a little bit into a bowl and refrigerating it for a few days. If it forms "crystals," it's probably extra-virgin cold-pressed; if it becomes like butter, it's probably "pit oil"; if it turns into a block, it's most likely industrial, chemically refined oil.

In general, olive oil should be kept in an opaque bottle, tightly capped, in a dark place, away from heat. It is not recommended that it be refrigerated. *Don't* keep it on your stove!

Olive oil is probably the best all-around cooking oil to use, not only for its taste, but because it is very stable at high temperatures and therefore not as prone to oxidation and the promotion of those pesky free radicals that can apparently cause us so many health problems. I even use it instead of ghee (clarified butter) in Indian cooking or lard in Mexican cooking. However, since most North Americans (myself included) don't do enough hard labor or other exercise to work off the calories provided by liberal use of olive oil, I am quite conservative in its use.

As for other cooking fats, canola and peanut oil are two neutral-tasting oils that are also largely monounsaturated (canola is 62% and peanut 49% monounsaturated), and therefore reasonably safe at high temperatures. Sesame and nut oils are also good to use as flavorings in small amounts. According to David Steinman (author of *The Safe Shopper's Bible* and *Diet for a Poisoned Planet*), these oils (and olive oil) contain virtually no pesticide residues. Nevertheless, if you can afford them, you should try to buy organic oils bottled by such reputable companies as Omega Nutrition and Flora. According to my research, these two brands are the only ones at this time that are actually pesticide-free.

I use good tasting, additive-free, soft dairy-free margarine where a butter-like taste is absolutely essential. It's true that margarine is not an ideal fat, but I refuse to get hysterical over the very small amount that I use.

You will probably obtain most of the essential fatty acids you need—omega 3s and omega 6s—from a low-fat vegetarian diet high in leafy green vegetables, grains, soyfoods, and other legumes and seeds. However, you might wish to sprinkle 1 or 2 tablespoons of freshly ground flaxseed on your breakfast cereal, just to be sure. Flax seeds are the richest vegetarian source of omega 3s, and full-fat soy products and sesame seeds are the richest vegetarian sources of omega 6s. Seeds should be ground to be properly assimilated, and you should drink plenty of water when you eat flaxseed. Soybean oil is not recommended since it usually contains dieldrin residues (according to Steinman) and is high in polyunsaturates, and therefore prone to oxidation, especially at high temperatures.

Tomatoes and Tomato Products

"Pomodori" translates as "golden apples," and, indeed, some old-style tomatoes were bright yellow in color. The favorite Italian tomato is the plum-type or San Marzano. Only use fresh tomatoes when they are bright red, ripe, and above all, tasty. There is no advantage to cooking with pale, tasteless, "fresh" tomatoes—it's a contradiction in terms! You are better off with good-quality canned tomatoes. Some people prefer only tomatoes canned in Italy, but there are some excellent domestic brands of plum tomatoes and diced tomatoes in juice, which are very convenient. Experiment with different brands in your area to see which you prefer. (There are a couple of very good organic brands of canned tomatoes, tomato pulp, and tomato paste on the market, but they are expensive.)

I almost never use canned tomato sauce. I prefer to purée canned or fresh tomatoes in a mouli (hand-crank food mill) or food processor and cook it down (with a little tomato paste, if the flavor is lacking). (See the Pizza Sauce recipe, p. 203, for example.) However, if you can or freeze your own sauce, by all means use it.

Tomato paste (estratto, conserva, or concentrato di pomodoro) can be a controversial ingredient—some cooks claim they would never use it. However, a couple of tablespoons of good tomato paste can rescue a so-so tomato sauce or add a lift to a soup. In North America, it comes in little cans, and it can be thick, rich, and delicious or thin and not very tasty. Again, you'll have to try different brands to see which you prefer. Italian tomato paste comes in tubes, and although it's expensive, it's more concentrated and flavorful than the domestic type, so you can use less. It's also easier to store this way after it's opened.

Homemade Purée of Sun-Dried Tomatoes: You can buy a delicious purée of sun-dried tomatoes (which are called "pomodori secchi" in Italian) to use in place of tomato paste. However, it's easy to make your own. Use rinsed sun-dried tomatoes in oil, or soak any amount of dried tomatoes you wish in boiling water or vegetarian broth to cover about 30 minutes, or until soft and pliable; drain well. To quick-soak, simmer them for 10 minutes. Drain them and discard any tough membrane, seeds, or peel. Chop them in a mini-processor or food processor, then add an equal amount of good-quality commercial tomato paste and a dribble of extra-virgin olive oil. Blend until thick and smooth. Place in a small container, cover the top with olive oil, seal, and keep refrigerated.

Browning Tomato Paste: While we're on the subject of tomato paste, try browning it to get deeper flavor and color. When you have sautéed the garlic and onions in a recipe in a little olive oil, add the tomato paste that the recipe calls for, and stir it over medium heat until the tomato paste darkens—this takes about 10 minutes. Then add the remaining ingredients, and carry on with the recipe.

Note: To soften dried tomatoes, soak them in boiling water or vegetarian broth to cover about 30 minutes, or until soft and pliable; drain well. *To quick-soak dried tomatoes,* simmer them for 10 minutes.

To peel or not to peel tomatoes; to seed or not to seed: Most modern recipe books tell you to peel tomatoes by plunging them into boiling water for a minute, then peeling the skins off. (The skins will also come off raw tomatoes easily when the tomatoes have been frozen first.) This practice is rarely mentioned in old cookbooks. I don't think it's necessary to peel tomatoes unless the skin is extraordinarily thick or you want a very velvety-smooth sauce.

I don't seed tomatoes either, and I think it's one of those unnecessary steps that everybody does but doesn't know why. The only reason for seeding, in my opinion, is if the tomatoes are very acidic.

I like the idea of retaining the seeds and skin of the tomatoes for fiber and nutrition, so I often add the pulverized skin and seeds back to the pot after running the tomatoes through the food mill (mouli).

Salt

Salt is a much-maligned, but essential, ingredient in cooking. Salt, used in moderate quantities, enhances and brings out flavors (even sweetness). It also affects the way foods smell and brightens colors. If you sniff two identical glasses of wine, but salt one, the one with salt will have a stronger aroma.

Salt is also an essential ingredient in breads, strengthening the gluten and regulating the growth of the yeast. Saltless bread can taste flat, look gray, and fall after rising.

Marcella Hazan refers to salt as a "magnet," drawing fragrance and flavor from food, and she writes, "To shrink from an adequate use of salt is to leave unmined the deep-lying flavors of food." (*Marcella's Italian Kitchen*, New York: Alfred A. Knopf, 1986).

Food essayist Robert Farrar Capon calls salt "the indispensable bass line over which all other tastes and smells form their harmonies."

Mimmetta Lo Monte, author of *La Bella Cucina* (New York: Beaufort Books, 1983), writes: "Food in Italy is well seasoned with salt, either added in the kitchen while cooking, or sprinkled on afterward and given time to sink in. Salt at the table is used sparingly.

"In the U.S. I have found that food gets to the table undersalted. . . Sprinkling it from a shaker will keep the taste of salt right on the surface; it will be the first taste to greet you and will overpower the other tastes of the dish."

This is an excellent point—I can't remember the number of times I have been served undersalted dishes and watched my fellow diners liberally sprinkle salt over their plates after the first taste, masking instead of enhancing the intended flavor of the dish. How much better if the cook had salted the dish properly in the first place!

It's easy to learn how to salt properly; taste the unsalted food first. Salt a little and taste again. You should not taste salt, but the underlying flavors in the dish should be enhanced and harmonized. If you actually taste the salt, you have overdone it. In soups and stews, cooking a potato in the mixture will draw out some of the salt.

What about the alleged harm to health by

including salt in the diet? Now some experts are telling us that we should eat more salt, especially if we are very active and likely to get dehydrated. As usual, moderation is the sensible answer.

Some studies say as much as 75% of the sodium in our diets comes from sodium compounds added to processed foods and the natural and added salts found in dairy products, *not* from moderately salted home-cooked foods.

Vegetarians eat less salt in general because they don't eat meat—carnivores ingest sodium from the blood and tissues of the animals they eat (and usually add salt on top). Dairy products also contain natural sodium, and quite a bit of salt is added to cheeses. And, according to Dr. Michael Klaper, vegans have a more favorable potassium/sodium balance, which is probably a major factor contributing to the low-to-normal blood pressure that most vegans enjoy.

Dr. Andrew Weil, in his book *Natural Health, Natural Medicine* (Boston: Houghton Mifflin Co., 1990), writes: "How harmful is salt? It is very harmful to some people and probably not harmful to most of us." He goes on to say that restricting sodium may not result in much improvement in conditions such as high blood pressure.

Other experts tell us that a low-fat, high-fiber diet can lower blood pressure by as much as 10%, even without restricting salt intake. Losing as little as 10 pounds often helps, as does eating more soy products and vitamin C.

If you follow a vegan diet, you'll have no problem doing away with the salt in processed foods and cheese. You won't be ingesting the natural sodium in meats and dairy products. You can use light (low-salt) soy sauce and restrict your intake of such salty foods, such as pretzels, chips, olives, sauerkraut, and salted nuts and seeds. This should allow you to moderately salt your homemade foods so that they are enhanced in flavor, aroma, and color. You can remove the salt shaker from your table and replace it with a pepper mill!

I use sea salt when cooking because it does not contain anti-caking chemicals, and I dry herbs with coarse salt.

Balsamic Vinegar

A few years ago very few North Americans had heard of balsamic vinegar—now it seems that half the items on any restaurant menu are prepared with it!

True balsamic vinegar is aged for many, many years in wooden casks. It is made only in Modena or Reggio nell'Emilia in the Emilia-Romagna region of northern Italy from cooked grapes (not from red wine) under strict government controls. True aged balsamic is rich, sweet, and syrupy, achieved by years of shifting to smaller and smaller casks, evaporating from one hundred liters to fifteen litres in twelve years! This is why the "real thing," aged between twenty and thirty years, costs so dearly and why the residents of Emilia-Romagna don't splash it all over everything in sight. They use red wine vinegar, in most cases, and save the balsamic for flavoring well-aged wine vinegar, for drinking (yes, indeed!—usually as a splash in a cocktail or other cold drink), or sprinkled over ripe, in-season strawberries.

Because of the phenomenal demand for balsamic vinegar, which cannot be met by the old way of producing it, the Italian government has sanctioned the sale of a cheaper balsamic vinegar known in Italy as "Industriale." It is a blend of high-quality wine vinegar, cooked-down grape must, young balsamic vinegar, and perhaps some caramel flavoring. It should be aged in casks with balsamic must in them. It does not have the complexity of a true, aged balsamic vinegar, but it is a pleasant, rich-tasting vinegar which should not taste raw and acidic.

You can tell a true balsamic by these things: the word "tradizionale" on the bottle; the bottle is never over 100cc, or 3.3 ounces; it must have the seal of the Consortium of Producers of the Traditional Balsamic Vinegar of Modena; it is extremely viscous—a dark brown syrupy liquid that coats the neck of the bottle when tilted; and that small bottle will cost you well over a hundred dollars!

"Industriale" is available in varying degrees of quality and price; as with olive oil, you'll have to taste and experiment. Usually you get what you pay for, but not always. Taste the vinegar from a spoon—if it burns your throat and makes you choke, try another. When you are satisfied with a particular brand, you may wish to enrich it as suggested by Lynn Rosetto Kasper, author and expert on the foods of Emilia-Romagna, by adding a generous pinch of brown sugar per tablespoon of good-quality "Industriale."

There is also a white balsamic "Industriale" on the market now, which is milder-tasting than the red and the color is less intrusive.

Herbs

It's a real asset to Italian cooking to have your own herb garden and to have a few pots of winter herbs indoors, but it's beyond the scope of this book to give you gardening advice. Most supermarkets carry at least a small selection of fresh herbs year-round. When you buy them, place them in a jar of water (just like a bouquet of flowers), and keep them on the kitchen counter (depending on how fast you use them up). Treat parsley and basil this way too.

When you use dried herbs, be sure that they are not old and stale. They should have a good color and aroma—if they don't, throw them out. Where you would use 1 tablespoon of fresh, chopped herb, use 1 teaspoon dried. Where you would add a fresh herb toward the end of the cooking time, add the dried herb at the beginning, so that it has time to rehydrate and exude its flavor.

It's preferable to use fresh or frozen basil and parsley whenever possible, but most other herbs for Italian cuisine (bay leaves, mint, oregano, thyme, sage, rosemary, and marjoram) can be used dried if they are of good quality.

A very old Italian way of preserving herbs is to salt-dry them. Place a layer of coarse salt in a gallon jar and lay clean, fresh herbs on top. Add another layer of salt and continue, ending with salt. The herbs stay quite flexible this way, with good color and aroma. I particularly like to preserve sage this way.

Fresh garlic, thyme, and rosemary can be preserved in jars of oil in the refrigerator. Most herbs can also be successfully frozen in plastic bags (chop parsley first), or hung in bunches in brown paper bags to dry.

Basil takes some special consideration, because it can easily turn black and very unappetizing. It can be frozen in whole leaves in a plastic container to be used in soups, stews, etc., where color doesn't matter. To keep the color when freezing, the leaves should be plunged first into boiling water, dried, and then rolled up on sheets of waxed paper placed inside of plastic bags, or dipped in cooking oil and treated the same way. Another way to freeze basil is as a basil paste (see page 30).

Equipment

We tend to have fantasies about the way Italians cook, but Italian housewives no longer stay in the kitchen all day—most of them work outside the home! They purchase prepared salads and antipasti, use good-quality bouillon cubes and canned tomatoes, pressure cookers, and even instant polenta. They no longer have long, five-course midday dinners, except perhaps on weekends. But they still insist on the freshest, in-season produce, fine olive oil and pasta, and freshly baked bread. We can do the same, using modern appliances to our advantage to produce wonderful food, despite our crowded lives.

That is not to say that we shouldn't slow down whenever we can and prepare things in the slow, old-fashioned way, if that is what we enjoy. Some people garden to reduce stress—I make ravioli. But not everyone is going to agree with me that making ravioli is relaxing. It's smart to only add cooking chores that are enjoyable and manageable. If that means using a microwave oven for the things that it really does well to cut down on preparation and cooking time, then do so. Ditto for food processors, pressure cookers, bread kneaders, etc. The object is to have the best-tasting, best-quality food possible with the money, time, and materials at your disposal, and to *not* resort to fast foods and frozen dinners on a regular basis! You can put love and thought into the food you serve, whichever way you choose to you chop it or cook it.

That said, I give you as many options within a recipe as I can so if you feel like stirring, you can stir—if not, you can use a microwave or pressure cooker. If you feel like chopping by hand, go ahead—otherwise, use your food processor. If a low-tech implement will work better or just as well as a high-tech one, I'll tell you so. A rotary food mill, for instance, is better than a blender for many recipes, because it does not totally purée the foods or cause them to foam up, and it strains out seeds and peels at the same time.

Other than the rotary food mill or mouli mentioned above, you probably have everything you need if you have a reasonably well-equipped kitchen (with sharp knives!). Sure, it's great if you have Italian ceramic casseroles, a mezzaluna (half-moon shaped knife with a handle on each end, used for chopping), a big mortar and pestle, and various types of ravioli cutters, but these really aren't necessary.

A hand-cranked pasta machine is a big help if you intend to make your own pasta or ravioli on a regular basis. Don't bother with fancy, expensive electric machines, especially the extruder type. Extruded pasta is best left to the manufacturers of commercial pasta; the homemade kind is usually inferior. If you don't want to invest in ravioli molds or rollers, you can simply use a fluted pastry wheel or inexpensive ravioli stamps (round or square).

If you intend to make Italian breads, you might consider investing in a baking stone, but this is only big enough for one loaf and quite expensive. I get chipped, unglazed ceramic tiles for pennies and line my oven rack with them. Or, invest in the very heavy, blue steel baking pans from restaurant supply houses—these can be used for pizza and bread.

For bread, I really love my Bosch 4-in-1 heavy-duty kitchen machine for kneading those sticky Italian doughs. But you can do smaller quantities by hand, in an automatic bread machine, a good food processor, or a smaller all-purpose kitchen machine.

For vegetarian cooking, I think a blender and a food processor are essential because you will be doing so much puréeing. A food processor is also handy for chopping large quantities of onions and other vegetables.

A hand or immersion blender is not a necessity, but I have recently acquired one and find it wonderful for small blending tasks. I can do it right in the mixing container and then just rinse off the "wand" of the blender—no extra containers to wash. I also like to have a mini-chopper for mincing quantities of garlic or fresh herbs and an electric coffee/spice mill for grinding spices and seeds. (None of these items need to be the expensive type.) And don't forget a nutmeg grater.

A good kitchen scale is a necessity, in my opinion, especially for converting and adapting recipes.

Tupperware has a great little gadget called a Quick Shake, in two sizes, that quickly mixes batters, salad dressings, etc. with a few shakes of your hand—quiet, low-tech, and efficient!

A pressure cooker is another handy piece of equipment, much used by Italian home cooks. You can cook beans, broth, stews, vegetables, polenta, and other dishes quickly. The new designs are safe, attractive, and made from stainless steel with thick, stick-resistant bottoms. I just purchased a new Lagostina pressure cooker and, to my delight, it makes wonderful risotto in 8 minutes!

Make sure that you have a large stockpot for cooking pasta, one that holds at least 8 quarts (or two 4-quart ones). If it has a heavy bottom, it can also be used for large quantities of soup.

Other pots and pans can be made from a variety of materials, but I think you should have at least one 10-inch cast-iron skillet and one good-quality 10- or 12-inch nonstick skillet. I have a 14-inch cast-iron skillet and two 10-inch ones; 12-inch, 10-inch, and 6-inch nonstick skillets; and a 10-inch stainless steel skillet with an aluminum bottom, which is great for shallow-frying.

A microwave oven is *not* a necessity and is not used much in Italy. But wait until the Italians try microwave risotto, pioneered by *Gourmet* food columnist and cookbook writer Barbara Kafka! It is also wonderful for making polenta (without stirring—and so much better than the instant or pre-cooked variety!), and it is also good for sauces, puddings, and pastry cream.

One piece of inexpensive equipment that I highly recommend is one of the new pump oil sprayers. You put your oil in the container (even olive oil) and work the pump up and down until it is firm. It sprays a very fine mist of oil, just like the commercial pan sprays, but with no propellant, no bad smell, and you can use the finest-quality oil. Best of all, no cans to throw out! I recommend having two—one for olive oil and one for your favorite neutral-tasting cooking oil.

Last, but not least, you *must* have a good pepper mill, or two (one for black pepper and one for white). If you don't believe that freshly ground pepper tastes better, do your own taste test. It is even possible to buy peppercorns that have not been irradiated. (Most spices and many dried herbs are irradiated in their country of origin.)

Here are some recipes and techniques that you will be using throughout the book. Most of them can be made up once a week or so, if you use them regularly.

I have provided as many soy-free recipes as possible in this section, so that people with soy allergies are not so limited in their choice of recipes. Most of them take a little more effort to make than the ones that use soy products, but that's a small price to pay if you have been trying to live a dairy-free lifestyle without soy for any length of time!

I also wanted to provide cooks the choice of making their own dairy substitutes if they don't like, can't afford, or can't obtain the commercial types.

Meat substitute recipes are provided on pages 169-92.

Two Italian terms you should know are *battuto* and *soffritto*.

A battuto is a mixture of fat with minced onion and/or garlic, sometimes with celery, herbs, parsley, carrots, etc. A battuto is sometimes added to dishes raw *(a crudo)*, but it is usually sautéed gently in a little olive oil. This sautéing transforms it into a soffritto, an important component of many Italian dishes.

III
Basic Recipes and Techniques
FONDAMENTALI

"Young women of rank [in Italy] actually eat—you will never guess what—GARLICK. Our poor friend Lord Byron is quite corrupted by living among these people."
—Percy Bysshe Shelley, letter to a friend, 1818

Homemade Low-Fat Mayonnaise
MAIONESE WITH AGLIATA VARIATION
(can be soy-free)

Yield: about 2 cups

¾ teaspoon agar powder, or 1½ tablespoons agar flakes

½ cup plus 2 tablespoons cold water

3 tablespoons cornstarch or wheat starch, or 4½ tablespoons white rice flour (other starches don't work well)

1 cup soymilk or other nondairy milk

2 tablespoons apple cider vinegar, white wine vinegar, or lemon juice

1½ teaspoons salt

¾ teaspoon dry mustard

A few grindings of white pepper

¼ cup extra-virgin olive oil (no substitutes)

Soak the agar and water together for a few minutes. In a small

Here is the perfect alternative to fat-laden egg mayonnaise, as well as commercial low-fat and fat-free versions. This delicious recipe contains a small amount of olive oil, but the recipe contains only about 1 g fat per tablespoon, in comparison with "light" mayonnaise, which contains 5 g per tablespoon, and real mayo, which contains about 11 g per tablespoon. The extra-virgin olive oil is so flavorful that this small amount still flavors the mayonnaise beautifully.

Garlic Mayonnaise (*Agliata or Ligurian Aioli*)

To make a delicious garlic dip for cold, steamed vegetables and artichokes, omit the dry mustard from the Homemade Low-Fat Mayonnaise, use lemon juice instead of vinegar, and add 4 peeled cloves of garlic while blending.

You can also add 2 tablespoons fresh herbs of choice, or 2 tablespoons capers with 1 tablespoon of tarragon.

Basil Agliata

To the basic Agliata, add 4 cups loosely packed fresh basil leaves, or use only 2 tablespoons of oil in the Agliata, and add ¾ cup Basil Paste for Freezing, p. 30.

Sun-dried Tomato Agliata

To the basic Agliata, add about 16 dried tomatoes which have been soaked in hot water until soft and then squeezed dry and chopped. Or use sun-dried tomatoes packed in oil, rinse as much of the oil off as you can, then chop them.

saucepan, stir together the cornstarch or rice flour and dissolved agar over high heat until thick and translucent.

Microwave Option: Place the above ingredients in a bowl, soak them for a few minutes, then microwave on high for 30 seconds. Whisk and repeat three times, or until very thick and translucent—not white.

Place the cornstarch mixture and all the other ingredients, except the oil, in a blender or food processor, and combine well. Slowly add the oil through the top while the machine is running. Blend until the mixture is very white, frothy, and emulsified and you can't see any oil globules. Pour into a clean jar, cover, and refrigerate. This keeps several weeks.

Allergy Note: You can make this mayonnaise with *any* nondairy milk.

Per tablespoon: Calories: 21, Protein: 0 g, Carbohydrate: 1 g, Fat: 1 g

Basil Paste for Freezing
(soy-free)

Yield: 1½ cups

This is an easy way to prepare large quantities of basil for freezing, and it keeps the bright green color. You can make pesto with this paste (page 51). I prefer doing this to making large quantities of pesto for freezing, because the flavors are better preserved.

8 cups loosely packed fresh basil leaves
¼ cup extra-virgin olive oil
2 tablespoons lemon juice

In a food processor, blend the ingredients to a paste.

To Store: Method #1—Pack into containers that will hold the quantity of paste you will use most often, or freeze in ice cube trays (placed inside plastic bags). After freezing, pop the cubes out into storage bags. One cube contains about 2 tablespoons paste, so each cube is equal to about ⅔ cup of loosely packed fresh basil leaves.

Method #2—Spread the paste out thinly on sheets of waxed paper or heavy plastic wrap, and then roll them up like jelly rolls. Pop the rolls into plastic bags, and freeze them. Then you can unroll just a little at a time and break off small quantities to use in recipes that call for fresh basil. One teaspoon of paste equals about 2 tablespoons chopped, fresh basil.

Per tablespoon: Calories: 23, Protein: 1 g, Carbohydrate: 1 g, Fat: 2 g

Bread Crumbs
PANGRATTATO O MOLLICA

For fresh bread crumbs, save any unused ends, crusts, and uneaten pieces of plain bread. (Just toss them in a bag in the freezer if you have no time to deal with them immediately.) Grind the bread to crumbs in a food processor, then store in a bag or plastic container in the freezer.

To toast bread crumbs ("mollica arrostiti"), cook about 1 cup of bread crumbs at a time in a dry heavy skillet over medium heat, stirring often and watching constantly, until they are golden. Cool thoroughly and store in a covered container. You can also brown them in 2 tablespoons extra-virgin olive oil with a whole clove of peeled garlic. Discard the garlic after browning the crumbs.

For dried bread crumbs ("mollica secchi"), save the bread in a paper bag, letting it get stale until hard and dry. Grind as above. When it is very dry, it will keep indefinitely in a dry, covered container.

Cooked Rice for Blended Mixtures

Yield: about 1 cup

This is used to thicken some of the soy-free cremes in this chapter and in some of the desserts.

½ cup short grain white rice

1 cup water

Mix the rice and water in a small pot with a tight lid, and bring to a boil. Cover and turn down to low. Cook 20 minutes.

Italians never waste bread. (That would be a sacrilege.) So bread crumbs have become an essential ingredient in their cuisine. Italian cooks have created many tasty ways of using stale bread: in salads (see Panzanella, p. 61); stuffing vegetables; breading vegetables, cutlets, and croquettes; thickening soups and sauces; sprinkled on casserole dishes to keep food from sticking; added to vegetable patties and dumplings; scattered on top of gratins and other casseroles; and even in pasta dishes to replace grated cheese, especially in southern Italy.

For extra fiber in your diet, use a whole grain Italian-style bread and/or add some wheat bran to the crumbs.

"Cheesey" Bread Crumbs

These are excellent for breading oven-fried vegetables. Mix 1 pound fine fresh bread crumbs with ¾ cup Soymage Parmesan substitute, or soy-free alternative, p. 37, 1½ teaspoons salt, and ½ teaspoon freshly ground pepper. Keep frozen.

Cheese Substitutes for Italian Recipes

Seasoned Bread Crumbs

Add to the "Cheesey" Bread Crumbs 2 tablespoons dried parsley, 1½ tablespoons dried oregano, ½ tablespoon dried basil, and ¼ teaspoon garlic granules.

As I mentioned on page 17, there are not many satisfactory vegan substitutes for Italian cheeses that would please the Italian palate, particularly the melted types. I use Dairy-Free Bechamel or White Sauce, p. 46, in lasagne and other recipes where a creamy texture and flavor is needed.

I do like the Soymage vegan Parmesan substitute, which can be purchased quite cheaply in bulk (see page 250 for address). If you prefer, you can simply use Seasoned Breadcrumbs, at left, ground, lightly toasted nuts, a drizzle of good extra-virgin olive oil, or a combination of any of these as a topping. In some recipes where you need a stronger flavor and you can't use the Soymage product due to a soy allergy, use Cashew Sprinkle, p. 37, a tasty combination of ground cashews and nutritional yeast with a tiny bit of miso.

The following recipes for alternatives to soft Italian cheeses, ricotta, and mascarpone, are essential to many recipes in the book. I think you'll find them delicious and use them often. I have provided both soy-based and nut-based versions.

Tofu Ricotta

RICOTTA DI SOYA

Yield: about 3½ cups

2 (12.3-ounce) boxes extra-firm *silken* tofu, crumbled
½ cup plus 2 tablespoons raw cashew pieces, finely ground in a
    coffee/spice mill or mini-chopper
2 tablespoons plus 1 teaspoon fresh lemon juice
½ teaspoon salt

This mixture is very similar to the creamy full-fat ricotta used in Italy, which bears little resemblance to the watery, grainy ricotta available to most North Americans. It's so creamy that you can use it as a spread on bread, as a filling for crepes (*crespelle*), p. 105, or even in desserts.

In a food processor, combine about 3 cups of the crumbled tofu, the ground cashews, lemon juice, and salt until they are *very* smooth. Then crumble in the remaining tofu and process again. The resulting mixture should be mostly smooth, but with a little graininess—it doesn't have to be like cream cheese.

Scoop the "ricotta" into a plastic container, and refrigerate. It firms up when chilled.

Per ¼ cup: Calories: 40, Protein: 1 g, Carbohydrate: 2 g, Fat: 4 g

Tofu Mascarpone
MASCARPONE DI SOYA
Yield: about 2 cups

Mascarpone is a very rich triple cream cheese, mild and a bit more yellow than cream. It is often used as a substitute for whipped cream on Italian desserts. In North America, ordinary cream cheese is often substituted. If you can obtain it, Tofutti's Better Than Cream Cheese also makes a good substitute. Otherwise, try this easy version.

1 (12.3-ounce) box extra-firm *silken* tofu
½ cup plus 2 tablespoons raw cashew pieces, finely ground in a coffee/spice mill or mini-chopper
6 teaspoons fresh lemon juice
Pinch of salt

Combine all of the ingredients in a food processor at high speed for several minutes. Be patient—it has to be *very* smooth. You may have to stop the machine a couple of times to scrape the sides and push the ingredients that have accumulated under the blade or at the bottom towards the middle. When the mixture is as smooth as possible, scoop it into a container, cover, and refrigerate. It will firm up considerably.

Per tablespoon: Calories: 24, Protein: 1 g, Carbohydrate: 1 g, Fat: 2 g

thi
las
dish
fresh
firm   .at if
desire   with 6 table-
spoons soymilk, nut milk, or rice milk, and ½ tea-spoon salt. This makes 2 generous cups.

Seasoned Flour
Use this simple recipe for dredging slices of marinated tofu, seitan, textured soy protein chunks, vegetables, etc.

Mix together 2 cups whole wheat or other whole grain flour, ¼ cup nutritional yeast flakes, 1 teaspoon salt, and freshly ground pepper to taste. Store in a tightly covered container in the refrigerator.

Don't substitute white flour for the whole grain unless you absolutely have nothing else in the house. Not only is whole wheat flour nutritionally superior to white, it tastes much better in this recipe. If you are allergic to wheat, you can use brown rice, spelt, teff, or kamut flours, or use fine crumbs made from a natural crispy brown rice cereal, or even fine cornmeal. Makes 2½ cups.

Tofu Ricotta Salata

RICOTTA SALATA DI SOYA

Yield: about 1½ cups

Ricotta salata is a pressed and lightly salted sheep's milk cheese that is something like feta cheese, but not as salty. It is often grated into pastas. This quick and easy recipe for a nondairy version is excellent for use in salads and pasta dishes, and it even melts! It's also a delicious addition to an antipasto plate. You can use reduced-fat tofu, if you prefer.

Note: The oil that the finished "cheese" is stored in can be rinsed off before serving, and it can be used again for storing the "cheese," if you carefully pour off the clear oil on top, and discard the oil on the bottom that contains any residue.

1¼ cups (6 ounces) crumbled firm tofu
2 tablespoons water
1 tablespoon light-flavored cooking oil
1 teaspoon agar powder, or 2 tablespoons agar flakes
1 teaspoon salt
½ teaspoon unbleached sugar
3 tablespoons lemon juice
½ tablespoon light miso

Combine the tofu, water, oil, agar, salt, and sugar in a food processor until the mixture is as smooth as possible. Scrape this mixture into a small saucepan, and stir over medium-high heat until the liquid starts boiling. Turn down and simmer for about 3 minutes, stirring frequently.

Microwave Option: Scrape the mixture into a medium-size, microwave-safe bowl, and microwave on high for 2 minutes. Whisk, then cook on high for 1 minute more.

Whisk in the lemon juice and miso. (Do not add the lemon juice to the mixture while it cooks, or the acid will interfere with the jelling of the agar.) Scrape the mixture into a square, rigid plastic container with a lid, and refrigerate until it is cool and firm, at least one hour.

Cut the firm "cheese" into whatever size slices you find convenient. To store for more than a few days, place the slices in a wide-mouth jar, and cover with a light-flavored cooking oil, such as canola. (Don't use olive oil because it hardens up when chilled.) Rinse the oil off before use. If you like, you can add bay leaves, Italian olives, dried red peppers, sprigs of thyme, rosemary, and other herbs, etc., to make an attractive presentation. Keep refrigerated. It will keep about 1 month.

Per 2 tablespoons: Calories: 12, Protein: 0 g, Carbohydrate: 0 g, Fat: 0 g

Almond Ricotta

RICOTTA DI MANDORLE

(soy-free)

Yield: about 2½ cups

1 cup hot water
½ cup whole blanched almonds
1 cup cold water
4 teaspoons fresh lemon juice
4 tablespoons cornstarch or wheat starch, or 6 tablespoons white
   rice flour
1 tablespoon light-flavored cooking oil
1 teaspoon maple syrup
½ teaspoon salt

Place the hot water and almonds in a blender, and combine until the mixture is very smooth and creamy—be patient. It cannot be grainy. Add the rest of the ingredients, and blend again well.

Pour the mixture into a medium, heavy-bottomed saucepan, and stir constantly over medium-high heat until it thickens and comes to a boil. Turn the heat down to medium, and cook 1 minute more, stirring constantly.

Microwave Option: Pour the mixture into a large, microwave-safe bowl or beaker. Microwave 2 minutes on high. Whisk and microwave 1 to 2 minutes more, or until thickened.

Scrape the mixture into a container, and let it come to room temperature. Beat it with a whisk or electric mixer, cover, and chill. When it is chilled and firm, mash and stir it with a fork until it has some texture. Refrigerate.

Per ¼ cup: Calories: 70, Protein: 1 g, Carbohydrate: 5 g, Fat: 4 g

This is a tasty, vegan ricotta; the almond milk has a clean, mild flavor. The inspiration for this recipe was the Incredible Almond Creme Cheeze in *Vegan Vittles* by Joanne Stepaniak.

Making Broth from and Reconstituting Dried Boletus or Porcini Mushrooms

As I've mentioned before, dried porcini mushrooms (cepes, in French) are prized by Italians. Even though they are very expensive in North America, it's best to get the Italian ones (which are light brown to cream in color) for use in cream sauces and where they are a primary ingredient. The less expensive South American boletus are also useful and make a very tasty broth. They are darker in color than the Italian mushrooms, but brown rather than black, and they should still be flexible and not woody, crumbled, dusty, or desiccated chips.

If you absolutely can't find dried porcini or boletus mushrooms, use the milder flavored dried shiitake mushrooms.

Soak each ounce of the dried mushrooms for about half an hour in about 1 cup of warm water. Fish out the mushrooms, rinsing if they are sandy, squeeze dry, chop, and add to your recipe. Strain the broth through a coffee filter and save for flavoring soups, sauces, meat substitutes, etc.

Quick-Soaking Dried Mushrooms

You can quick-soak dried mushrooms if you can't wait 30 minutes by covering them with hot water and simmering them on the stove for 10 minutes or in the microwave for 5 minutes (covered, in a bowl large enough so that the liquid doesn't boil over).

Soy-Free Almond Ricotta Salata
RICOTTA SALATA DI MANDORLE

Yield: about 2½ cups

This feta-like variation on the soy-free ricotta recipe can be sliced or crumbled to use in salads, antipasto plates, or on pasta.

Make the Almond Ricotta, p. 35, using ¼ cup lemon juice, 2 teaspoons of salt, and adding ¾ teaspoon agar powder or 4½ teaspoons agar flakes. Add the lemon juice after cooking the mixture. Pour the blended mixture into a flat container, cover, and let chill until firm.

If you wish, store in oil as instructed in the Tofu Ricotta Salata recipe on page 34.

Per 2 tablespoons: Calories: 38, Protein: 1 g, Carbohydrate: 4 g, Fat: 3 g

Cashew Mascarpone
MASCARPONE DI ANACARDI
(soy-free)

Yield: 1 cup

Cashews are used in this recipe, which is very similar to the Almond Ricotta but much richer. They provide a sweet, buttery flavor.

1 cup plain commercial rice milk

¼ cup raw cashews

4 teaspoons fresh lemon juice

2 tablespoons cornstarch or wheat starch, or 3 tablespoons white rice flour

2 tablespoons light-flavored cooking oil

¼ teaspoon salt

Place the rice milk and cashews in a blender, and combine until *very* smooth—there should be no graininess at all. Add the remaining ingredients and blend well.

Pour into a small, heavy-bottomed saucepan, and stir constantly over medium-high heat until it thickens and boils. Lower the heat to medium, and cook for 1 minute, stirring constantly.

Microwave Option: Pour the mixture into a medium, microwave-safe bowl or beaker, and microwave for 2 minutes. Whisk well.

Scrape the mixture into a container, and let cool to room temperature. Whisk or beat with an electric beater until smooth, then cover and refrigerate. Before using, beat it again with a whisk or electric beater. If it's too thick, thin it with a little rice milk or nut milk. Refrigerate.

Per tablespoon: Calories: 41, Protein: 0 g, Carbohydrate: 4 g, Fat: 3 g

Cashew Sprinkle
SOY-FREE PARMESAN ALTERNATIVE
Yield: about 1 cup

⅔ cup raw cashews
⅓ cup nutritional yeast flakes
Optional: 1 teaspoon calcium carbonate powder
1 teaspoon light miso (chick-pea miso for soy-free version)
¼ teaspoon salt

If you have a soy allergy, this is an easy and tasty alternative to the Soymage Parmesan substitute. Use it either as a topping or as an ingredient in certain recipes.

Use a food processor, mini-chopper, or spice mill for this recipe, rather than a blender, so that the cashews won't be blended into butter.

Process the ingredients until as fine as possible. Stir to get rid of any lumps. Place in a covered container or shaker, and keep refrigerated.

Per tablespoon: Calories: 42, Protein: 2 g, Carbohydrate: 3 g, Fat: 4 g

Vegan Butter and Cream Substitutes

As I mentioned on page 17, I like to use Canoleo margarine wherever olive oil or other oils aren't appropriate. It contains more liquid oil than hydrogenated margarine, no preservatives or colors, is 100% nondairy, and has a wonderful flavor and texture. (It does contain some soy protein and lecithin.)

There are other brands of nondairy margarine in different parts of the U.S. and Canada which I have not been able to sample—some of these may be excellent too. Just make sure that you use a margarine that really tastes good by itself. I don't use it a lot in my recipes, but when I do, it's because I want a "buttery" flavor, not just tasteless grease.

If you still prefer not to use margarine, try using Spectrum Naturals Spread which is like a soft margarine but has no hydrogenated oil. Very expensive, but tasty, nut oils, such as walnut, hazelnut, and almond, can also be used judiciously in place of butter.

For savory dishes, you can try the delicious Roasted Garlic-Olive Oil "Butter," below, which, amazingly, does not taste garlicky, but rather "buttery." It is a great spread and can also be used in pasta dishes that call for butter.

To cut down on the fat in pasta dishes, I often use some olive oil and/or margarine and substitute Jelled Broth, p. 118, for the rest of the fat. This gives delicious flavor, gloss, and substance to a low-fat vegetable sauce.

I also offer you two excellent recipes for vegan "creams" for cooking—one made with cashews or almonds and another with soy. You can substitute either of these equally for dairy cream.

Italians don't use butter on their bread, as a general rule, but most North Americans like some sort of spread on bread or toast. And you may like an alternative to the butter used in some pasta sauces, as well.

This simple invention is a delicious one. Because roasting mellows the garlic considerably, this "butter" doesn't even taste garlicky. The smooth, buttery, roasted garlic melds with the olive oil and hardens just enough in the refrigerator to spread with a knife. It's great on Bruschetta, p. 53.

Roasted Garlic-Olive Oil "Butter"

(soy-free)

Yield: a generous ½ cup

1 whole head roasted garlic, p. 72
½ cup extra-virgin olive oil
Pinch of salt

Squeeze all of the garlic out of the peels into your blender, mini-processor, or hand blender, and add the olive oil and salt. Blend until creamy. Pour into a small, covered container, and refrigerate until it firms to a spreadable consistency. (This might take 2 days or so.) All of the garlic will go to the bottom, so when it is firm, stir the mixture until it is homogenous, then smooth the top and keep refrigerated.

If you like, add fresh herbs to the mixture.

Per tablespoon: Calories: 124, Protein: 0 g, Carbohydrate: 1 g, Fat: 13 g

Homemade Reduced-Fat Margarine

(Can be soy-free, depending on the margarine used)

Yield: 1¼ cups

¼ cup plus 1 tablespoon water

¼ cup plus 1 tablespoon soymilk or rice milk

½ teaspoon agar powder, or 1 tablespoon agar flakes

½ cup plus 2 tablespoons very cold good-tasting dairy-free
   margarine

¼ teaspoon lemon juice

⅛ teaspoon salt, or to taste

Mix the water, milk, and agar together in a small saucepan. Let set for a few minutes, then bring it to a boil while stirring. Simmer for 2 or 3 minutes, then remove from the heat.

Microwave Option: After letting the mixture sit for a few minutes, microwave on high in a medium, microwave-safe beaker or bowl for 2 minutes.

Pour the hot mixture into a food processor or blender, and combine for 1 minute. When still warm but not yet becoming firm (this is important), add the cold margarine, lemon juice and salt, and process until very smooth. You can also pour the mixture into a mixing bowl and beat the margarine in with an electric mixer or hand blender. Scoop into a container, cover, and refrigerate for 1 to 2 hours until firm.

Per tablespoon: Calories: 52, Protein: 0 g, Carbohydrate: 0 g, Fat: 6 g

Most reduced-fat margarines have a disagreeable taste and mouth feel and many contain gelatin. This is delicious if you use a good-tasting margarine.

I have made this only with Canoleo dairy-free margarine, but if you have another favorite margarine, try it with this recipe. You can use reduced-fat soymilk, if you prefer.

Easy Tofu Creme for Cooking
CREMA DI SOYA FACILE PER CUCINA

When you need some "heavy cream" for adding to a recipe—say, as a binding in a ravioli filling, "creaming" a soup, or thickening a vegetable pasta sauce—make sure you have some nondairy milk and a box of extra-firm *silken* tofu on hand. (You can use rice milk, soymilk, almond milk, oat milk, or whatever kind you prefer, as well as reduced-fat tofu.) Just blend equal parts of the nondairy milk and silken tofu in a blender or food processor until it is very smooth. (You can even use a mini-processor or a hand blender for small amounts.) Add the mixture to your recipe. With this formula you don't have to make up a whole recipe ahead of time and, perhaps, have half of it hanging around in the fridge waiting to be used.

For instance, if you need ½ cup "cream" for your recipe, blend ¼ cup nondairy milk with ¼ cup extra-firm *silken* tofu.

Don't worry about seasoning the creme; you can add more seasoning to the food you are adding it to.

Steam-Frying

If you prefer to "sauté" without oil, try a method I call "steam-frying." Use a heavy skillet, either non-stick or lightly oiled by brushing on about ½ teaspoon oil with your finger tips or using an oil pump sprayer.

Heat the skillet over high heat, and add your vegetables for sautéing with 1 or 2 tablespoons of broth, wine, or water. Cook over high heat until the liquid evaporates, stirring often. Keep adding just enough liquid to prevent sticking, and cook until the vegetables are tender and beginning to brown. Don't add too much liquid or the mixture will stew rather than sauté.

If you want a well-browned or caramelized mixture, keep adding liquid after the natural sugar in the vegetables begins to brown on the bottom of the pan, scraping up the brown bits to mix in with the vegetables. Be careful not to burn or scorch the vegetables.

Easy Cashew or Rice Creme for Cooking
CREMA DI ANACARDI O RISO FACILE PER CUCINA
(soy-free)

If you are allergic to soy, this is a soy-free variation on the Easy Tofu Creme recipe on page 39. Use three parts nondairy milk other than soymilk (such as commercial reduced-fat rice or almond milk) and one part raw cashew pieces. For a very low-fat version, use one part well-cooked white short-grain rice (page 31) instead. (Middle-of-the-roaders can use ½ part rice and ½ part cashews!) Blend until *very* smooth, preferably in a blender. If you are doing just a small amount, use a small jar attachment on your blender.

For instance, if your recipe calls for ½ cup heavy cream, use 6 tablespoons rice or almond milk and 2 tablespoons cashew pieces or cooked rice (or 1 tablespoon of each).

If you need a rich milk, blend 2 to 3 tablespoons raw cashew pieces with 1 cup commercial reduced-fat rice milk or almond milk until smooth.

Note: One-quarter cup cashew pieces contains about 12 g fat, compared to ½ cup extra-firm lite silken tofu, which contains about 1 g of fat.

Salse is the general Italian term for sauces (singular-*salsa*), and a *salsa di pomodoro*, or tomato sauce, usually refers to a tomato sauce with flavorful additions, such as vegetables or wine.

"*Sughi*" (singular—*sugo*) are very simple tomato sauces with a few basic ingredients—olive oil, onions, garlic, salt, and pepper, perhaps carrots, celery, and/or basil. They can be used alone on pasta, pizza, fritatte, "meatballs," vegetables, fritters, croquettes, etc., or as components of other recipes. Both of these types of sauces are cooked in about 35 minutes or less.

Use very ripe, fresh plum tomatoes or good-quality canned tomatoes in purée or juice. (See page 23 for notes on canned tomatoes, and "To peel or not to peel tomatoes; to seed or not to seed" on page 24.) If you use canned tomatoes in juice and they lack depth of flavor, you can add 2 or 3 tablespoons of good-quality tomato paste to the sauce. *Don't* use "fresh" tomatoes that are pink and tasteless—good canned tomatoes make a much better sauce than pale winter tomatoes and are perfectly authentic. There are a couple of good organic brands available now. Don't add sugar or other sweeteners to these quick-cooking sauces, and don't use strong-flavored ingredients such as green peppers and oregano. Fresh basil is the herb most commonly used (added at the end of cooking) or possibly fresh sage or rosemary. Aside from canned tomatoes, use only fresh ingredients, and use good-quality extra-virgin olive oil. You can use a good-tasting nondairy margarine instead, if you wish.

As I explain in the recipes for Neapolitan and Bolognese *ragù* (meat-style sauces), southern and northern Italian ragù are very different from one another, but they have one thing in common—a much longer cooking time than the tomato sauces described before. They also generally contain wine (my husband's doesn't, however). It is perfectly acceptable to use dried herbs in ragù.

The long cooking time was originally used to tenderize cheap cuts of meat, but I use this same technique in the following three vegetarian ragù to achieve the rich quality and depth of flavor that you might think only a meat sauce could deliver. I know that, traditionally, vegetarian sauces are quick-cooked, but vegetarians sometimes long for a heavier, richer sauce as well.

At the end of the chapter you'll also find a recipe for a rich-tasting Dairy-Free Bechamel or White Sauce *(besciamella)*, which is used extensively in Italian cooking (and I often use instead of melted cheese in casseroles such as lasagne). There is a "butter" sauce lightened with

IV
Sauces
SALSE, SUGHI E RAGÙ

"The relationship between them [the Italians], their food, and their land has not yet been ruined by industrial revolution. They enjoy, appreciate and respect good food and they conserve with pride the regional differences in their cooking . . . "
—Elizabeth Romer
Italian Pizzas and Hearth Breads
(New York: Clarkson Potter, 1987)

Neapolitan-Style Tomato Sauce

To the Marinara Sauce, add 2 stalks celery. Toward the end of cooking, add a small handful of fresh basil leaves and maybe a handful of chopped Italian parsley and/or some chopped fresh sage leaves. If you like, you can add a pinch of red chile pepper flakes. Leave the sauce chunky.

Winter Tomato Sauce

Use the onion, carrot, and garlic, plus 2 stalks celery, chopped, and a handful of chopped Italian parsley. When this *soffritto* (cooked vegetable mixture) is soft, add ¾ cup of red wine, and let it evaporate while stirring over high heat. Use canned plum tomatoes—imported San Marzanos, if possible, or the best domestic brand you can find. Drain the tomatoes and add 1 cup of vegetarian broth. Simmer about 35 minutes. Add a few chopped, fresh basil leaves. You can use the sauce chunky or puréed.

Porcini Mushroom and Tomato Sauce

To the Winter Sauce, add 2 ounces dried porcini or boletus mushrooms, soaked and chopped, pp. 35-36 Use the mushroom soaking water in place of the vegetarian broth.

reduced vegetable broth for using on pasta and a light, but authentic, vegan version of basil pesto, with a few variations.

With this repertoire of Italian sauces, you will never again have to resort to cans, bottles, or packages from the store, and your Italian cooking will taste truly authentic.

Light Tomato or Marinara Sauce

SALSA ALLA MARINARA

(soy-free)

Yield: a scant 2 quarts

"Marinara" just means something cooked the way sailors do—Italian sailors, of course! To many of us, a marinara sauce just means a lightly cooked tomato sauce. Here is a good, tasty basic sauce.

2 tablespoons extra-virgin olive oil

1 medium onion, chopped

1 medium carrot, minced

Optional: **1 stalk of celery, chopped**

2 cloves garlic, minced or crushed

About 5 pounds very ripe plum tomatoes, chopped,
    or 2 (28-ounce) cans plus 1 (14-ounce) can chopped or diced
    plum tomatoes

1 teaspoon salt, or to taste

Freshly ground black pepper

In a heavy pot, heat the olive oil over medium-high heat. Add the onion, carrot, celery, and garlic, and sauté until the onions are soft. Add the tomatoes and tomato juice, salt, and black pepper. Simmer for about 20 minutes if using fresh tomatoes and 35 minutes for canned. If you have a food mill (*mouli*), run the sauce through. You can also use a hand-blender or a food processor, but the sauce should be velvety—not full of bubbles. Taste for seasoning and reduce it over medium heat if it is too thin, stirring occasionally.

Per ½ cup: Calories: 187, Protein: 4 g, Carbohydrate: 25 g, Fat: 2 g

Ragù alla Napoletana

(can be soy-free)

Yield: about 6 cups (enough for one 9 x 13-inch lasagne)

Battuto (vegetable mixture):

1 large onion

1 small carrot, peeled

3 large cloves garlic, peeled

1 stalk celery with leaves

1 tablespoon olive oil

Sauce Ingredients:

1 cup dry red wine or nonalcoholic equivalent

2 pounds ripe plum tomatoes, or 1 (28-ounce) can plum tomatoes and juice, passed through a food mill or processed briefly in a food processor or blender

½ (6-ounce) can tomato paste

1 ounce dried porcini or boletus mushrooms, soaked ½ hour in 2 cups warm water, drained and chopped (reserve and strain the liquid)

¼ pound fresh white or brown mushrooms, chopped

¼ cup chopped fresh Italian parsley

1 bay leaf

2 teaspoons salt, or to taste

½ tablespoon dried basil

½ tablespoon dried oregano

½ teaspoon dried rosemary

½ teaspoon unbleached sugar

Optional: ¼ teaspoon red chile pepper flakes

Freshly ground pepper, to taste

Optional for lasagne: ¾ cup textured soy protein granules, rehydrated in ⅔ cup boiling water, or ¼ to ½ pound more chopped fresh mushrooms, or about 1 cup vegetarian hamburger replacement "crumbles," or ground seitan beef, p. 178, or seitan veal, p. 180

Fresh Summer Tomato Sauce

Use very ripe plum tomatoes only. You can either use just basil and 4 cloves of garlic as the seasoning, or use the onion, garlic, carrot, and celery, and add a handful each of chopped fresh basil and Italian parsley at the end. This can be used chunky or puréed.

Creamy Tomato Sauce

Purée the Fresh Tomato Sauce, and add about ½ cup of Easy Tofu Creme, p. 39, or Easy Cashew or Rice Creme, p. 40. Use white pepper instead of black.

This very tomatoey Ragù alla Napoletana was originally flavored with meat, but I use dried porcini mushrooms instead, with great success.

It is a wonderful winter sauce for pasta and ravioli—rich and deeply satisfying—and is my favorite for lasagne, as well. Actually, it's worth your while to double or triple the recipe and freeze some. You'll find many uses for it.

To make the battuto, chop the vegetables finely with a sharp knife or food processor, then heat the olive oil in a large, heavy-bottomed pot. Add the chopped vegetables and cook over medium heat, stirring often, until they are soft. Add the remaining ingredients, including the strained porcini soaking broth, and bring to a boil. Turn down the heat and simmer, partially covered, for about 2 hours, or until the sauce has cooked down, stirring every so often. Taste for seasoning.

Per ½ cup: Calories: 80, Protein: 1 g, Carbohydrate: 10 g, Fat: 1 g

Brian's Wine-Free Mushroom Tomato Sauce
RAGÙ ALLA BRIAN
(soy-free)

Yield: 2 quarts

This ragù is my husband Brian's standard spaghetti sauce, and it is one of the most delicious I have ever tasted, despite the fact that he uses no wine (which makes it less expensive, by the way). He freezes tomatoes in bags in late summer and early fall to use in his sauce. When they are partially thawed, the skins peel off easily, and the tomatoes can be chopped with a sharp knife.

3 tablespoons extra-virgin olive oil

1 medium onion, minced

1 whole head garlic, peeled and crushed

1 large green pepper, seeded and chopped

4 pounds ripe plum tomatoes (peel if you like), chopped,
    or 2 (28-ounce) cans Italian plum tomatoes, chopped, or diced
    tomatoes, with their juice

1 (6-ounce) can good-quality tomato paste

1¾ cups water

1 large bay leaf

1 tablespoon salt

1 tablespoon dried oregano

1 tablespoon dried thyme

1 tablespoon dried basil

1 small dried red hot pepper

2 cups sliced button, crimini, or other mushrooms

In a large heavy pot, heat the olive oil. Add the onion, garlic, and green pepper, and sauté for several minutes, until the onion starts to soften (don't brown the garlic). Add all of the remaining ingredients *except* the mushrooms. Bring to a boil, then turn down, cover, and simmer for 4 to 6 hours, stirring every half hour or so. During the last half hour, remove the lid, add the mushrooms, and simmer uncovered until serving time. Serve over any type of hot pasta, polenta, or even gnocchi.

For a classic "meat" sauce, add 12 to 16 ounces of your favorite commercial hamburger replacement "crumbles" or ground seitan beef,p. 178, or seitan veal, p. 180, along with the mushrooms.

Note: To cook in a slow-cooker, omit the water and sauté the mushrooms along with the onions, etc. Place these in a large slow-cooker, and add the rest of the ingredients. If you are adding hamburger replacement, add it along with the tomatoes. Cook on high for 1 hour, then on low for 10 to 12 hours.

Per ½ cup: Calories: 60, Protein: 1 g, Carbohydrate: 7 g, Fat: 2 g

Ragù alla Bolognese

(can be soy-free)

Yield: about 5 cups

2 tablespoons extra-virgin olive oil

2 teaspoons roasted sesame oil

1 medium onion, minced

1 carrot, minced

1 stalk celery, minced

2 cloves garlic, minced

1 (14- to 16-ounce) package vegetarian "hamburger crumbles" or ground seitan veal, p. 180 (about 2 cups)

⅔ cup dry red or white wine (can be nonalcoholic), or use ⅓ cup dry white wine and ⅓ cup marsala, dry sherry, or madeira

1½ cups vegetarian broth

1½ cups chopped fresh, ripe plum tomatoes, or lightly drained chopped or diced canned plum tomatoes

2 cups nondairy milk (can be reduced-fat), heated

4 fresh sage leaves, chopped

Optional: **1 teaspoon dried rosemary**

Salt and freshly ground black pepper, to taste

As Lynn Rosetto Kasper wrote in her book, *The Splendid Table* (recipes from the rich cuisine of Emilia-Romagna), "Ragù is *not* a tomato sauce with meat. It is a meat sauce sometimes flavored with tomato." The Bolognese ragù is very different from the rich tomato sauce called a ragù in Naples and other parts of southern Italy. Traditionally, a *soffritto* (sautéed vegetables) of onion, carrot, and celery is browned slowly in butter and bacon fat *(pancetta)*. Then wine and stock are reduced with the mixture, to which ground veal and a bit of tomato are added. The whole thing is bound with cream and cooked for at least 2 hours. Lighter, more contemporary sauces use olive oil and milk.

This sauce employs a ground meat substitute, such as vegetarian "hamburger crumbles" that you can buy in many supermarkets and health food stores. If you are allergic to soy, use the soy-free ground seitan veal. Roasted sesame oil takes the place of bacon fat.

The traditional seasonings for this sauce are lemon zest and nutmeg, but I prefer the "gamier" rosemary and sage.

Ragù alla Bolognese is the traditional topping for tagliatelle (long, wide noodles) and tortellini, but you can use it on any pasta, or on polenta, gnocchi, "cheese" ravioli, or in a Lasagne Al Forno Bolognese, p. 113.

In a medium-sized heavy pot, heat the oils together over medium-high heat. Add the onion, carrot, celery, and garlic, and sauté until the vegetables are soft, stirring frequently. Add the "burger" and cook for a few minutes. Add the wine and cook over high heat until it has almost evaporated. Add the broth and cook it over high heat until it reduces by at least half.

Add the tomatoes and herbs to the sauce, and cook for a few more minutes. Slowly stir in the heated milk, then reduce the heat to a mere simmer, uncover, and cook for about 2 hours. Add salt and pepper, to taste.

Per ½ cup: Calories: 127, Protein: 11 g, Carbohydrate: 6 g, Fat: 5 g

Dairy-Free Bechamel or White Sauce

SALSA BESCIAMELLA

(can be soy-free)

Yield: 2 cups

This rich-tasting sauce, used frequently in Italian cooking, is actually quite low in fat. It is a key ingredient in dishes such as lasagne. Bechamel Sauce can be used as an all-purpose white sauce in all of your cooking and as a topping for Greek dishes, such as vegetarian moussaka.

I think this formula is a great improvement upon vegan white sauces made completely with soymilk, which I find too sweet. The tofu and broth cube add richness without much fat. You can also use reduced-fat soy products if you prefer.

Blended mixture:
1 cup soymilk or rice milk
½ cup crumbled extra-firm *silken* tofu or regular medium-firm tofu
½ cup water
1 chicken-style vegetarian broth cube, crumbled (enough for 1 cup liquid)
½ teaspoon salt

2 tablespoons good-tasting dairy-free margarine or extra-virgin olive oil
1½ to 3 tablespoons unbleached flour (depending on desired thickness)
Large pinch of freshly grated nutmeg
Large pinch of white pepper

Place the soymilk, crumbled tofu, water, broth cube, and salt in a blender, and combine until *very* smooth. Set aside.

Melt the margarine in a medium-size, heavy saucepan, and whisk in the flour. Continue whisking it over medium-high heat for a few minutes, but remove it from the heat before it starts to change color. Scrape this into the blended mixture, and process for a few seconds, then pour the mixture back into the pot. Stir over medium-high heat until it thickens and boils; turn down and simmer on low for a few minutes. Whisk in the nutmeg and white pepper.

Microwave Option: Melt the margarine in a large, microwave-safe bowl or 1-quart Pyrex measuring beaker on high for 45 seconds. Whisk in the flour and microwave on high for 2 minutes. Scrape this into the blended mixture, process briefly, then pour it back into the bowl or beaker. You can also pour the blended mixture into the beaker and mix with a hand immersion blender until smooth. Microwave on high for 2 minutes, then whisk. Microwave for 2 more minutes, then whisk again. Microwave for 2 minutes more, then whisk in the nutmeg and pepper.

To make this sauce soy-free, omit the tofu and use ¼ cup more rice milk (1¼ cups total) and ¼ cup raw cashews. Because the cashews have a thickening effect, use only 1 to 2 tablespoons of flour. Use only 2 teaspoons soy-free, dairy-free margarine or olive oil.

To make this sauce wheat- and corn-free, add the melted margarine directly to the blended mixture, along with 1 to 4 tablespoons white rice flour or sweet/glutinous rice flour *(mochiko flour),* instead of the wheat flour. (You omit the first cooking step.) Four tablespoons makes a very thick sauce. Sauces made with mochiko flour are excellent for freezing because they will not separate when thawed. This makes them ideal if you use them in a lasagne you will be freezing before you bake it.

Per ½ cup: Calories: 109, Protein: 5 g, Carbohydrate: 5 g, Fat: 8 g

Mushroom Sauce
(Salsa di Funghi)

To the basic Basic White Sauce (whatever thickness you prefer), add about ½ pound sliced, fresh mushrooms which have been briefly sautéed in 1 to 2 tablespoons of extra-virgin olive oil or good-tasting dairy-free margarine. You can use any kind of mushroom: button, cremini, chanterelle, oyster, fresh stemmed shiitake, portobello, etc. Add about ¼ cup Soymage Parmesan substitute, or soy-free alternative, p. 37.

If you like, add about 1 ounce dried porcini or boletus mushrooms that have been soaked (see pages 35-36). Use the strained mushroom soaking broth instead of the water.

Reduction "Butter" Sauce

(can be soy-free)

Yield: 1½ cups

3½ cups unsalted or very lightly salted vegetarian broth
¼ cup good-tasting, dairy-free margarine or extra-virgin olive oil
**¼ teaspoon agar powder, or 1½ teaspoons agar flakes, dissolved
   in 2 tablespoons cold broth or water**
Salt and freshly ground pepper, to taste

In a small sauté pan or wide saucepan, reduce the broth over high heat until it measures 1¼ cups. Pour it back into the pan, and whisk in the margarine, along with the dissolved agar. Simmer for 3 to 4 minutes; season to taste with salt and pepper.

Note: Do not use bean or chick-pea broth—it gets too cloudy and sweet-tasting when it is reduced.

Per ¼ cup: Calories: 77, Protein: 1 g, Carbohydrate: 1 g, Fat: 7 g

This delicious, velvety sauce makes a light alternative to melted butter on anything from steamed vegetables to pasta, ravioli, tortellini, etc. You must use a very tasty margarine, such as Canoleo, or you can use extra-virgin olive oil. Vegetable Broth, p. 117, is preferable.

Walnut Sauce

SALSA DI NOCI

(can be soy-free)

Yield: about 2 cups

¾ cup chopped walnuts
2 cups soymilk or rice milk (reduced-fat, if desired)
**1 chicken-style vegetarian broth cube, crumbled (enough for 1 cup
   broth)**
1 small clove garlic, crushed
Optional: **1 to 2 teaspoons chopped fresh marjoram**
¼ teaspoon freshly ground nutmeg
**2 tablespoons Soymage Parmesan substitute, or soy-free
   alternative, p. 37**
Salt, to taste

Heat a cast-iron skillet or other heavy pan over high heat. Add the walnuts and reduce the heat to medium. Toast the walnuts, stirring frequently and watching them constantly, until they just begin to

This is a modern, lighter version of a very ancient Ligurian sauce to serve on flat pasta, such as *tagliatelle* or fettuccine, or *pansotti* (a type of stuffed pasta, see pages 92 and 102). Very simple to make!

Note: Traditionally, pepper is not used in this sauce.

darken and smell toasty. Remove them from the pan. Place the toast-ed nuts in a mini-chopper, electric spice and seed grinder, or food processor, and process them until they are almost ground.

Combine the milk, broth cube, garlic, and walnuts in a heavy, medi-um-sized saucepan or sauté pan. Bring to a boil over medium-high heat, and keep at a low boil until it has reduced somewhat and thick-ened to a sauce consistency. Remove from the heat and add the mar-joram, nutmeg, and soy Parmesan. Taste for salt. (Do not add pep-per.) Heat gently before serving.

Per ¼ cup: Calories: 99, Protein: 4 g, Carbohydrate: 3 g, Fat: 8 g

About Pesto

Pesto, formerly a specialty known only in Liguria, is now as equal-ly popular as marinara sauce in all corners of the Western world. But it has been badly bastardized—made with cilantro, for instance, an herb which most Italians abhor. And most American pestos are far heavier on the garlic than Ligurian pesto—it is the basil you should smell, not the garlic.

This pesto recipe is pretty standard, except that I use Soymage Parmesan substitute instead of dairy cheese. (There are also some variations for those who do not wish to use, or cannot obtain, soy Parmesan.) Use the freshest, most aromatic, basil you can find; that is the soul of pesto.

If you have a bumper crop of basil in the late summer, consider making Basil Paste for Freezing, p. 30, and using that in your winter pesto, instead of freezing the pesto itself. I think that this method pre-serves the color and flavor better.

Although the Genoese insist that using a mortar and pestle (from which the name "pesto" originates) is the *only* way to make authentic pesto, I must confess that I probably wouldn't make it very often if that were my only recourse. And I suspect that many Italian cooks would agree—certainly most North Americans would! I don't think you will have any complaints about this food processor method, but if you want to try it the old-fashioned way, place the finely chopped garlic, nuts, and a pinch of coarse salt in a large mortar, and crush it with the pestle to make a smooth paste. Add the basil, a little at a time, and crush it to a coarse paste, adding a little more salt if needed.

Gradually crush in the soy Parmesan, then drizzle in the olive oil, and work it until it is very smooth.

Pesto without the cheese is stirred into Minestrone, p. 122; otherwise, it is used on wide, flat pastas and Gnocchi, pp. 92-98. Ligurians don't use it as freely as North Americans, but I must confess that I do love it on Grilled Mushrooms, p. 73.

Pesto Genovese

(can be soy-free)

Yield: about 1½ cups

To serve pesto with pasta, dilute it with a little of the water the pasta was cooked in and toss it with the pasta. See some of the variations that follow for making either soy-free or low-fat pesto. If you are allergic to nuts, you can omit them, or use shelled, lightly toasted sunflower and/or pumpkin seeds instead.

You can also halve or even quarter this recipe, if you don't want any leftover pesto.

4 cups packed fresh basil leaves

⅓ cup Soymage Parmesan (omit this if the pesto is to be used in soup)

½ cup extra-virgin olive oil

¼ cup lightly toasted pine nuts, chopped walnuts, filberts (hazelnuts), almonds, or Brazil nuts

2 to 4 cloves garlic

1 teaspoon salt

Optional: **½ tablespoon lemon juice, to preserve the color**

Place everything in a food processor, and process until a paste forms. Place the paste in 2 or 3 small containers. (The less air the pesto is exposed to, the better.) Cover the pesto with a thin film of olive oil or place a piece of plastic wrap directly on the pesto to prevent discoloration. Cover tightly, refrigerate, and use this up within 2 or 3 days. After that, you should freeze it in small containers or make frozen cubes. Don't leave it in the freezer for more than a month or so, or it loses flavor.

Per tablespoon: Calories: 54, Protein: 1 g, Carbohydrate: 1 g, Fat: 6 g

Soy-Free Yeasty Pesto

Replace the soy Parmesan with ¼ cup nutritional yeast flakes, 1½ tablespoons chicken-style broth powder, and 1 tablespoon lemon juice.

Miso Pesto

Replace the soy Parmesan with 2 tablespoons light soy or chick-pea miso. Omit the salt.

Low-Fat Pesto

Omit all or some of the oil, and substitute an equal quantity of one of the following or a mixture: medium-firm or *silken* tofu; mashed, cooked cannellini beans; chick-pea or white bean broth.

Winter Pesto

This is an authentic method for stretching expensive, store-bought fresh basil during the winter months. In the basic recipe or any of the variations, use 2 cups fresh basil and 2 cups fresh Italian parsley leaves, instead of 4 cups basil. Add about 2 tablespoons chopped fresh marjoram, if you can find it.

Pesto made from frozen Basil Paste

Instead of fresh basil in the Basic Pesto or any of the variations above, use 1 cup thawed Basil Paste for Freezing, p. 30. Omit 2 tablespoons plus 2 teaspoons olive oil. For Winter Pesto, use ½ cup of the Basil Paste instead of the 2 cups fresh basil, and omit 4 teaspoons of olive oil.

V
Appetizers, Vegetable Side Dishes, and Salads

ANTIPASTI,
CONTORNI,
E INSALATE

"A real greengrocer is a treasure beyond price, and the closest thing you will ever discover to a secret ingredient in Italian cooking."

—Tom Maresca and
Diane Darrow
La Tavola Italiana
(New York: William
Morrow, 1988)

I am including "appetizers" or "starters" (antipasti), vegetable side dishes (contorni), and salads (insalate) all in one chapter, because they can be interchangeable, depending on the size of the serving. In larger helpings, some of these dishes can also be served as secondi, or what we think of as main dishes.

Antipasti are so diverse and so numerous that one can make a whole meal of them. (This is actually a good option for vegetarians in an Italian restaurant.) Try serving one simple antipasto dish at the beginning of any family meal—like grilled mushrooms or crostini with fresh tomatoes and olive oil. It makes the meal seem more special and helps you resist the temptation to overeat during the rest of the meal.

For a company dinner, serve two or three antipasti. Many of them can be made ahead of time. Your guests will then have an opportunity to try even more of the diversity of Italian cuisine, and the meal will be pleasantly drawn-out and relaxed.

Small servings of salads make excellent antipasti, or you can serve a larger helping after the main meal as a *contorno* (literally "that which rounds out"—the meal, that is!). Italians believe that eating a salad made from raw vegetables at the end of a meal aids digestion.

Side dishes can be served with main dishes, but should be placed in separate serving bowls.

These are some of our very favorite Italian dishes and serve as mere examples of the imaginative use of vegetables in Italian cookery.

Hot Garlic Dip for Raw Vegetables

BAGNA CAUDA

(can be soy-free)

Yield: almost 2 cups

¾ cup soymilk or rice milk

6 tablespoons extra-firm *silken* tofu (For a soy-free version, substitute 3 tablespoons raw cashews.)

6 tablespoons water

2 tablespoons light soy or chick-pea miso

1 vegetarian broth cube, crumbled (enough for 1 cup liquid)

¼ cup extra-virgin olive oil

6 cloves garlic, thinly sliced
Freshly ground black pepper, to taste

In a blender, combine the soymilk or rice milk, tofu or cashews, water, miso, and broth cube until very smooth. Set aside.

In a small skillet or sauté pan, heat the olive oil over medium heat. Add the garlic and sauté slowly until golden; don't brown it. Remove the garlic and whisk the blended mixture into the oil. Heat the sauce slowly and add black pepper to taste. Keep the sauce warm as you would a fondue, in a heat-proof bowl over a small candle or other warming device.

Per 2 tablespoons: Calories: 42, Protein: 1 g, Carbohydrate: 1 g, Fat: 3 g

Hazelnut Bagna Cauda

Use hazelnut or filbert oil instead of the olive oil, and add ¼ cup ground toasted hazelnuts or filberts.

To skin hazelnuts and almonds

Skin both hazelnuts and almonds *before* toasting.

For hazelnuts, bring 2 cups water to a boil with 3 tablespoons baking soda. Add the nuts and blanch for 3 to 4 minutes. Drain and rinse in a colander under cold running water; the skins will slide off.

For almonds, place them in boiling water for about 1 minute, drain, and plunge them into cold water. Squeeze each almond between your thumb and forefinger, and the almond will pop out of the skin. (Be careful it doesn't shoot across the room!)

Bruschetta
TOASTED ITALIAN BREAD
(soy-free)

Choose the best crusty bread you can find (white or whole wheat)— chewy with a porous texture and a crackly crust. Cut the bread into ½- to ¾-inch slices. The traditional way to prepare the bread is to grill it or broil it 4 to 6 inches from the heat, one side at a time, until it is golden and crunchy, but you can cheat and use a toaster or toaster oven! (cont.)

Bagna cauda means "hot bath." It's a very old sauce from Piedmont, although it is eaten all over Italy now. It was popular as far back as the 16th century, and today, as then, it makes a wonderful communal antipasto.

Some recipes mix butter and olive oil; some mix cream and olive oil. I have improvised on the cream-based sauce to make a lower-fat version that is creamy, garlicky, and luscious. (Miso stands in for the usual anchovies.) Serve the sauce with a platter of raw bell pepper slices, cabbage wedges, celery, and fennel stalks. Cold cooked artichokes and other lightly steamed vegetables are also good with bagna cauda. You also might like to serve some crusty bread to mop up the last traces of the sauce.

Bruschetta (pronounced broos-kéh-tah) is trendy in North America, but it is no more than toasted rustic Italian bread which serves as a base for various tasty antipasto toppings.

Crostini

Italians don't eat "garlic bread" with their meals like we do, but they do have a type of crusty bread with garlic called "crostini," which is used as an antipasto and bears no resemblance to the soft bread dripping with garlicky butter that is popular in North America.

The process is pretty much the same as for making Bruschetta, p. 53, but use a long, thin loaf of crusty bread, like a French baguette or baton, and slice the bread about ½ inch thick. After toasting to a golden brown, scrape one surface of each piece with a peeled clove of garlic; the garlic will rub off onto the rough surface of the toast. One clove should cover about two pieces of bread. Brush the crostini with a little extra-virgin olive oil—a nice fruity, green variety, if possible. That's it! Serve the crostini with various antipasti, or top it with something simple that isn't infused with garlic, such as chopped fresh, ripe tomatoes and basil, sun-dried tomatoes in oil, plain sautéed greens, grilled mushrooms, etc.

When it's done, try the traditional topping of diced fresh, ripe plum tomatoes seasoned with salt and freshly ground black pepper, a little fresh garlic, and plenty of fresh basil; or sautéed greens with olive oil and garlic (pages 74-75). Or try any one of the following toppings:

Sun-dried tomatoes in oil
Truffle-Style Mushrooms, p. 68
Raw Tomato Sauce with Black Olives, p. 86
Grilled Mushrooms, pp. 73-74
Roasted or Grilled Peppers, p. 74
Peperonata, p. 69
Marinated Grilled Eggplant or Zucchini, p. 71
Eggplant Relish (Caponata), p. 56
Puréed Beans with "Wild" Greens (La Capriata), p. 161
Beans in a Jug (Fagioli in Fiasco), p. 161

Raw Tomato Sauce with Black Olives
SALSA CRUDA CON OLIVE
(soy-free)

Yield: about 2 cups

This is a delicious topping for bruschetta or piadine (Italian flat bread, p. 208), but it can also be served with crackers, on hot pasta, or with plain sliced seitan, pp. 178-81, or Breast of Tofu, p. 170.

2 pounds firm, but ripe, Roma (plum) tomatoes, cut into chunks, or 1 (28-ounce) can diced tomatoes, well-drained
40 black calamata olives, pitted
6 cloves garlic, crushed
6 tablespoons chopped fresh basil
½ teaspoon salt
Freshly ground black pepper, to taste
Optional Additions:
2 to 4 tablespoons extra-virgin olive oil
1 red or sweet onion, finely chopped

½ cup minced fresh Italian parsley
½ to 1 cup chopped marinated artichoke hearts

If you have no food processor, chop the tomatoes quite small, and mince the onions and olives finely with a sharp knife. Mix them all together in a small bowl with the olive oil and salt and pepper to taste (and any optional additions desired). Cover and chill until serving time.

If you have a food processor, pulse the onion and olives a few times to mince them, then add the tomato chunks and pulse until coarsely chopped. Pour into a small bowl, and toss with the olive oil and salt and pepper to taste.

Per ½ cup: Calories: 48, Protein: 1 g, Carbohydrate: 4 g, Fat: 4 g

Chick-Pea "Pancake"
FARINATA, CALDA CALDA, OR CECINA
(soy-free)

Yield: one 14-inch farinata (8 servings)

1½ cups water
1½ cups chick-pea flour or plain *besan* (Indian chick-pea flour)
2 tablespoons extra-virgin olive oil
¾ teaspoon salt
Freshly ground black pepper, to taste
Optional: 2 teaspoons crushed garlic

Mix the water and chick-pea flour in a medium bowl, cover, and let stand in a cool place for 2 hours.

Preheat the oven to 475°F (450°F if using a convection oven). Coat a 14-inch pizza pan or cookie sheet with 1 tablespoon of the olive oil.

Stir the salt, pepper, and garlic, if using, into the batter, which should be like a pancake batter. Add water if the batter is too thick. Pour the

Farinata is a Ligurian specialty. My father referred to it as "fai'na," in the Genoese dialect. A similar recipe is called Socca in Monaco and Nice. In Tuscany, they call it calda calda (meaning "hot, hot") or cecina. Whatever you call it, it's a delicious snack food and very nutritious. This is a thin version, which I prefer. You can sprinkle the top with chopped garlic and rosemary, thyme, or sage before baking, if you like. Ligurians, who eat fai'na with a knife and fork, sometimes also top it with thinly sliced onions or green onions, or even slices of baby artichoke. In Nice, the street vendors top it with lots of freshly ground black pepper, and it's eaten like chips from a paper cone. I like the leftovers cold too. *Note:* If you use besan (Indian chick-pea flour), be sure that it is plain and doesn't contain spices.

batter into the pan, and drizzle with the remaining oil. If you like, sprinkle with some of the items suggested in the recipe comments.

Bake for 10 minutes, then place under the broiler for a few minutes to brown the top. Grind more pepper on top, if you wish, and cut into wedges to serve. Serve hot.

Per serving: Calories: 105, Protein: 5 g, Carbohydrate: 13 g, Fat: 3 g

Eggplant Relish
CAPONATA OR GABOLADIN
(soy-free)

Yield: about 3 cups

Extra-virgin olive oil for brushing or spraying

1 pound eggplant, cut into ¾-inch cubes

2 large stalks celery, diced

1 small onion, chopped

2 large cloves garlic, minced or pressed

2 tablespoons extra-virgin olive oil

1 (15-ounce) can tomato purée (2 cups)

½ cup sliced pitted Italian green olives, pimiento-stuffed green olives, or pitted calamata black olives

½ cup dry red wine (can be nonalcoholic)

2 tablespoons drained capers

2 tablespoons red wine vinegar

1 tablespoon unbleached sugar

Salt and freshly ground black pepper, to taste

There are as many versions of this relish as there are southern Italians, but it always contains eggplant, tomato, onions, capers, green and/or black olives, and celery in a slightly sweet and sour sauce. Sometimes pine nuts are added. Some people add peppers, parsley, hot pepper flakes, even raisins.

Serve it at room temperature with crostini or crackers or in pita pockets or crusty rolls as a sandwich. You might even like to try it hot on pasta. (By the way, Sicilians call it *caponata*, and many Apulians call it *gaboladin*.)

Optional (use any or all):
¼ cup lightly toasted pine nuts
2 tablespoons raisins
½ teaspoon dried red pepper flakes
1 or 2 bell peppers (any color), roasted, seeded, trimmed, and chopped
¼ cup chopped Italian parsley

Preheat the oven to 400°F.

Brush or spray a cookie sheet with olive oil, and place the eggplant cubes on it. Spray or brush with a little more olive oil. Bake the eggplant for 30 minutes, or until soft and browned on the bottom.

Meanwhile, in a large, heavy skillet, sauté the celery, onion, and garlic in the 2 tablespoons olive oil over medium heat until the celery has softened, stirring often.

Add the baked eggplant to the celery mixture along with the tomato purée, capers, olives, vinegar, sugar, wine, and any optional ingredients you are using, except the parsley. Cook, uncovered, stirring occasionally, until the mixture is thick, about 30 minutes. Add salt and pepper to taste. Add parsley at this time, if you are using it.

Serve hot or at room temperature. If you store it in the refrigerator, let it come to room temperature or heat it before serving.

Per ¼ cup: Calories: 79, Protein: 1 g, Carbohydrate: 9 g, Fat: 3 g

Salads

INSALATE

There are no ironclad rules for salads in Italy, except that the greens should be very fresh—the best you can pick or buy. An *insalata verde* is a green salad. Usually, this consists of predominantly one variety of lettuce (*not* iceberg), plus one or two other greens, usually of a sharp or bitter variety. Bitter salad greens could be curly endive (*cicoria*), escarole, young dandelion greens, young mustard greens, arugola (*rucola*), sorrel, radicchio, or even young kale.

Mixed salad (insalata mista) may be as simple as lettuce with ripe tomatoes, but it usually contains two or three types of greens, some sweet onion slivers, and tomato wedges. (Pale winter tomatoes will not do here.) Cooked vegetables might also be used in a mixed salad—cold roasted beets, p. 72, cooked asparagus, carrots, artichoke hearts, potatoes, squash, etc. These cooked vegetables can either be grilled or steamed until crisp-tender.

In Italy, the salad will most likely be served as a *contorno*, along with the main dish (*secondo*) or after, as it is believed to aid digestion. If a small salad is served at the beginning of dinner, then it qualifies as an antipasto. A large salad might be the main dish at lunch.

There are other types of salads in Italy—rice salads, potato salads, bread salads, and bean salads. Rarely are there pasta salads— although you might be served a pasta dish at room temperature during hot weather. These hearty salads would not be eaten as a salad course after the meal, as a green salad would, but could be the main dish of a light meal, an antipasto, or part of a buffet. I have given a few examples (my favorites) of this type of salad, and some ideas for variations on these.

Cold cooked vegetables, dressed with vinegar or lemon juice and olive oil, qualify as salads (as well as antipasti) and make beautiful additions to a buffet table when arranged artistically on platters. Almost any fresh, seasonal vegetable can be treated this way. Simply cook until just tender, and drizzle with a little extra-virgin olive oil and red wine vinegar, white balsamic vinegar, or fresh lemon juice, or, in some cases (particularly on roasted beets), red balsamic vinegar. Then sprinkle with salt and freshly ground pepper. Herbs are not usually added, but you could garnish the plate with them. You can treat many vegetables this way—artichokes, asparagus, green beans, carrots, fennel, mushrooms, fresh fava or broad beans, cooked chard or other greens (such as beet tops), cauliflower, broccoli, roasted peppers, and onions—*and, if you mix several cooked vegetables together in a salad, it's called insalatone.*

Italian potato salads can be made the same way, preferably with new, waxy potatoes, such as the red-skinned varieties. The salad can simply consist of sliced, cooked potatoes or potatoes mixed with green onions, marinated artichokes, cooked green beans, raw or roasted fennel, roasted beets, cannellini beans, chick-peas, and celery, etc. Basil or other fresh herbs can be added, and perhaps a splash of marsala.

For crisp salad greens and lettuce: As soon as you pick the greens or bring them home from the market, separate the leaves (discarding any bad ones), and soak them in cold water for 15 minutes. Dry the leaves in a salad spinner, or lay the leaves on a large, clean towel, roll the towel up loosely, then spin the towel roll around, holding tightly to both ends. Another old-fashioned way of drying salad greens without bruising them is to place them in a clean, old pillow case. (Using two pillowcases, one inside the other, provides more absorption capacity.) Stand outside and whirl it around like mad!

Remove the leaves, wrap them in moist, clean tea towels, and place them in plastic bags. There are special plastic bags available now that keep vegetables fresh longer—look for them in the vegetable section of your market. You can also use special plastic refrigerator containers for salad. Lettuce and other greens will keep crisp and fresh longer if you take a few minutes to do this, and they will be ready at a moment's notice. This method can also be used to revive wilted lettuce.

Dressing a salad: Regardless of how the salad is made, or when it is served, in Italy, it is always dressed at the table, just before serving, with a generous amount of olive oil and a judicious amount of either red wine vinegar or fresh lemon juice and salt. Red balsamic vinegar is rarely used; when it is, it is mixed with red wine vinegar. White wine vinegar or white balsamic vinegar are also used infrequently. Pepper is optional—you can just grind it over the salad, if you wish. Fresh herbs, such as a little basil, oregano, parsley, or onion, are also up to you.

Garlic is rarely used on a salad in Italy, so I depart from tradition by adding garlic to my dressing—a California affectation, I admit, but I love it! You can leave it out with good conscience, if you prefer.

I have given you the choice of either substituting cannellini (white bean) or chick-pea broth (see pages 119-20) for some of the oil (if you wish to cut down on fat). The bean broth is light-colored, tasty, and viscous enough to cling to the leaves; just a little olive oil will add flavor.

You can simply sprinkle the dressing ingredients over the salad and "eyeball" the amounts, but, for those who like accurate measurements, I have provided a couple of simple dressing recipes. They are so easy to make and so inexpensive that I hope you will never feel the need to buy a prepared "Italian" dressing again.

Note: I advise you to make the dressing fresh each time you make a salad because olive oil crystallizes when it's refrigerated. If you prefer to make a larger amount ahead of time, use the bean broth only and add a little olive oil when you dress the salad. A good method for mixing larger amounts of dressing is to place all of the ingredients (along with any crushed garlic) in a Tupperware Quick Shake container or a jar with a tight cover. Shake until well mixed.

My mother never bought prepared salad dressing, and neither do I. This is my version of the one we had on our big daily bowl of salad greens when I was growing up. We ate it first, American-style, but my father ate his salad portion as the last course of the meal, Italian-style.

My mother never measured, but I have figured out a formula for those who like to use exact amounts.

This method of mixing is easy and convenient for small amounts made just before dressing the salad. See note above for advice on making larger amounts ahead of time.

My Mother's Lemon Salad Dressing
(soy-free)

Yield: a scant ½ cup (enough for 4 servings)

¼ teaspoon salt
1 small clove garlic, minced or crushed
5 tablespoons extra-virgin olive oil
2 tablespoons fresh lemon juice

With the back of a teaspoon in a small, round-bottomed bowl or with a medium-sized mortar and pestle, mash together the salt and garlic until it is like a paste. (The salt grains will help mash the garlic to a paste, and the garlic juice will dissolve the salt.) Whisk in the olive oil (and/or broth—see note below) and lemon juice with a fork or small wire whisk.

Note: To reduce fat and calories, substitute chick-pea or cannellini (white bean) broth, pp. 119-20, for up to 4 tablespoons of the olive oil. Use at least 1 tablespoon olive oil to impart a good flavor.

Per serving: Calories: 151, Protein: 0 g, Carbohydrate: 1 g, Fat: 15 g

Italian Wine Vinegar Dressing

Yield: a generous ⅓ cup (enough for 4 servings)

¼ teaspoon salt
1 small clove garlic, crushed or minced
5 tablespoons extra-virgin olive oil
1 tablespoon good-quality red wine vinegar
1 teaspoon red or white balsamic vinegar

With the back of a teaspoon in a small, round-bottomed bowl or with a medium-sized mortar and pestle, mash together the salt and garlic until it is like a paste. (The salt grains will help mash the garlic to a paste, and the garlic juice will dissolve the salt.) Whisk in the oil and vinegar (and any broth you are using—see note below) with a fork or small wire whisk.

Note: To reduce fat and calories, substitute chick-pea or cannellini (white bean) broth, pp. 119-20, for up to 4 tablespoons of the olive oil. Use at least 1 tablespoon of olive oil to impart good flavor.

Per serving: Calories: 149, Protein: 0 g, Carbohydrate: 0 g, Fat: 15 g

Panzanella

TUSCAN BREAD SALAD

(soy-free)

Yield: 4 servings

4 cups cubed heavy, slightly stale Italian bread
Double recipe Italian Wine Vinegar Dressing, above
2 cups diced fresh, ripe tomato
½ cup chopped red onion or green onion
½ cup chopped fresh basil or marjoram, or 1 cup chopped Italian parsley
Freshly ground black pepper, to taste
8 crisp romaine lettuce leaves to serve the salad on

This is a basic formula for an Italian-style salad dressing. Remember that you can leave out the garlic if you don't like it, and that freshly ground pepper and chopped fresh herbs are optional items that you can sprinkle over the salad while dressing it. This method of mixing is easy and convenient for small amounts made just before dressing the salad. See page 60 for advice on making larger amounts ahead of time.

This rustic salad is also called pan molle or pan-bagnato and is made not only in Tuscany, but all over central Italy. More recently, it has enjoyed popularity in all parts of Italy, and in North America, as well. It is obviously a thrifty invention of "la cucina povera" (cuisine of the poor), for Italians would never waste even stale bread. It reminds me of Lebanese fattoush, a salad made of stale pita bread, tomatoes, and greens.

It's important to use a good, heavy Italian or sourdough bread—a few days old, but not all dried out. A light airy bread will turn to mush when treated this way.

Optional Additions (any or all):
Up to 2 cups diced cucumber
Up to 2 cups diced bell pepper (any color)
A few sliced, pitted green Italian olives
1 or 2 stalks celery, sliced
A few capers

Place the bread in a salad bowl with ½ cup of the Wine Vinegar Dressing, and let set for ½ hour. Just before serving, add the remaining ingredients, including the remaining salad dressing. Toss well and serve over the lettuce leaves.

Per serving: Calories: 407, Protein: 4 g, Carbohydrate: 22 g, Fat: 31 g

Sicilian-Style Fennel and Orange Salad
INSALATE DI FINOCCHIO E ARANCE

Yield: 6 servings

This a very delicious, colorful, and unusual salad.

1 head romaine lettuce, washed, dried and crisped
4 medium navel oranges, peeled and sliced
2 large bulbs fennel, washed, trimmed, and thinly sliced
1 medium red onion, thinly sliced
1 recipe Italian Wine Vinegar Dressing, p. 61, without garlic
Freshly ground black pepper
Optional: **A few black calamata or Sicilian olives**

Arrange the crisp lettuce leaves on a cold platter. Arrange the orange and fennel slices artistically over the lettuce, alternating fennel with orange. Scatter the red onion slices over this, drizzle with the dressing, and grind black pepper over it. Arrange the olives over the salad, if you like. Serve within 30 minutes.

Per serving: Calories: 161, Protein: 1 g, Carbohydrate: 13 g, Fat: 10 g

Piedmontese Rice Salad

INSALATA DI RISO

Yield: 8 to 12 servings

2½ cups light vegetarian broth, or 2½ cups water with broth cubes
  for 2 cups liquid
1½ cups brown basmati, white basmati, or other long-grain rice
½ pound fresh asparagus, cut into 1-inch pieces*
4 green onions, chopped
1 (7-ounce) jar marinated artichoke hearts, rinsed and sliced
2 roasted red peppers, chopped (see pages 74-75 for roasting
  instructions or use canned roasted red peppers)**
2 stalks celery or fennel, chopped
½ cup sliced, pitted green Italian olives
2 tablespoons capers
2 tablespoons chopped Italian parsley
2 tablespoons chopped fresh basil

Dressing:
1 head roasted garlic, squeezed out of the peels, p. 72
½ cup chick-pea broth, pp. 119-20, or other vegetarian broth
¼ cup extra-virgin olive oil
¼ cup white wine vinegar or white balsamic vinegar
1 teaspoon Dijon mustard
½ teaspoon salt
¼ teaspoon freshly ground pepper

¼ cup toasted pine nuts or slivered almonds

**For a heartier dish, add some strips of crispy, fried Breast of Tofu,
  p. 170, or seitan chicken, p. 181**

*You can substitute 1 cup shelled fresh or thawed frozen petit pois (baby peas) for the asparagus, if you wish.

**If you have no red peppers, use a chopped green pepper and about 6 sliced sun-dried tomatoes in oil.

There are many, many versions of this delicious salad, some with a mayonnaise-type dressing and some with a vinaigrette. I have combined vegetarian broth and roasted garlic with a small amount of olive oil in the salad dressing to produce a creamy product with a fraction of the oil and all of the flavor.

This salad makes a wonderful late spring or summer luncheon dish, or it can be the star attraction at a buffet or potluck.

To cook the rice, bring the broth or water and broth cubes to a boil in a medium saucepan with a tightly fitting lid. Slowly add the rice in a stream, bring back to a boil, cover, and reduce the heat to the lowest setting. Cook white rice for 15 minutes and brown rice for 30 to 45 minutes. Fluff with a fork and let set a few more minutes before scraping into a large salad bowl.

Meanwhile, steam the asparagus until crisp-tender, and rinse under cold running water to stop cooking. Drain very well. Prepare the other vegetables and herbs.

Blend the dressing ingredients together in a blender or mini-chopper until smooth. Toss with the warm rice, and add the asparagus, remaining vegetables, optional tofu or seitan (if using), and herbs. Cover and refrigerate no more than 4 hours. (The rice kernels harden if refrigerated too long.) Serve at room temperature, with the nuts sprinkled on top.

Per serving: Calories: 159, Protein: 3 g, Carbohydrate: 18 g, Fat: 7 g

Other Bean Salads

• Dress cooked or canned romano, borlotti, cranberry, or pinto beans with Italian Wine Vinegar Dressing, p. 61, and serve with strips of radicchio or curly endive.

• Dress cooked or canned chick-peas or brown lentils with either My Mother's Lemon Dressing, p. 60, or Italian Wine Vinegar Dressing, p. 61. Mix with chopped green or red onions and fresh Italian parsley.

Bean Salad
INSALATA DI FAGLIOLI
(soy-free)

Yield: 6 servings

If you must refrigerate this salad, bring it to room temperature before serving.

3 cups cooked or canned cannellini (white kidney or Great Northern) beans

3 tablespoons extra-virgin olive oil

3 tablespoons vegetarian broth or chick-pea or cannellini broth, pages 119-20 (Do not use the liquid from canned beans.)

1 tablespoon red wine vinegar

2 teaspoons light soy or chick-pea miso

1 green onion, chopped

1 tablespoon chopped fresh sage or basil
¼ cup chopped Italian parsley
Salt and freshly ground black pepper, to taste

Warm the beans slightly in their juice, then drain well. Place them in a serving bowl. Blend the oil, broth, vinegar, miso, green onion, and sage or basil until creamy, and pour over the beans. Add the parsley and salt and pepper to taste.

Per serving: Calories: 168, Protein: 6 g, Carbohydrate: 20 g, Fat: 7 g

Roasted Vegetable Salad
INSALATA DI VERDURI AL FORNO

This is one of the most delicious salads in Italy.

Roasted vegetables, prepared according to the directions on page 73
Other options:
   Roasted Beets, p. 72, Roasted Garlic, p. 72, Grilled Mushrooms, p. 73, Roasted or Grilled Peppers, pp. 74-75, and Marinated Grilled Eggplant or Zucchini, without the lemon dressing, p. 71.

Arrange the vegetables artistically on a plate or platter, and drizzle with My Mother's Lemon Salad Dressing, p. 60. Let set at least 1 hour at room temperature.

Vegetables

I don't have the space to cover all the details of Italian vegetable cookery in this book. I urge you to find a copy of *From an Italian Garden* (also published under the title *Cooking Vegetables the Italian Way*) by Judith Barrett (New York: MacMillan, 1992). Ms. Barrett set out to discover why Italian vegetables taste so good and how they can be prepared authentically in North American kitchens with North American vegetable varieties.

I would like to discuss two popular Italian vegetables that North American cooks may not be familiar with—eggplant (melanzane) and artichokes (carciofi).

Italian artichokes are elongated, often purple-tinted, and less fibrous than our round green ones. The Italian variety is spineless, so it has no tough, woody, inedible parts. In Italy, it's also possible to buy small artichokes the size of an egg (carciofini), and you may be able to find these in farmer's markets on the west coast of the U. S.

In order to make something resembling an Italian artichoke out of a North American one, you must trim away the tough membranes. It may seem like you are wasting a lot, but it would be discarded eventually anyway. Have a bowl of cold water ready with a few tablespoons of lemon juice in it. Peel away the dark outer leaves of each artichoke, and then start breaking off the top two-thirds (fibrous part) of the leaves. Don't use scissors or a knife until you come to the tender, yellowish inner leaves. Cut off the top 1 or 2 inches of the artichoke with a sharp knife, peel the stem, and trim the base neatly. Scrape out the fuzzy "choke" from the middle. Place each one in the lemon water while you finish the rest to prevent the edges from browning.

To use in sautéed dishes, cut the prepared artichokes into quarters lengthwise. To use cooked in tarts and other dishes, poach them in vegetarian broth until tender, about 10 minutes.

Large, untrimmed artichokes can be steamed or boiled for about 35 to 45 minutes, or until a leaf can be pulled out easily and the "meat" at the base of the leaf is tender. (Some people recommend microwaving artichokes, but I find they come out tough and dry.) The leaves can be plucked off one by one and dunked in a savory dip (sugges-

An Easy Way to Pit Olives:

If the olives are going to be sliced or chopped, this is the easiest way to pit them—it's the same procedure as peeling a clove of garlic. Simply place the olive on a board, and put the wide part of a chef's knife flat down on it. Strike the flat of the knife with your fist, and the pit practically pops right out!

tions follow). The tender part at the base of each leaf is scraped off with the teeth. The more tender leaves in the center can be pulled out as one and nibbled all around until you come to the fibrous part. If you have not already scraped out the "choke" from the center before cooking, scrape it off with a spoon—the "heart" that remains is the prized part.

Hot artichokes can be served with Hot Garlic Dip, p. 52, or melted, good-tasting, nondairy margarine infused with garlic. Cold artichokes can be served with Agliata (Ligurian Garlic Mayonnaise), p. 30, Italian Wine Vinegar Dressing, p. 61, or Hot Garlic Dip, p. 62.

Because in most areas of North America artichokes are expensive out of season (and the season is short), I have not given many artichoke recipes here, but this does not accurately reflect the Italian love affair with artichokes (or my own!). They are baked, fried, stuffed, pickled, and enjoyed in many other ways in every region of the country.

In North America, large purple *eggplants* are the most common ones, but you can often find small Japanese purple or white ones, too—any of these will work in Italian recipes.

Most recipes for eggplant will instruct you to salt the eggplant pieces, drain them in a colander for about half an hour, then rinse them and pat them dry. This is done to draw out any bitter juices and so that the eggplant absorbs less of the oil it is cooked in. There is no need to salt the eggplants if they are young, small, or very fresh, and even large ones do not necessarily need to be salted if you are baking, grilling, or steaming them, and you're in a hurry.

One more vegetable I want to mention especially is *fennel* (finnochio), which you will often find mistakenly labeled "anise" in supermarkets. It does smell a little like anise or licorice, but it is a whitish-green bulbous vegetable with stalks growing out of it somewhat like celery, except that it has green, feathery fronds instead of leaves. It is delicious raw, cut into thin slices for *pinzimonio* (sliced raw vegetables, including fennel, celery, carrots, green onion, red bell pepper, and romaine lettuce, etc.). These are served with a bowl of very good extra-virgin olive oil, salt, and freshly ground pepper for dipping (and a glass of white wine for sipping!). Fennel is also good in salads, or it can be braised or added to stews and gratins for wonderful flavor. It is rather expensive, but is easily grown in the garden.

Baked Artichokes
CARCIOFI ARROSTO
(soy-free)

Yield: 4 servings

This is a common way of preparing artichokes in Italy, but North Americans may find it unusual.

For Stuffed Baked Artichokes, you may use a simple herb and bread crumb mixture, perhaps with some Soymage Parmesan substitute added, the stuffing for Stuffed Vegetables, pp. 166-67, or just crushed garlic and fresh parsley and other herbs. Press any of these mixtures down into the center and between the leaves of the artichokes before drizzling on the olive oil.

4 large globe artichokes
4 cloves garlic, peeled and crushed
¼ cup extra-virgin olive oil

Preheat the oven to 375°F.

Remove the tough leaves from around the base of the artichokes. Cut off the stems and trim the bases. Snap off the tough tips of the leaves as directed on page 66. Press down on the tops of the artichokes with the palm of your hand to cause the leaves to separate. Scrape out the choke. Place a garlic clove in the center of each artichoke where the choke was. Place the artichokes in a deep baking dish, and drizzle with the olive oil. Cover the dish tightly and bake about 45 minutes, or until tender.

If the artichokes are stuffed (see the sidebar at left), uncover the dish for 10 to 15 minutes before the end of the baking time.

Per serving: Calories: 138, Protein: 1 g, Carbohydrate: 4 g, Fat: 12 g

Truffle-Style Mushrooms
FUNGHI TRIFOLATI
(can be soy-free)

Yield: 6 servings

This is delicious on crostini or polenta or as a vegetable dish. If all you have are cultivated mushrooms, the addition of a little miso adds rich flavor.

Note: The amounts of seasonings listed here are approximate. You can adjust to suit your taste.

Up to ¼ cup extra-virgin olive oil
3 cloves garlic, minced
3 tablespoons minced fresh Italian parsley
1½ pounds mushrooms, sliced (any kind, but preferably a mixture of cremini [small brown], portobello, chanterelles, and shiitake, etc.)
Salt and freshly ground black pepper, to taste

1 tablespoon light soy or chick-pea miso (use if all you have are white cultivated mushrooms)

In a large, nonstick skillet, heat 2 tablespoons olive oil with the garlic. Cook and stir until the garlic becomes pale gold in color. Add the parsley and the mushrooms, along with a little more olive oil, if you wish. Add salt and pepper to taste, and stir-fry the mushrooms until they are tender, adding a little water, if necessary, to keep them from sticking. (If you are using miso, mix it with a tablespoon of water, and add at this point. Stir over high heat until absorbed.) Serve hot or at room temperature.

Per 2 tablespoons: Calories: 106, Protein: 3 g, Carbohydrate: 13 g, Fat: 5 g

Peperonata
PEPPER AND TOMATO "STEW"
(soy-free)

Yield: 4 to 6 servings

¼ cup extra-virgin olive oil
2 large onions, thinly sliced
1 clove garlic, minced
2 large red bell peppers, seeded and cut into strips*
2 large yellow or green bell peppers, seeded and cut into strips
Salt and freshly ground black pepper, to taste
5 large, ripe plum tomatoes, or 10 canned Italian plum tomatoes, chopped
Optional: 1 to 2 tablespoons chopped fresh Italian parsley
  1 tablespoon red wine vinegar or ½ tablespoon balsamic vinegar (Add this if you plan to keep the peperonata refrigerated for a few days.)

*If you have no fresh red peppers, or they are very expensive, use roasted red peppers from a jar, rinsed well.

In a large, heavy saucepan or sauté pan with a lid, heat the olive oil. Add the onion and sauté for about 10 minutes over medium heat, or until soft—do not brown. Add the garlic and peppers, and salt to

Sweet and Sour Grilled Peppers

"Agrodolce" is a very old Sicilian way of flavoring many foods. It is also used on browned baby onions (cipollini). Cook grilled peppers, pp. 74-75, or browned baby onions in a sauce of ¼ cup dry white wine, ¼ cup crushed tomatoes or tomato pulp, 2 tablespoons red wine vinegar or white balsamic vinegar, 1 tablespoon extra-virgin olive oil, and 1 tablespoon unbleached sugar for 5 to 10 minutes. Add salt and freshly ground pepper to taste, and sprinkle with chopped Italian parsley.

Peppers were considered strictly peasant food in Italy until the 1920s, when cooking writer Ada Boni published several recipes using them in her book *Il Talismano della Felicit*. Now, as with so many European peasant foods, peppers are a necessity in modern cooking.

This typically Mediterranean dish has its origins in southern Italy, but is now popular all over Italy. The recipe changes slightly with each region and each cook, so feel free to make your own adjustments to my recipe.

Serve Peperonata on crusty bread as a sandwich, on pizza or focaccia, rolled up in piadine (Italian flat bread, p. 208), on meat alternatives, pp. 169-92, on fritatte and tortini, p. 142, on polenta, pp. 130-32, on crostini, p. 54, as a sauce on hot pasta, or just by itself as an antipasto dish.

Italians are very fond of batter-fried vegetables, which they call fritto misto. A much easier, less messy way to prepare them is to oven-fry them, breaded with "Cheesey" Bread Crumbs. Even "eggplant-haters" love it fixed this way! Because this method uses less oil, it makes the vegetables more digestible than if they were deep-fried.

Main Dish Ideas

Meat alternatives, such as seitan, your favorite commercial vegetarian cutlet, textured soy protein chunks, and marinated tofu or tempeh can also be prepared this way.

taste. Cook 10 minutes more, stirring frequently. Add the tomatoes; when they come to a boil, turn down to a simmer. Cover and cook about 25 minutes more, stirring every so often to make sure the mixture doesn't stick. The mixture should be fairly soft, but not soupy. If too much liquid remains, take the cover off and cook for a few more minutes until the liquid has almost evaporated.

Taste and add more salt, if needed, and pepper, if desired. Add the optional parsley and vinegar at this point, if using.

Per serving: Calories: 155, Protein: 2 g, Carbohydrate: 12 g, Fat: 10 g

Breaded, Oven-Fried Vegetables or "Cutlets"

VERDURE IMPANATA

Yield: 6 servings

Have ready:

1 cup plain flour

1 cup soymilk or nut milk, curdled with 2 teaspoons lemon juice or vinegar

2 to 3 cups "Cheesey" Bread Crumbs, p. 31

4 to 6 cups eggplant, zucchini or other squash, onions, large mushroom caps, or other fairly soft, quick-cooking vegetables, cut in ½-inch thick slices (Harder, longer-cooking vegetables should be partially cooked before breading and oven-frying.)

Preheat the oven to 400°F. Lightly oil two or three dark-colored cookie sheets. (Foods brown better on dark sheets).

Dip each piece of vegetable into the flour, then the soured milk, then coat all over with the "Cheesey" Bread Crumbs. Place them on the cookie sheets. If you have an oil spray pump (see page 28), spray them with a fine mist of extra-virgin olive oil.

Bake the vegetables for 10 to 15 minutes per side, or until they are soft in the center and golden on both sides. (Test one to see if it is done in the center.) If they are browning too fast, move them to a higher oven rack and/or reduce the heat a little. Serve hot.

Per serving: Calories: 162, Protein: 7 g, Carbohydrate: 29 g, Fat: 2 g

Marinated Grilled Eggplant or Zucchini
MELANZANE O ZUCCHINI A SCAPICI
Yield: about 4 servings

1 large eggplant or 2 medium zucchini (I like to do some of each)
Salt for coating the eggplant
2 tablespoons extra-virgin olive oil
1 tablespoon fresh lemon juice
Freshly ground black pepper, to taste
Optional: **Fresh mint or basil, chopped**

If using eggplant, slice it about ½-inch thick. Salt it liberally and leave it to drain for half an hour in a colander. If using zucchini, slice it ¼-inch thick and don't salt it.

Rinse and pat the eggplant dry. Brush both the eggplant and zucchini with 1 tablespoon of the oil, and grill or broil it on both sides about 3 to 4 inches from the heat source, or until slightly browned and soft. (This takes just a few minutes per side.)

Cut the vegetables into thick strips, and arrange on a serving platter. Drizzle them with the remaining olive oil and the lemon juice. Sprinkle with pepper to taste, and salt the zucchini lightly (salt isn't necessary for the eggplant). If you like, sprinkle also with chopped fresh mint or basil.

Per serving: Calories: 97, Protein: 1 g, Carbohydrate: 9 g, Fat: 7 g

"A scapici" is a southern Italian version of the Spanish or Caribbean "escabeche," cooked fish pickled in a vinegar sauce, or the Latin American "seviche," a method of "cooking" fish with the acid of lime or lemon juice. (Seviche is a very typical dish in Peru, where my father was born—now I make seviche with mushrooms.) In Italy, many vegetables are also prepared a scapici.

Some versions use vinegar instead of lemon juice, add garlic, use other herbs (such as sage), and fry the vegetables in olive oil. I like this version made with fresh lemon juice. It's such a simple recipe that you might tend to overlook it, but it is one of my absolute favorites! The eggplant melts in your mouth, and the zucchini is juicy and sweet.

Also try spreading grilled eggplant slices thinly with pesto, p. 49-50, roll up, and serve hot or at room temperature.

Roasted Potatoes with Rosemary
PATATE AL FORNO CON ROSMARINO
(soy-free)

Yield: 6 servings as a side dish

This may serve 6 as a side dish, but these are so delicious you may decide to eat nothing but the potatoes and a bit of salad for your whole meal!

3 pounds Yukon Gold or red-skinned potatoes, scrubbed
¼ cup extra-virgin olive oil
2 tablespoons chopped fresh rosemary
Salt and freshly ground black pepper, to taste

Preheat the oven to 450°F.

Cut the potatoes into small wedges or chunks. Pat them dry on clean tea towels. Place them in 2 large, shallow baking pans or jelly roll pans (cookie sheets with sides), and toss each half with 2 tablespoons olive oil and 1 tablespoon rosemary. Salt them lightly.

Bake the potatoes for about 30 minutes, turning them with a spatula from time to time and salting them. When they are tender inside and golden brown on the outside, grind fresh pepper over them and serve immediately.

Per serving: Calories: 275, Protein: 3 g, Carbohydrate: 46 g, Fat: 9 g

Roasted Beets, Italian-Style

Once you taste roasted beets, you'll never boil a beet again! Roasted beets are so sweet, with a slightly smoky taste.

To roast beets, wrap small beets or unpeeled chunks of large ones in two layers of aluminum foil. Bake them on a cookie sheet at 400°F for about two hours, or until tender when pierced with a fork. If you have a wood stove or wood heater, you can place the foil packets of beets right in the coals of your fire—this gives them an extra-special flavor.

Our favorite way to serve them is to peel them under cold running water and slice them while they are still hot. The beet slices are spread out on a platter

Roasted Garlic

Roasted garlic has many uses—squeeze the soft, buttery cloves out of the skins right onto crusty bread, crackers, or bruschetta; make Roasted Garlic-Olive Oil "Butter," p. 38, for a spread; use it in salad dressings for a mellow garlic flavor and creamy consistency (see the dressing for Piedmontese Rice Salad, p. 63), or squeeze the cloves onto roasted vegetables, p. 73, or mashed potatoes. I usually roast about four heads at a time. They will keep a week in the refrigerator in a tightly covered container.

Heat the oven or toaster oven to 400°F. Cut large garlic heads in half horizontally. Place them on foil in a baking pan, and drizzle them with about 1 teaspoon extra-virgin olive oil per half. Pull the foil up and crinkle it shut. Bake for about one hour, or until the garlic is soft.

Oven-Roasted Vegetables

Vegetables roasted at a high heat are sweet and intensely flavored. The basic method is to heat the oven to 500°F, and spread about 1½ to 2 pounds of vegetables (prepared as instructed below) in a single layer on a baking sheet, and brush them with about 2 to 4 tablespoons of extra-virgin olive oil. Sprinkle them with salt and roast them in the top half of the oven for 10 to 15 minutes, depending on their thickness and the degree of doneness that you prefer. The vegetables should be tender when pierced with a fork and just starting to brown a little.

Serve the hot vegetables plain, with salt and freshly ground pepper, with a little melted, good-tasting, nondairy margarine, or with a squirt of fresh lemon juice or balsamic vinegar. They can be served as antipasti or side dishes (contorni) or used in crusty bread or focaccia with Basil Mayonnaise, p. 30, for a delicious sandwich.

Also try Roasted Beets, p. 72, Roasted Garlic, p. 72, Grilled Mushrooms, p. 73, Roasted or Grilled Peppers, pp. 74-75, and Marinated Grilled Eggplant or Zucchini, p. 71.

Vegetables to roast:

Plum tomatoes, cut in half lengthwise

Asparagus (this is so delicious!), bottoms trimmed and tips well coated with oil

Green or wax beans, ends trimmed

Carrots, peeled and cut diagonally into ¼-inch-thick slices

Parsnips, salsify, or kohlrabi, peeled and cut into "fingers"

Baby onions (cipollini) or shallots, with skins left on

Large onions, peeled and cut into wedges

and drizzled with extra-virgin olive oil, salt, freshly ground pepper, and chopped fresh Italian parsley or mint. Add a little balsamic vinegar, too, if you like. Serve at room temperature.

Grilled Mushrooms with Pesto

I know that it is considered near-heresy in Liguria to use pesto for anything other than pasta or soup, but I can't resist passing on this very simple, but absolutely delicious, idea.

Take the stems off any number of large mushroom caps (criminis are delicious, but the white ones are fine). Fill the caps with pesto, pp. 49-51, and place them on an oiled cookie sheet. Place them about 4 inches under the broiler of your oven, and cook them until the mushrooms are a little browned around the edges and the pesto is bubbling. Serve warm with a knife and fork—they tend to be juicy.

Roasted or Grilled Peppers

Bell peppers come in a myriad of exquisite colors now—green, red, orange, yellow, purple, and brown. Roasted peppers are a frequent ingredient in modern Italian recipes, but they have always been eaten with a little olive oil as a side dish (contorno) or antipasto or have been stuffed or added to salads and sandwiches (panini).

You can buy jars of roasted red peppers in supermarkets now, and the quality of these is usually very good. In some areas, and at some times of the year, red peppers are actually cheaper to buy this way than fresh. Feel free to use these when I call for roasted or grilled peppers in my recipes, unless I specify only freshly grilled ones.

To roast your own at home, the peppers must be blackened over or under hot coals or flames. You can do this on a grill, in a broiler very close to the heat, or with a barbecue fork over an open gas flame. This takes a little patience and some watching, but it doesn't take long. Placed the blackened peppers in paper bags for 15 minutes to soften, and then peel the blackened

Grilled Portobello and Other Mushrooms

Portobello mushrooms are not Italian. (You'll get blank looks if you ever ask for them in a market in Italy!) They are actually a very large version of the domestic, cultivated North American brown or crimini mushroom, but they have a meaty texture and a rich flavor reminiscent of European mushrooms. You can use either crimini, portobello, or fresh shiitake instead of the hard-to-find and very expensive fresh porcini or cepes mushrooms so prized in European cooking.

Portobellos are available in most supermarkets across North America now, but if you can't find them, use the smaller brown or crimini, oyster, or fresh shiitake mushrooms. These aren't as dramatic-looking as the portobellos, which are often as big as a small steak—and can be served instead of one!—but they still taste delicious.

To grill, barbecue, or broil them, wash them *just* before cooking and pat them dry with paper towels. Remove the stems; you can chop them up to use in other dishes. Brush the mushrooms with an extra-virgin olive oil or a good homemade, low-fat vinaigrette, p. 61, or lemon salad dressing, p. 60. Grill or broil on a rack about 4 inches from the heat source for about 6 minutes per side, or until very tender and juicy when pierced and very well-browned on the outside.

Grilled portobellos can be sliced and used instead of meat, textured vegetable protein chunks, or seitan in many recipes, or eaten as an antipasto or side dish (contorno). Try them sliced on crostini or bruschetta—wonderful!

Italian Greens

This ubiquitous Italian vegetable dish can be served on bruschetta, p. 53 or crostini, p. 54, rolled in piadine, p. 208, served by itself as a side dish (contorno), or with white beans and crusty bread as a full meal.

Wash and trim about ½ pound of greens per person, at least—most greens cook down considerably. You can use kale, collards, rapini or Chinese broccoli (very similar), mustard or turnip greens, curly endive, Swiss chard, beet greens, spinach, arugula, young dandelion greens, or French sorrel (sourgrass), etc. Even thawed frozen greens, squeezed dry and sliced, can be used.

Drain the washed greens well. Take a bunch that you can hold down with one hand, and slice the greens into thin ribbons. Repeat with the rest of them.

In a large, heavy pot or skillet, heat 1 to 4 tablespoons of extra-virgin olive oil. Add several cloves of chopped garlic, and cook for just a few seconds—don't brown it. Then add the greens and toss them around. If you are using only very tender greens, such as spinach, arugula, sorrel, etc., just wilting them will be enough. Tougher greens will need to be cooked for up to 10 minutes. I cook them over high heat with a lid on, checking them every minute or so. Usually there is no need to add liquid, because they give off plenty, but if by some chance they dry out, add just a little bit of water or broth. Season the greens with salt (or use a little light soy or chick-pea miso) and freshly ground pepper to taste.

Some cooks like to add pancetta or prosciutto (Italian unsmoked pork products) to the greens. You can add a smoky flavor by drizzling some roasted sesame oil over the greens before serving and/or adding some chopped vegetarian Canadian or "back" bacon or "ham" when you sauté the garlic.

Other additions can be a sprinkling of red chile pepper flakes or some toasted pine nuts and plumped raisins, a Sicilian touch. Plain greens with garlic can also be topped with fresh lemon juice, a splash of balsamic vinegar, a sprinkling of Soymage Parmesan substitute, or soy-free alternative, p. 37, or toasted plain, "Cheesey," or Seasoned Bread Crumbs, p. 32. Use crusty bread to sop up the nutritious, garlicky juices.

skins off under cold running water. Remove the seeds and stems, and sprinkle the peppers with a little extra-virgin olive oil.

If you are lucky enough to have an abundance of peppers to roast, they can be frozen (after roasting and peeling) in rigid freezer containers with waxed paper between the layers.

Italian Broccoli

Break heads of broccoli into flowerettes, and cut them into thin slices. Peel and thinly slice the stalks. Proceed as for Italian Greens, but you'll have to add about ½ cup of water, broth, or wine while it cooks, and watch it carefully so that it doesn't dry out completely before it is cooked. Most of the liquid should be cooked off before serving, however.

Green Beans, Italian-Style

There are several simple ways to prepare green beans (string beans, snap beans, young runner beans, etc.). The basic recipe is to use about 1 pound for 4 people. Trim and string if necessary. Cut them only if they are very long. Steam them for about 5 minutes, drain, and immerse in very cold water to stop the cooking. Drain again. If you have no fresh green beans, use frozen, whole small green beans or romano beans, thawed but not cooked.

For each pound of beans, heat 1 to 2 tablespoons extra-virgin olive oil over medium-high heat in a large, nonstick skillet. You can use half good-tasting nondairy margarine, or add 1 teaspoon of roasted sesame oil for a smoky flavor. Add 2 cloves chopped garlic, and sauté just until they begin to turn golden. Add the beans, salt, and freshly ground pepper to taste, and toss the beans until well coated with oil and heated through.

Extra Additions (per pound of green beans):
2 tablespoons chopped fresh basil, oregano, marjoram, chives, or Italian parsley, or ½ tablespoon chopped fresh rosemary (add at the end of cooking)
1 small onion, thinly sliced (sauté a little before adding the garlic)
1 teaspoon crushed anise seeds
¼ cup dry white wine or crushed tomatoes (evaporate juices)
2 teaspoons light soy or chick-pea miso (omit salt)
¼ to ½ cup chopped vegetarian Canadian or "back" bacon, sautéed with the garlic

VI
Making
Fresh Pasta
LA PASTA FATTA
IN CASA

"The Etruscans, who inhabited part of Italy, had special implements to shape pasta and were even growing a harder wheat for it in the fourth century B.C. . . . Ancient Romans liked to fry their wheat noodle dough and sauce them with interesting ingredients such as honey or fish sauce. Sometimes their laganum, the word used for their dough strips, were baked before being used in soup.

By the thirteenth century, even before Marco Polo left for his great journey, noodles were a staple in Italy, Asia, the Middle East, and North Africa . . ."
—Linda Merinoff
The Glorious Noodle
(New York: Poseidon
Press, 1986)

It's not easy to find fresh, egg-free pasta, despite the fresh pasta craze that hit North America in the '80s. You may be able to find fresh tofu pasta in some health food stores, and there may be the odd fresh pasta producer who uses only durum semolina wheat flour and water, but most fresh pasta contains eggs (or even dried eggs). This doesn't necessarily guarantee that the pasta is tender. Much fresh pasta sold in North America is of inferior quality—rubbery and thick—and you are better off using a good-quality dry pasta instead. (See more about good dry pastas on page 83.)

If you would like to enjoy fresh pasta at its best, with light or creamy sauce or stuffed with various fillings, it's easy to make your own vegan pasta. Lasagne made with homemade pasta is very different than that made with commercial dry pasta—it just melts in your mouth!

In the following recipe, first developed for an article I wrote for *Vegetarian Times* magazine (June 1995), I use soy flour or chick-pea flour to replace part of the wheat flour and water as the liquid. The protein, fats, and lecithin in the bean flours tenderize the dough just like eggs do, coating the gluten in the wheat flour. The golden color of the bean flours also lend a pleasant golden color to the noodles.

It is possible to make noodles using only flour and water, but they don't hold up as well or have as much flavor as this version. Commercial pasta makers who use only flour and water in fresh pasta use high-protein durum semolina wheat flour, which is much tougher and requires special machines to make properly. You can also use tofu as an egg substitute, but it's more expensive, complicated (you have to blend the tofu first), and does not lend a golden color to the noodles.

In Liguria, interestingly enough, there is a type of pasta made only with flour and white wine. This is a very delicate pasta, used primarily for fazzoletti or "handerkerchiefs," very thin pasta squares which are either served with a simple sauce or rolled or folded around a savory filling, like crepes (pp. 105-07). I wouldn't recommend trying this wine pasta dough if you are a novice pasta maker, but an experienced cook might like to give it a go. You can make fazzoletti with regular pasta dough if you prefer, rolling it as thinly as possible and cutting the dough into 4-inch squares with a fluted pastry or pasta wheel cutter.

Modern chefs make herbed fazzoletti by sandwiching a few whole herb leaves and edible flowers in an artistic arrangement between two sheets of fazzoletti, which are then run through the pasta machine once more or rolled with a rolling pin to seal. The herbs and flowers make a beautiful pattern through the thin pasta when they are cooked. You can use the basic pasta dough, or try the white wine dough, if you like. Sage and basil leaves and nasturtium flowers make lovely "pictures" within the sheets of thin pasta.

Vegan Homemade Pasta
LA PASTA FATTA IN CASA VEGAN
(can be soy-free)

Yield: about 1 pound (3 to 4 servings)

1⅔ cups unbleached white flour, or 1 cup unbleached white flour and ⅔ cup whole wheat flour

½ cup chick-pea flour or full-fat soy flour

⅔ cup water

Optional: **½ to ¾ teaspoon salt**

Notes: If you are making pasta for ravioli or other stuffed pasta, add 1 tablespoon olive oil or neutral cooking oil to the dough, to make it more flexible.

Also, the amount of salt in pasta dough is variable. Some Italians never add salt to the dough, but they generally salt the cooking water more heavily than North Americans do. Eggs also contain sodium, so eggless pasta can taste flat without a bit more salt added. This is a matter of personal taste, so I have made the salt optional—however, I do add it myself.

To make the dough by hand, mix the flour, chick-pea or soy flour, and salt, if using, in a medium-sized bowl. Pour in the water and stir with a fork until the dough comes together in a ball. Knead the dough on a lightly floured surface for about 10 minutes, or until the dough is smooth. (You can also knead the dough, especially larger amounts, in a heavy-duty kitchen machine with a dough hook.) Place the dough in a plastic bag, and let it rest for at least 10 minutes.

To make the dough in a food processor, mix the dry ingredients in a dry processor bowl, then add any moist ingredients through the top with the motor running. Process for about 30 seconds or until a smooth ball forms. (The dough may seem a bit sticky, but you'll be flouring it as you work.) Place the dough in a plastic bag, and let it rest for at least 10 minutes. (cont.)

Pasta Machines

If you quiz experienced pasta makers about their favorite pasta machine, invariably they will choose the inexpensive, hand-cranked roller machine. There are electric roller-types, but they are more expensive and I don't really see the point—it's not that hard to crank the hand-driven ones (kids love to help with this!).

Extruder pasta machines were all the rage in the '80s, and most of them languish in garages and bottom cupboards for the simple reason that they produce inferior pasta. Leave extrusion pasta to the experts, the commercial dry pasta makers—that's what Italians do! Only rolled pasta is served fresh.

Never wash your pasta machine or get it wet! I just shake it and brush it with a clean pastry brush, then store it in dry plastic bags. When breaking in a new machine, throw away the first piece of dough after rolling it through the rollers several times.

To make the dough in a bread machine, place the wet and dry ingredients in the bread container according to the directions for your machine, and begin the dough cycle. Unplug the machine when it finishes kneading. Oil the dough lightly, place it in a plastic bag, and refrigerate it for at least half an hour.

To roll and cut the dough by hand, divide the dough into eighths, keeping the portion you aren't working with in the plastic bag. Roll each piece out on a floured surface until it is about 1/16th of an inch thick, flouring as you go to prevent sticking. If you like, hang the rolled-out portions of dough over the backs of chairs or on a pasta rack to dry for 5 to 10 minutes before cutting. This makes the dough a bit easier to handle.

Flour the pasta well and roll each portion up loosely like a little jelly roll. If the portions seem too long, you can cut them in half across, to make shorter noodles. Cut them into the desired widths (1/2 or 1/4 inch) with a sharp knife. Shake the noodles out and either hang them up until ready to cook, or flour them lightly and swirl them into little pasta "nests" on floured cookie sheets.

To roll and cut with a hand-crank pasta machine or electric pasta-rolling machine, divide the dough into eighths, keeping the portions you aren't working with in the plastic bag. Flour the dough well and run it through the first setting of the machine. Flour it lightly again, fold it into thirds, and run it through the first setting again. Do this until the dough looks smooth. Then flour the dough and run it through each successive setting twice, until it is the desired thickness.

I like the pasta best at the third-to-the-last setting (number 5 on my machine) and the second-to-the-last setting for stuffed pasta. This is pretty standard for the inexpensive hand-roller machines. The very expensive ones are better-aligned, so you can more easily use the last, very thin setting, if you wish.

If you like, hang the rolled-out dough to dry as instructed above. Flour each portion of dough well, and run it through whichever cutters you desire. (If the portions seem too long to you, cut each across in half to make shorter noodles.) Either hang the noodles as above until ready to cook, or flour them lightly and swirl them into little pasta "nests" on floured cookie sheets.

Note: High humidity will make the dough harder to roll out, regardless of which rolling method you use.

To cook fresh pasta, have your sauce ready and use 4 to 6 quarts of boiling salted water in a large pot over high heat. Drop in the pasta, shaking off any excess flour first (do not thaw, if frozen), and stir it gently with a fork or spaghetti rake. Cover the pot until it comes to a boil again, then remove the cover. Then count from the second the water comes to a boil again. *Be vigilant!* Very fine noodles take only about 5 seconds, thicker noodles take about 15 seconds. Very soft noodles may need to be removed as soon as the water comes to a boil again. (Thoroughly dried pasta and frozen pasta may take somewhat longer, but test one minute after the second boil.)

Some recipes for fresh pasta tell you to cook one to three minutes; this amount of time is counted from the moment the pasta is dropped into the pot, not from the second boil. Otherwise, the pasta would be overcooked. I think it is more accurate to count after the water boils, because it may take more or less time to come to a boil again depending on the temperature of the dough, how much you put in, etc.

Drain the pasta and serve immediately with your favorite sauce. (Some cooks drain the pasta over the serving bowl so that the hot water heats the bowl.) You can serve the sauce ladled individually over each serving of pasta, or toss the whole recipe with the sauce in a hot serving bowl.

Per serving: Calories: 247, Protein: 9 g, Carbohydrate: 51 g, Fat: 1 g

Storing, Freezing, and Drying Homemade Pasta

If you plan to refrigerate or freeze fresh noodles, spread them out on clean dry tea towels or hang them on drying racks or the backs of chairs for 15 to 20 minutes. You can also buy folding pasta-drying racks or improvise with dowels hung from hooks below your kitchen cupboards.

Some cooks freeze pasta uncooked, but others recommend "blanching" the pasta in boiling salted water for 15 seconds, then immersing it in ice water immediately. The drained noodles are then frozen in plastic bags. This blanching method is also recommended for frozen ravioli and other stuffed pasta.

Either way, the frozen pasta is dropped into boiling, salted water and cooked just until the pasta floats, then drained and served immediately.

Cook lasagne or cannelloni noodles before freezing or refrigerating. (Cannelloni are simply 4-inch squares of pasta that are rolled around a filling.) Cook as directed in the recipe for making pasta, then drain and immerse immediately in ice water. Drain and dry briefly on

farfalle

penne rigati

clean tea towels. Layer the noodles with waxed paper in rigid plastic containers and cover tightly. These will keep refrigerated for almost a week, or can be frozen a couple of months.

If you want to dry your homemade pasta, drying racks are the best way to insure even drying, which is an absolute necessity to prevent molding. You will have to dry it for at least 24 hours. When you are sure that the pasta is dry all the way through, you can store it in metal cookie tins or rigid plastic storage containers for about a month. Dried homemade pasta takes only a few seconds longer than fresh pasta to cook.

I prefer freezing, because the pasta is more like the fresh product. But I usually make pasta fresh each time because it's a treat, and it really doesn't take very long to make once you get the hang of it.

Making Pasta for Ravioli and Other Stuffed Noodles

Do not allow the strips of rolled-out pasta to dry out; cover them with a clean, damp tea towel while you work. Do not allow any tears in the dough, or the filling will seep out. If you find a tear or hole, fold it up and pass it through the rollers again. Roll the dough out as thinly as your machine will allow; this means the second-to-the-last setting for most inexpensive machines.

Traditional Variations on Vegan Homemade Pasta

Buckwheat Pasta *(Pizzoccheri, a specialty of Lombardy)*

Use ½ cup buckwheat flour and 1 cup plus 3 tablespoons unbleached white flour, as well as the chick-pea or soy flour. Roll the dough as thinly as possible and cut into fettuccine; then cut the noodles in half, on the diagonal, to make them shorter. These are traditionally served with cabbage or chard, leeks, potatoes, and sage in a "butter" sauce, but they can be served with any simple vegetable sauce.

Whole Wheat Pasta *(Bigoli, a specialty of Veneto)*

Use 1 cup whole wheat flour and ⅔ cup unbleached white flour, along with the chick-pea or soy flour. Traditionally, bigoli is pressed through a special extruder, not a common piece of equipment in most homes. As an alternative, roll the dough as thinly as possible, and cut into tagliatelle, a flat noodle of various widths. Serve with simple "butter" sauces and onions.

radiatorre

rigatoni

Colored Pastas

Chocolate Pasta (*Pasta al Cioccolato*)

Add about 4 teaspoons cocoa powder to the dough. This pasta was traditionally served with sweet and sour sauces containing nuts, raisins, and spices (and dates back to the Renaissance!), but for the modern palate, it is best served with mushroom sauces.

Yellow Pasta *(Pasta Gialla)*

Add ¼ teaspoon Spanish saffron threads to the water, and let it soak for several minutes (until the color comes out) before you add it to the dough. Serve with Creamy Tomato Sauce, p. 42, or Ragù alla Bolognese, p. 45.

Green Pasta *(Pasta Verde)*

Use ⅓ cup puréed cooked spinach (even processed spinach for babies or toddlers) and ⅓ cup water for the liquid.

Red-Orange Pasta *(Pasta Rossa)*

Use 1 tablespoon tomato paste plus enough water to make ⅔ cup liquid. Serve with simple "cream" sauces.

Pink pasta *(Pasta Rosa)*

Use 1 tablespoon puréed cooked beets plus enough water to make ⅔ cup liquid. (You can use the puréed beets for babies that comes in jars) Serve with "cream" or "butter" sauces or green vegetable sauces.

shells
(small=conchigliette
large=conchiglioni)

tortellini

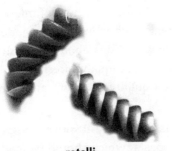

rotelli

rotini

ziti

VII
Pasta in Sauce
PASTE ASCIUTTE

"Seven days without a plate of spaghetti drops me into a deep, dark well of physical anxiety."
—Mario Puzo, author of *The Godfather*

I had thought this would be one of the longest chapters in this book when I first started writing, but pasta with a sauce is one of the most easily adapted foods for the vegan diet, and there are several books on the market on vegetarian pasta alone. One of my favorites is called *Pasta e Verdure* (140 Vegetables Sauces) by Jack Bishop (New York: Harper Collins, 1996). Just look up the vegetable, and there are several delicious sauces for pasta to make with it. Most are fairly low in fat, and you can easily substitute soy Parmesan and some of my homemade ricotta substitutes and nondairy cremes for the dairy products. I often use Jelled Broth, p. 118, in place of some of the butter called for in this type of recipe, which adds wonderful flavor, body, and glisten to the dish. (Add it at the end of cooking.) Check your library or bookstore for this book or several others in a similar vein.

What follows in this chapter are my favorite pastas with sauce, ones that I cook over and over again. (See also the sauces and ragù on pages 42-51.)

Cooking Dry Pasta

You can serve these dishes with your own homemade pasta (pp. 77-81), but you are going to find it difficult to purchase commercial, fresh vegan pasta in most places. The town where I do my shopping has an establishment run by expatriate Italians which makes wonderful eggless pasta, but it is an exception! You may be able to find tofu pasta in some natural food store refrigerator cases, but don't think you are necessarily getting a product superior to a good dry pasta.

When the fresh pasta craze hit North America a few years back, many mistakenly thought that they were being "authentic" by always using the fresh product, not realizing that much of it was of inferior quality; commercial fresh pasta is often rubbery, instead of tender, and cut too thick. Italians have no compunctions about using dry pasta—in fact, southern Italians prefer it! Good-quality fresh pasta is really a different food product from good-quality dry pasta, and comparison is unfair.

Fresh noodles are lighter than dry pasta and easily absorb sauces, so they are best with creamy sauces. Dry pasta, which should be made from nothing more than water and the best durum semolina wheat (a high-protein wheat), is more suited to robust sauces with stronger flavors—ideally suited to the flavors of southern Italy.

Although pastas are somewhat interchangeable, there are a few guidelines to remember when matching sauces to pasta. Simple tomato, "cream," or "butter" sauces go well with any type of pasta. Delicate sauces made with finely diced ingredients can be used on long, thin pastas. Chunky sauces are better served with large tubular pastas or shapes such as shells. Very small pastas are generally served in soup.

Cook dry pasta in a large pot with *lots* of boiling, salted water—about 4 to 6 quarts of water per pound of pasta. Italians *always* add salt to the pasta water, using about 1½ tablespoons salt per pound of pasta to be cooked and adding the salt just before adding the pasta. If you don't normally salt the water, try it—you'll notice a great difference! You *do not* need to add oil to the pot to keep the pasta from sticking—plenty of rapidly boiling water will keep it well separated. Furthermore, oil makes the pasta slick. Properly cooked pasta should have a light film of starch that helps bind the sauce to it. Oil does the opposite.

Stir the pasta well with a pasta rake or long-handled fork as soon as you drop it in to keep it from sticking together. Cook the pasta until "al dente," which means "to the tooth" or tender but still chewy. Cooking times are different according to the thickness and shape of the pasta. The recommended times listed on packaging are usually too long, so test the pasta by tasting it about 5 minutes before the suggested time. If the pasta is to be baked, undercook it.

Don't overdrain the pasta—it should still be a little wet when sauced. Drain the pasta over the serving bowl; this heats the serving bowl and allows you to save some of the pasta cooking water, which may be needed to thin the sauce or moisten the pasta, should it dry out. Some cooks add a couple of tablespoons of melted butter or olive oil to the drained pasta to keep it from sticking, but I don't find it necessary to add more fat if the pasta is served right away. Sauce the pasta immediately, either tossing all of it with the sauce in the hot serving

Most of the major Italian restaurants in North America use dry pastas made by such reliable companies as De-Cecco and Del Verde, and these brands are recommended by Italian food experts, such as Lynn Rosetto Kasper. If you prefer a whole grain pasta, choose one that is a light beige in color and made with whole durum semolina wheat, not brown pasta made from ordinary whole wheat flour, which will taste muddy and pasty. Catelli makes a good product, but they only make a few shapes, such as lasagne, spaghetti, and macaroni.

For celiacs and people who are allergic to wheat, there are now some excellent Italian-style rice pastas. Good brands are Pastariso and DeBoles.

Italians usually eat a small portion of pasta as a primo or first course, but having a larger portion of pasta as the entire meal is becoming more popular for either the midday or evening meal. Count on using 2 to 3 ounces of dry pasta per serving for a primo and 4 to 6 ounces for a main course.

bowl or filling individual heated plates or pasta bowls with pasta and topping with the sauce. (Don't drown the pasta in sauce.) Italian cooks expect you to be ready and waiting when the pasta is about to be drained!

To cook the pasta ahead of time, use the "al segreto" method, cooking the pasta for 2 minutes less than you would to make it "al dente." Drain, but don't rinse it. When you are ready to serve it, add the pasta to some of the heated sauce in a skillet, and cook it over low heat for 2 or 3 minutes, then place in a heated bowl with more of the sauce on top.

Spaghetti per Mimi

(soy-free)

Yield: 4 servings

Mimi is one of my husband's stepdaughters. I made this for her when we visited her near Montreal a few years ago, and it has remained a favorite. This chunky vegetable sauce is easily and quickly made with ingredients that you probably always have in your cupboard and refrigerator.

3 tablespoons extra-virgin olive oil
1 large green pepper, thinly sliced
1 medium onion, thinly sliced
3 cloves garlic, chopped
½ pound fresh mushrooms, sliced
½ cup sliced, pitted black calamata olives
1 handful fresh basil, chopped, or 1 tablespoon dried basil plus a handful of fresh Italian parsley, chopped
3 large, dried tomato halves or oil-packed, sun-dried tomato halves, chopped
½ teaspoon dried rosemary
2 pounds ripe plum tomatoes, chopped, or 1 (28-ounce) can good-quality diced tomatoes with juice
½ cup dry red wine, or 6 tablespoons water plus 2 tablespoons balsamic vinegar
1 teaspoon salt
½ teaspoon unbleached sugar
Freshly ground pepper, to taste
Soymage Parmesan substitute, or soy-free alternative, p. 37
1 pound spaghetti

Put a large pot of water on to boil for the spaghetti.

In a large, heavy skillet, heat the olive oil, then add the green pepper, onion, garlic, mushrooms, olives, basil, dried tomatoes, and rosemary. Sauté over medium-high heat until the onions are limp.

Add the tomatoes and juice, wine, salt, sugar, and pepper. Cook this uncovered over medium-high heat until it has cooked down to a sauce consistency, about 10 minutes Meanwhile, cook the spaghetti until al dente, salting the water first. Drain the spaghetti and top immediately with the sauce and soy Parmesan.

Per serving: Calories: 407, Protein: 9 g, Carbohydrate: 52 g, Fat: 14 g

Spring Vegetable Pasta
PASTA ALLA PRIMAVERA
(can be soy-free)

Yield: 6 servings

1 recipe medium-thick Dairy-Free White Sauce, p. 36

1 pound dry egg-free fettuccine "nests," or linguine, spaghetti, or other favorite pasta

1 medium onion, sliced

2 large cloves garlic, chopped

1 pound thin asparagus, trimmed and cut diagonally into slices

½ pound button or crimini mushrooms, sliced

2 small zucchini or other summer squash, cut into ¼ -inch rounds

1 small carrot or 4 baby carrots, peeled, halved lengthwise, and sliced diagonally ⅛ inch thick

6 ounces cauliflower, cut into small slices

1 to 2 tablespoons extra-virgin olive oil

1 cup petit pois, or 2 cups edible-pod peas, sliced 1 inch wide

5 green onions, chopped

2 tablespoons chopped fresh basil

Salt and pepper, to taste

Soymage Parmesan substitute, or soy-free alternative, p. 37

Make the white sauce, then put the pasta on to cook in a large pot of boiling salted water.

My version of this famous spring vegetable pasta dish is gorgeously creamy, but is much lower in fat than most recipes. Broiling the vegetables first adds a delicious flavor. You can substitute any other vegetables that seem appropriate or that proliferate in your garden or produce store.

Place all of the vegetables except the peas and green onions, in a large, shallow roasting pan, and toss with the olive oil. Place the pan 3 or 4 inches under the broiler of your oven, and roast the vegetables until they are slightly charred. Turn them over with a spatula, add the peas and green onions, and broil them until they are crisp-tender and have some slightly charred edges. This process should take only about 10 minutes. Add the basil and white sauce to the vegetables, and stir gently. Add salt and pepper to taste. When the pasta has cooked to al dente, drain it and add to the sauce. Toss well and serve hot, with soy Parmesan or soy-free alternative.

Per serving: Calories: 294, Protein: 11 g, Carbohydrate: 41 g, Fat: 8 g

Pasta with Raw Tomato Sauce
PASTA AL POMODORO CRUDO
(soy-free)

Yield: 6 servings

This is one of the fastest and most delicious recipes in the book (sort of an Italian salsa cruda), but you must have good, ripe tomatoes (preferably Italian plum tomatoes) and fresh basil; save this for late summer meals.

Traditionally, this not eaten with any kind of cheese on it.

1 pound rotelle, fusilli, rigati, rigatone, or radiatore pasta
6 cloves garlic, peeled
6 tablespoons chopped fresh basil
2 pounds ripe tomatoes (preferably plum-type), chunked
2 to 4 tablespoons extra-virgin olive oil
1 to 2 teaspoons salt
1 teaspoon freshly ground black pepper
12 pitted black calamata olives

Cook the pasta in a large pot of boiling, salted water.

Place the garlic and basil in a food processor, and pulse until finely chopped. Add the remaining ingredients, and pulse quickly.

Drain the pasta and immediately toss with the uncooked sauce. Serve right away with salad and crusty bread.

Per serving: Calories: 210, Protein: 5 g, Carbohydrate: 29 g, Fat: 8 g

Pasta with Spicy Eggplant Sauce
PASTA CON SALSA DI MELANZANE
(soy-free)

Yield: 4 servings

1 pound penne rigate or other favorite pasta

2 tablespoons extra-virgin olive oil

1½ pounds eggplant, cut into large dice

8 large cloves garlic, minced

¼ to ½ teaspoon dried red pepper flakes

2 pounds ripe plum tomatoes, chopped, or 1 (28-ounce) can diced
   tomatoes and juice

1 teaspoon salt

½ teaspoon unbleached sugar

¼ cup chopped fresh Italian parsley

Optional: Soy Parmesan, or soy-free alternative, p. 37

Some people prefer spaghetti, ziti, fusilli, or other pastas with this typical southern Italian sauce, but penne is my favorite. Penne is a tubular pasta with pointy ends, a perfect foil for this *very* quick and wonderful eggplant sauce.

Put on a large pot of salted water for the pasta. Broil the eggplant chunks on both sides in the oven broiler until softened. Set aside.

In a large, nonstick or lightly oiled pot, heat the olive oil and sauté the garlic and red pepper flakes lightly. Add the tomatoes, broiled eggplant, salt, and sugar. Simmer over medium-high heat, and begin cooking the pasta.

Drain the pasta when it's done, and add the parsley to the sauce. Serve the sauce over the hot pasta with soy Parmesan on the side.

Per serving: Calories: 319, Protein: 8 g, Carbohydrate: 54 g, Fat: 7 g

Penne all' Arrabbiata

"ENRAGED" PENNE
(soy-free)

Yield: 4 servings

This is a very simple dish, but spicy and satisfying. It's another of those great pasta dishes that can be ready in the time it takes to boil the pasta.

This dish is traditionally not eaten with cheese.

1 pound penne rigate or other tubular pasta
¼ cup extra-virgin olive oil
6 to 8 cloves garlic, chopped
¼ to ½ teaspoon dried red pepper flakes
2 pounds ripe plum tomatoes, or 1 (28-ounce) can Italian plum tomatoes
½ to 1 teaspoon salt
¼ cup chopped fresh Italian parsley

Put a large pot of salted water on to boil for the pasta.

In a large, heavy skillet or pot, heat the oil over medium heat. Add the garlic and hot pepper, and stir just until the garlic begins to change color. Remove from heat. If you have a manual food mill (mouli), you can set it right over the pot and grind the tomatoes and juice right into it with the coarse blade. If you don't have one, use a food processor, but pulse it and leave it a bit rough. You can also use a can of good-quality crushed tomatoes, but not puréed tomatoes.

Place the pan back on the heat, add the salt, and simmer uncovered while you cook the pasta to the al dente stage.

Taste the sauce for salt, drain the pasta, and add it to the sauce. Toss well and let it cook in the sauce for a minute or two. Sprinkle with the parsley and serve.

Per serving: Calories: 331, Protein: 8 g, Carbohydrate: 43 g, Fat: 14 g

Spaghetti Alla Puttanesca

(can be soy-free)

Yield: 4 servings

2 to 3 tablespoons extra-virgin olive oil
2 cloves garlic, sliced, or more to taste

1-inch piece dried hot red pepper

2 pounds ripe plum tomatoes, chopped, or 1 (28-ounce) can diced
   tomatoes, drained (save the juice)

⅔ cup pitted, sliced black calamata olives

Optional: 1 tablespoon capers

2 tablespoons light soy or chick-pea miso

Freshly ground black pepper, to taste

1 pound spaghetti

2 tablespoons chopped fresh Italian parsley

Put on a large pot of salted water to boil for the pasta.

In a large, heavy skillet or pot, heat the olive oil over medium heat.
Add the garlic and hot pepper, and cook just until the garlic starts to
change color slightly. Add the tomatoes, olives, and capers, and let
simmer while you cook the spaghetti to the al dente stage. If you are
using canned tomatoes and the sauce is too dry, add some of the
reserved tomato juice.

Mash the miso in a small bowl with some of the sauce, then add it
back to the sauce, and stir well. Add salt and pepper to taste. Add the
drained pasta, toss well, and cook for a minute. Sprinkle with parsley and serve immediately.

Per serving: Calories: 342, Protein: 8 g, Carbohydrate: 47 g, Fat: 14 g

This dish with the unre-
fined name "Spaghetti in
the manner of a prostitute"
is exceedingly popular—
perhaps because of the
speed and ease of its
preparation, or perhaps
because of the wonderful
flavors. Anchovies are
replaced by miso in this
version.

Traditionally this is
pasta dish is not eaten with
cheese.

Sicilian Pasta with "Fried" Eggplant

PASTA ALLA NORMA

(can be soy-free)

Yield: 4 servings

1 large eggplant, sliced ½-inch thick

Salt

Extra-virgin olive oil

Sauce:

2 tablespoons extra-virgin olive oil

You will find this pasta
dish , with minimal variations, all over Sicily.
Apparently, it was named
after the heroine of
Sicilian composer
Vincenzo Bellini's most
famous opera, "La
Norma," because he was
so fond of this dish.

Leftover Pasta

Reheating leftover pasta is frowned upon in Italy. Leftover pasta is usually used in fritatte or soup. However, fully cooked pasta can be successfully reheated in a microwave without drying it out or overcooking it. Cover the plate of pasta with another plate or a glass pie pan, and cook on high for about 1 or 2 minutes, depending on the quantity of pasta. You can also place the pasta in a bowl, and pour boiling water over it. Drain it as soon as it's as hot as you want it, and use immediately. This is a good method to use when someone is having seconds and the pasta has cooled off. You can also heat up leftover pasta in a glass pie pan covered with foil at 350°F in an oven or toaster oven for 15 to 20 minutes, but I wouldn't heat up the oven just for that.

Most Italians consider cold pasta "dead pasta," so you won't be served many pasta salads in Italy except in "touristy" areas. You may, however, encounter pasta dishes served at room temperature during the heat of summer.

1 large onion, minced

2 cloves garlic, minced

2 pounds fresh tomatoes, chopped, or 1 (28-ounce) can plum tomatoes, chopped, or diced tomatoes with juice

¼ cup tomato paste

2 sprigs fresh basil, chopped

1 teaspoon salt

Freshly ground black pepper, to taste

Flour

1 pound spaghetti or other long, thin pasta

1 cup crumbled Tofu or Almond Ricotta Salata, pp. 34-36

Sprinkle the eggplant slices liberally with salt, and let set in a colander to drain while you make the sauce.

Heat the olive oil in a medium-sized heavy saucepan over moderately high heat. Add the onion and garlic, and sauté until the onion softens. Add the tomatoes, tomato paste, basil, salt, and pepper. Simmer the sauce for about 20 minutes.

Preheat the oven to 400°F.

Rinse the eggplant well and pat it dry. Coat it with flour. Place it on a dark-colored cookie sheet coated with olive oil, and lightly brush or spray the top with a little more olive oil. Bake the eggplant slices for about 10 minutes, or until the bottom is golden. Turn the slices over and bake until the other sides are golden and the middles are soft. Keep warm while you boil the pasta until al dente.

For each serving, place some hot, drained pasta on a warm plate or pasta bowl, top with some of the eggplant slices, cover with some of the sauce, and sprinkle with some of the ricotta salata.

If you prefer, you can fry the eggplant in olive oil, as is traditionally done. But eggplant soaks up so much oil, I usually bake it instead.

If you have no soy or almond ricotta salata made, you can substitute Soymage Parmesan substitute, or soy-free alternative, p. 37.

Per serving: Calories: 380, Protein: 13 g, Carbohydrate: 58 g, Fat: 10 g

Fettuccine with Wild Mushrooms
FETTUCCINE CON FUNGHI FRESCHI
(can be soy-free)

Yield: 4 servings

1½ pounds fresh wild mushrooms

1 to 2 tablespoons extra-virgin olive oil or good-tasting nondairy
margarine

3 to 4 cloves garlic, minced

1 pound fettuccine (whole wheat or chocolate pasta, pp. 80-81, can
be used with this sauce successfully)

1¾ to 2 cups thin Dairy-Free White Sauce (can use soy-free
version), p. 36, Easy Tofu Creme, p. 39, or Easy Cashew or Rice
Creme, p. 40

Salt and freshly ground pepper, to taste

3 to 4 tablespoons chopped fresh Italian parsley

Soymage Parmesan substitute, or soy-free alternative, p. 37

Put a large pot of water on to boil for the fettuccine. Clean and slice the mushrooms thinly.

Heat the oil or margarine over high heat in a large, nonstick skillet. When bubbly, add the garlic and cook for just 30 seconds. Add the mushrooms. Stir-fry over high heat until the mushrooms have exuded their own juice and then evaporated most of it again, about 8 minutes.

Meanwhile, add the pasta to the boiling, salted water. Add the white sauce or creme to the mushrooms, and stir well. Add salt and freshly ground pepper to taste and the parsley. Keep warm over low heat until you drain the pasta. Toss the hot pasta with the sauce, and serve immediately with soy Parmesan or soy-free alternative.

Per serving: Calories: 352, Protein: 12 g, Carbohydrate: 46 g, Fat: 12 g

This is a treat in the autumn, when fresh wild mushrooms are to be found. We pick chanterelles (gallinaci) in September near our home, and this is the dish Brian always asks me to make first. In Italy, of course, fresh porcinis are used whenever possible. If you rely on a supermarket for mushrooms, you can use chanterelles, oyster mushrooms, fresh stemmed shiitakes, portobellos, or even the small brown domestic mushrooms, criminis. A combination would be excellent.

VIII
Stuffed Pasta

(DUMPLINGS, CREPES,
AND BAKED,
LAYERED, AND
MOLDED PASTA
DISHES)

PASTE RIPIENE
(GNOCCHI,
CRESPELLE,
E PASTICCI E PASTE
AL FORNO)

"Making love and cap-
pelletti are the paradise of
the poor."
        —Italian folk saying

There are so many imaginative Italian dumplings and stuffed pastas that a whole book could be devoted to them, so I'll pass along only my very favorite recipes here. The names of Italian dumplings, or gnocchi, vary from region to region, so the names I use here may be different than those you are familiar with.

Most gnocchi recipes come from the north and seem to be of Germanic origin, but "Strangolapreti" (priest-chokers) are potato dumplings of Neapolitan origin. Gnocchi, at first glance, seem to be a humble food, unpretentious and nourishing, made from such peasant staples as potatoes, bread crumbs, greens or squash, flour, even semolina flour or cornmeal (polenta). But, in fact, they have a delicate, sophisticated flavor and texture.

Gnocchi used to be referred to as ravioli in ancient times, and some gnocchi do resemble ravioli fillings without the pasta wrapping (see Spinach-"Ricotta" Dumplings or Gnocchi Verde, p. 93). What we now call ravioli, an envelope of pasta with a stuffing, used to be referred to as "tortelli" until the end of the 18th century. They were a clever and tasty way of using up leftovers and cheap cuts of meat, even meat juices eked out with bread crumbs. The term "ravioli" comes from "rabioli," meaning "things of little value." Three-inch rounds, squares, or triangles of pasta stuffed with a cheese and spinach filling are still called "tortelloni" in some areas, and smaller squares or half-moon-shaped pastas are called "tortelli."

Cappelletti and tortellini are two words for the same type of pasta which is stuffed and then rolled around the finger and pinched together at the ends. Tortellini, nicknamed "umbilichi sacri" or "sacred navels" in reference to Venus' navel, start out with circles of dough. Cappelletti start out with squares of dough which make little peaks when they are folded—thus the name, meaning "little hats." Cappellacci are larger versions of cappelletti, usually with a pumpkin stuffing. I have not given instructions for these rather more complicated and time-consuming shapes.

Two and one-half-inch squares or rounds of ravioli with almost any filling are called "agnolotti" (fat little lambs) in Piedmont, and slightly smaller squares or half-moons filled with cheese and/or vegetables are called "agnolini" or "anolini" in Lombardy. In Liguria, the local ravioli is called "pansotti" ("pansuti" in Genoese, and you will see many other spellings). These are fairly large triangular or round "potbellied" dumplings filled with cheese and green herbs.

In recent years, ravioli have become very trendy in both Italy and North America, stuffed with just about anything under the sun—

asparagus, eggplant, artichokes, radicchio, etc. So, feel free to experiment after you try these more "traditional" fillings. You will find suggestions for saucing various kinds of ravioli which can guide you in your own recipes.

Crepes, or crespelle, may not be the first thing that comes to mind when Italian food is mentioned, but they have been enjoyed for centuries in Italy, even by the Medicis (see notes with the recipe on pages 105-06), and you will find the Italian way of serving them ideal for simple family meals and for entertaining.

Spinach-"Ricotta" Dumplings

GNOCCHI VERDE

(can be soy-free)

Yield: 36 to 40 gnocchi

1 pound fresh spinach or Swiss chard, or 1 (10-ounce) package frozen chopped spinach
2 cups Tofu Ricotta, p. 32, or soy-free Almond Ricotta, p. 35
⅞ to 1 cup unbleached flour (use the lesser amount with Tofu Ricotta)
½ cup Soymage Parmesan substitute, or soy-free alternative, p. 37
1 teaspoon salt
Freshly ground black pepper, to taste
Pinch of freshly ground nutmeg
Reduction "Butter" Sauce, p. 48, Marinara Sauce, p. 42, or Dairy-Free White Sauce, p. 36
Soymage Parmesan substitute, or soy-free alternative, p. 37

Wash the spinach or chard well, then trim off the stems and steam in several inches of boiling water until tender, about 3 to 5 minutes. Drain it well, squeeze dry, and chop. If you are using frozen spinach, thaw it and squeeze dry. (You can quick-thaw it in the microwave right in the box for 5 minutes.)

Mix together the spinach or chard, ricotta, flour, Parmesan, salt, black pepper, and nutmeg in a bowl. Cover and chill for an hour or more.

These are a favorite of ours, and I was so pleased that they worked well without dairy products and eggs—they're still light and delicately flavorful. You can serve them with a light marinara (tomato) sauce or a thin white sauce, if you wish, but the traditional way is to serve them simply with melted butter and Parmesan cheese. Melted, good-tasting, nondairy margarine or Reduction "Butter" Sauce and Soymage Parmesan substitute (or a soy-free variation) are lighter vegan alternatives.

By the way, in Tuscany these are called "ravioli gnudi" or just "nudi," because they are like spinach ravioli filling without the dough—therefore naked! In Lombardy, they are called "strozza-preti," or "priest-chokers"!

Scoop spoonfuls of the mixture (about the size of a small walnut) onto a well-floured surface, and then form into balls with floured hands. Place on floured cookie sheets, and refrigerate until time to cook.

Preheat the oven to 400°F.

Bring a large pot of salted water to a boil. Drop the dumplings into the boiling water about 10 at a time, and boil gently for about 4 to 5 minutes. (The almond ricotta ones seem to need a little less cooking time than the tofu ricotta ones.) Scoop into a colander with a slotted spoon, drain, and place on a greased baking dish. Drizzle with a little bit of Reduction "Butter" Sauce (or ¼ cup of melted margarine, if you aren't worried about fat), and sprinkle with soy Parmesan or soy-free alternative. Bake the gnocchi for about 15 minutes, then serve hot with more Reduction "Butter" Sauce, Marinara Sauce, or Dairy-Free White Sauce.

Per gnocchi: Calories: 41, Protein: 2 g, Carbohydrate: 3 g, Fat: 2 g

Potato Dumplings or "Priest-Stranglers"
STRANGOLAPRETI O GNOCCHI DI PATATE
(soy-free)
Yield: 6 servings

2 pounds russet potatoes
1 teaspoon salt
Optional: **¼ teaspoon white pepper**
Up to 1¾ cups unbleached flour

Either bake the potatoes whole until they are very tender, or scrub them, cut into even-sized chunks, and steam on a rack over boiling water. You can also steam them in a covered glass pie dish with a couple of tablespoons of water in the microwave until they are tender. (This will take about 9 minutes.)

Whichever way you cook them, drain them well, if necessary, and peel them or scoop the insides out, scraping the skin well. *While still*

Evidently, these Neapolitan dumplings were a common dish to serve the hungry parish priest when he came to dinner, hence the name! Whatever the name, it is a comforting winter dish and a lot easier to make than it sounds. Forming the dumplings takes only about 15 minutes, and they take seconds to cook.

Some recipes include eggs, but eggs actually make a tougher dumpling. It is often recommended that "old" potatoes be used, as they make a drier dumpling. But I've found that using russets (baking potatoes) and either baking, steaming, or microwaving them works fine.

hot, mash the potatoes in a bowl with the salt (and optional pepper, if using). Slowly add the flour until a sticky but kneadable dough forms. (The less flour you have to add, the more tender the dumpling will be.) Knead the dough on a lightly floured surface for 2 or 3 minutes, then pat out into a ½-inch-thick rectangle. Cut the rectangle into 1-inch thick strips. Re-flour the surface lightly, and roll the strips with your hands into "ropes" ½ inch in diameter. Cut the "ropes" into ¾-inch sections. Have several cookie sheets ready sprinkled with flour.

To form the gnocchi, place each ¾-inch section of dough on the tines of a fork (in the inner curve, as illustrated), and press a deep indentation with your thumb. This makes a curved dumpling with a hollow center and a ribbed design on the outside. Place the finished gnocchi on the floured cookie sheets, not touching.

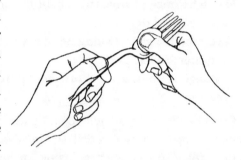

If you aren't going to cook them for a few hours, refrigerate the trays.

When ready to cook, preheat the oven to 350°F, and bring a large pot of salted water to a boil. Drop in the gnocchi into the boiling water, a few at a time. They are done when they rise to the surface. Scoop them out with a slotted spoon, and place in a colander to drain. Cook and drain the remaining gnocchi the same way. Place the gnocchi in one layer in a well-oiled oven-proof casserole. Cover with a little bit of whatever sauce you are using, and place the casserole in the oven for a few minutes, just to heat them up. Serve with more sauce and soy Parmesan or soy-free alternative.

Per serving: Calories: 233, Protein: 5 g, Carbohydrate: 52 g, Fat: 0 g

All Italian dumplings can be served with a marinara sauce, p. 42, melted margarine or Reduction "Butter" Sauce, p. 48, and fresh sage, or Walnut Sauce, p. 48, along with Soymage Parmesan substitute, or soy-free alternative, p. 37. Potato dumplings are also delicious with Ragù alla Napoletana, p. 43, any mushroom sauce (especially a porcini sauce!), Spicy Eggplant Sauce, p. 87, (omitting the hot pepper flakes), or with Pesto, p. 49-51, thinned with some of the water used to cook the dumplings. Potato Dumplings are also good with bitter greens or Savoy cabbage and a little chopped vegetarian Canadian or "back" bacon and garlic sautéed in olive oil and broth.

Baked Semolina Dumplings
GNOCCHI DI SEMOLINA
(can be soy-free)

Yield: 4 to 6 servings

This is perfect "comfort food" for a cold winter evening in northern Italy.

3½ cups reduced-fat soymilk or rice milk

1 cup semolina cereal ("Cream of Wheat" or "wheatlets")

3 cloves garlic, crushed

¼ teaspoon freshly grated nutmeg

Pinch of freshly ground black or white pepper

½ cup Soymage Parmesan substitute, or soy-free alternative, p. 37

Flour for dredging

¼ cup melted good-tasting nondairy margarine or Reduction "Butter" sauce, p. 48

Soymage Parmesan substitute or soy-free alternative, to sprinkle on top

Combine the milk, semolina, and garlic in a heavy-bottomed medium saucepan. Bring to a boil, stirring constantly, over high heat, then turn down to a simmer and cook for 5 to 7 minutes, or until quite thick.

Stir in the nutmeg, pepper, and soy Parmesan or soy-free alternative. Spread the mixture out on an oiled cookie sheet, and refrigerate until it is cool.

Preheat the oven to 425°F.

Shape the mixture into 1½-inch balls, and coat with flour. Flatten them slightly and overlap them in an oiled casserole. Drizzle with the melted margarine or Reduction "Butter" Sauce, and sprinkle with soy Parmesan or soy-free alternative. Bake for 10 minutes and serve hot.

Variation: Add a little chopped vegetarian Canadian or "back" bacon to the semolina mixture while it cooks.

Per serving: Calories: 304, Protein: 11 g, Carbohydrate: 37 g, Fat: 12 g

Pumpkin Dumplings
GNOCCHI DI ZUCCA
(soy-free)

Yield: 4 servings

10 ounces russet potato, baked, steamed, or microwaved until tender as directed for Potato Dumplings, p. 94
1 cup mashed baked butternut squash
1 teaspoon salt
¼ teaspoon freshly grated nutmeg
⅛ teaspoon white pepper
1 cup unbleached flour
Optional: **1 tablespoon organic grated lemon or orange zest**

Peel and mash the potato *while still hot*. Mash in the squash, salt, and seasonings. Slowly add the flour to make a sticky but kneadable dough. You can add up to ¼ cup more flour if necessary.

Follow the recipe for the potato dumplings, and serve as suggested in the comments at right.

Per serving: Calories: 182, Protein: 4 g, Carbohydrate: 41 g, Fat: 0 g

These dumplings are made in exactly the same way as the potato dumplings on page 94. They should be served with melted margarine or Reduction "Butter" Sauce with a few sage leaves or some chopped fresh rosemary heated in it, or with Walnut Sauce, p. 36—both with soy Parmesan, or soy-free alternative, p. 37.

Zucca, or Italian pumpkin, is actually more like our butternut squash than our pumpkin. You want it to be as dry as possible, so bake it until it's very tender (you can use leftover baked squash). The potato should be prepared as in the potato dumpling recipe.

Use organic citrus zest if you can buy organic fruit in your area. Pesticides become concentrated in citrus fruit peels.

Polenta Gnocchi

Make firm polenta, using broth and either the microwave version or the 6-serving pressure-cooker or double-boiler versions (see pages 130-32). Add 2 to 3 cloves crushed garlic, a few dashes of pepper, and ⅓ cup minced fresh Italian parsley. Pour the polenta into an oiled 11 x 15-inch cookie sheet with sides (or jelly roll pan), about ½ inch thick. Chill until firm—you can cool this quickly in the freezer.

To serve, cut into 2-inch squares, then cut the squares diagonally into triangles. Overlap the triangles in an oiled, shallow baking pan. Drizzle with melted nondairy margarine (with or without some fresh sage leaves) or Reduction "Butter" Sauce, p. 48. Sprinkle with Soymage Parmesan substitute, or soy-free alternative, p. 37, and/or drizzle with Dairy-Free White Sauce, p. 36. Bake at 400°F for 10 to 15 minutes.

Master Recipe for Stuffed Pasta Envelopes, Ravioli, Etc.

(can be soy-free)

Yield: 4 to 6 servings

1 recipe Homemade Vegan Pasta, pp. 77-81, made with either soy or chick-pea flour (Read the special notes in the pasta recipe which refer specifically to filled pasta.)

Filling of your choice (see pages 100-01), thoroughly chilled

To fill the ravioli, roll the dough out as instructed on page 78 to the second-to-the-last setting of your pasta-rolling machine or by hand about ⅟₁₆ inch thick. Place the dough on a lightly floured surface, and keep covered with a damp cloth when not working with it.

For tortelli or agnolini: Cut each length of dough into 2-inch wide strips. Cut into 2-inch circles or squares with a ravioli stamp, cookie cutter, or pasta or pastry cutter. Place a heaping teaspoon of filling in the center of half the rounds or squares. To seal, brush water around the edges of the filled dough discs or squares, and cover with the remaining discs or squares. For "half-moon" shapes, cut rounds and place a teaspoon of filling in the center of each one, moisten one edge, fold the dough over to make a half-moon shape, and seal the edges.

Don't over-fill the dough, and make sure that no filling gets into the seal on the edges, or it may break open when cooking. (If the dough is nice and moist, you don't need to moisten the edges to get a good seal.) Seal with fork tines, a pastry wheel, or a fluted pasta cutter.

For ravioli or agnolotti: Cut the lengths of rolled-out dough into 2½-inch wide strips, and cut 2½-inch squares or rounds with a ravioli stamp, cookie cutter, or pasta or pastry cutter. Fill half of them as directed above for tortelli, and cover them with the remaining squares or rounds, sealing as instructed.

For tortelloni: Cut the rolled-out lengths of dough into 3-inch strips, and cut it into 3-inch rounds or squares with a ravioli stamp, cookie cutter, or pastry or pasta cutter. Fill half of them as directed for tortelli, using about ½ tablespoon filling. Cover them with the remaining rounds or squares, and then seal as instructed for tortelli. For "half-moon" or triangle shapes, place about 1 teaspoon filling in the center of each round or square, moisten one edge, fold the dough over to make a half-moon shape or triangle, and seal the edges as instructed in the beginning of the recipe.

Cover cookie sheets with wax paper, and sprinkle with cornmeal or flour. Place the filled pasta shapes on the cookie sheets (not touching), and cover with dry, clean tea towels while a large pot of salted water comes to a boil. Turn the pasta envelopes frequently so they don't get soggy on the bottom and tear when you try to pick them up. (See page 100 about pre-cooking stuffed pasta.)

Have the serving platter and plates hot and your sauce warm before you start cooking the ravioli. Cook them in 2 or 3 batches, dropping them one at a time into rapidly boiling water. They need to cook no longer than 3 to 4 minutes once the water has come back to a gentle boil. (Don't let the water boil so hard that the dumplings come apart.)

Be ready to start cooking your stuffed pasta shapes as soon as they are stuffed—have a large pot of salted water ready to come to a boil, your sauce ready, and a platter warming up. To make ahead and serve later, read the notes on storing, pre-cooking, and freezing stuffed pasta on pages 79-80.

Note: You can make the pasta several hours ahead of time and keep it refrigerated in a plastic bag. Divide it into 8 pieces and keep covered. You can also make the filling several hours or days ahead of time and keep refrigerated.

Saucing the Ravioli
Top your homemade stuffed pasta with Reduction "Butter" sauce, p. 48, or any of the fresh tomato sauces on pages 42-51. You may also use a thin white sauce, p. 36, Mushroom Sauce, p. 47, or a Walnut Sauce, p. 48. "Cheese" ravioli may be topped with a ragù, pp. 45-46, for a hearty dish.

Porcini Filling

Use the Mushroom Filling, but use fresh porto-bellos, criminis, or shi-itakes, and add about 1 ounce dried porcini or boletus mushrooms which have soaked 45 minutes in hot water. Strain the broth and use it instead of the wine in the filling. Mince the soaked, dried mush-rooms very finely, and add to the filling.

Asparagus Filling

Use the Mushroom Filling with white button or oyster mushrooms. Add 1 cup of cooked fresh asparagus, cut in ½-inch pieces, and process in the food processor until the asparagus is well mixed with the mushrooms and no large chunks remain.

"Meat" Filling

Use the "Meat" and Spinach Filling for Canneloni on page 108, but grind it very finely in the food processor. If it still seems too crumbly, bind it with a little "cream," p. 32, or Dairy-Free White Sauce, p. 36.

"Ricotta" and Spinach Filling

Use the Spinach and "Cheese" Filling for Crepes on page 107, omit-ting the onions.

Watch over them and stir gently with a slotted spoon to make sure none have stuck to the bottom. When cooked, quickly lift them out with a slotted spoon and into the hot, oiled serving platter or bowl.

Drizzle each serving with warm sauce, and pass soy Parmesan or soy-free alternative, if desired (or a sprinkling of chopped, toasted nuts, if you prefer). I like to sprinkle on some minced parsley for color, as well.

Pre-Cooking and Storing Stuffed Pasta

Stuffed pasta should not be left on the flour or cornmeal-sprinkled cookie sheets for more than three or four hours, and then they must be turned frequently so that they dry out evenly and don't get soggy on the bottom. Otherwise they will tear when you pick them up.

You can refrigerate or freeze them uncooked, with sheets of waxed paper sprinkled with flour or cornmeal between layers in a rigid plastic container, but it's better to half-cook them first, drain them well, and then layer them.

Uncooked refrigerated ravioli needs 5 to 6 minutes to cook. (Time them from when the water comes back to a boil.) Uncooked frozen ravioli needs 7 to 8 minutes; half-cooked refrigerated ravioli needs 2 to 3 minutes; half-cooked frozen ravioli needs about 5 minutes.

Fillings for Stuffed Pasta Envelopes

Fillings should not be too wet, or they will make the dough soggy and easy to tear. Greens should be squeezed as dry as possible before using; mushrooms should be cooked until they absorb all the liquid that is exuded; if "ricotta" is watery, drain it well. Soy Parmesan will absorb some of the liquid. If a filling seems too wet, add some bread crumbs, 1 tablespoon at a time.

Mushroom or "Seafood" Filling for Ravioli

Yield: 4 to 6 servings

For Mushroom Filling:

1 pound fresh mushrooms, finely chopped

1 to 2 cloves garlic, chopped

1 tablespoon extra-virgin olive oil

½ cup dry white wine (can be nonalcoholic)

½ cup Tofu, Cashew, or Rice Creme, pp. 39-40, or ¼ cup extra-firm lite *silken* tofu, blended smooth with ¼ cup soymilk or rice milk

¼ cup Soymage Parmesan substitute, or soy-free alternative, p. 37

¼ cup minced Italian parsley

Salt and freshly ground white pepper, to taste

For "Seafood" Filling:

Use oyster mushrooms and add 3 tablespoons dulse flakes or nori flakes (1½ sheets nori, ground). Use the juice of 1 lemon in place of about 3 tablespoons of the white wine.

Sauté the mushrooms and garlic (and seaweed, if using) in the olive oil until the mushrooms have exuded their liquid and it evaporates. Add the wine and let that evaporate over high heat. Remove from the heat, and stir in the creme, soy Parmesan or soy-free alternative, parsley, salt, and pepper.

Per serving (mushroom filling): Calories: 112, Protein: 6 g, Carbohydrate: 6 g, Fat: 4 g

Per serving ("seafood" filling): Calories: 96, Protein: 6 g, Carbohydrate: 6 g, Fat: 4 g

"Cheese" Filling

Use the "Cheese" Filling for Crepes, on page 108.

Bean and Green Filling

Follow the recipe for Spinach and "Cheese" Filling for Crepes on page 107, but replace the "ricotta" with 1½ to 2 cups cooked or canned cannellini (white kidney), romano, or pinto beans, drained and mashed. Omit the onion and use 1 clove garlic.

Pumpkin Filling

Mix together well 1⅓ cups mashed, cooked butternut squash and/or orange sweet potato, ⅔ cup Tofu Ricotta, p. 32, or Almond Ricotta, p. 35, 2 tablespoons Soymage Parmesan substitute, or soy-free alternative, p. 37, ¼ teaspoon salt, and freshly grated white pepper and nutmeg, to taste.

To make an old-fashioned version of this filling, omit the "ricotta" and use 2 cups of mashed squash and/or sweet potato. Use ½ teaspoon salt. Add ¼ cup Amaretti Crumbs, p. 243, and the white pepper and nutmeg, to taste.

This recipe for large "cheese" and green herb-stuffed pasta is a very old one, and the walnut sauce is a Renaissance touch. In accordance with modern tastes, I have lightened the sauce considerably, eliminating the oil, cream, and bread crumbs, and reducing the amount of walnuts. It is still a rich and delicious sauce, but you can replace it, if you prefer, with a simple tomato sauce (see page 42) or Reduction "Butter" Sauce, p. 48.

The herb mixture in the stuffing is a very ancient Ligurian combination called "preboggion." Wild herbs and greens are the ideal (I use some nettles in the spring), You can mix bitter greens such as arugula, radicchio, dandelion, borage, Italian parsley, chicory, endive, mustard, broccoli rabe (or Chinese broccoli), turnip greens, etc., with chard, spinach (fresh or frozen), or beet greens. According to Coleman Andrews, in his book *Flavors of the Riviera* (New York: Bantam Books, 1996), in the hills above Chiavari and Rapallo, where my grandmother's family came from, women used a mixture of sow thistle, pimpernel, borage, chard, Italian

Ligurian Herb-Stuffed Pasta Triangles
with Walnut Sauce
PANSOTTI ANTICA CON SALSA DI NOCI
(can be soy-free)

Yield: 4 to 5 servings

1 recipe Homemade Vegan Pasta, p. 77, (made with either soy or chick-pea flour), for filled pasta

1 recipe Walnut Sauce, p. 48

Filling:

1¼ pounds mixed greens (spinach, chard, nettles, arugula, mustard greens, broccoli rabe or Chinese broccoli leaves, turnip or beet greens, collards, borage, chicory, endive, chervil, young dandelion leaves, radicchio, etc.), or use ¾ pound bitter greens and ½ (10-ounce) box frozen chopped spinach, thawed and squeezed dry

1 cup Tofu Ricotta, p. 32, or Almond Ricotta, p. 35

2 tablespoons chopped fresh basil or other fresh herbs of choice, or 1 tablespoon frozen basil paste, p. 30

2 tablespoons Soymage Parmesan substitute, or soy-free alternative, p. 37

1 tablespoon fresh lemon juice

½ teaspoon salt

⅛ teaspoon freshly grated nutmeg

Freshly grated pepper, to taste

Note: You can make the pasta several hours ahead of time and keep it refrigerated in a plastic bag. Divide it into 8 pieces, and keep covered. The filling can also be made several hours or days ahead and refrigerated.

To make the filling, clean the greens thoroughly, trim (use gloves when handling nettles), and plunge them into a pot of boiling water. Cook tender greens, such as spinach and arugula, just until wilted, and other greens until tender. If you are using a mixture, add them in order of cooking time, starting with the toughest ones. When they are cooked, drain them and rinse under cold water. Squeeze them very dry and chop them finely.

Mix the greens with the other ingredients in a medium bowl, except the Parmesan and Italian parsley for topping, combining thoroughly. If the filling is at all warm, refrigerate it until it is cold. (It can be made several hours or a couple of days ahead of time.)

To fill the pansotti, roll the dough out as instructed on page 78 to the second-to-the-last setting on your pasta-rolling machine, or by hand about ⅟₁₆ inch thick. Place the dough on a lightly floured surface, and keep covered with a damp cloth when not working with it. Cut the rolled-out lengths of dough into 4-inch strips, and then divide them into 4-inch squares.

Place a tablespoon of the filling in the center of each square, and fold the dough over to make a triangle. (Don't overfill and make sure that no filling gets into the seal on the edges, or it may break open when cooking.) If the dough is moist, you don't need to dampen the edges to get a good seal. Press the edges together with fork tines, a pastry wheel, or a fluted pasta cutter.

Cover cookie sheets with wax paper, and sprinkle flour or cornmeal over the paper. Set the filled pansotti on the sheets, and cover with dry, clean tea towels while a large pot of salted water comes to a boil. Turn the pansotti frequently so they don't get soggy on the bottom and stick when you try to pick them up.

Before you start cooking the pansotti, have the serving platter and plates hot, and warm the Walnut Sauce over medium heat, stirring frequently, or in the microwave for 2 to 3 minutes. Cook the pansotti in 2 or 3 batches, dropping them one at a time into rapidly boiling water. They need to cook no longer than 3 to 4 minutes once the water has come back to a gentle boil. (Don't let the water boil so hard that the dumplings come apart.) Stir gently with a slotted spoon to make sure none have stuck to the bottom. When cooked, quickly lift them out and place on the hot, oiled serving platter or bowl.

Drizzle each serving with warm Walnut Sauce, and pass soy Parmesan or soy-free alternative, if desired (or chopped toasted walnuts, if you prefer). I like to sprinkle on some minced parsley for color, as well.

parsley, and two dandelion-like plants in their local preboggion.

The cheese that was originally used in this recipe was a Ligurian variety called "prescinsena," a tangy, fresh full-fat curd cheese. These days ricotta is used, but it is not as acidic as prescinsena, so I add a bit of lemon juice to either the soy or almond ricotta to add some tang.

Pansotti (which literally means "pot-bellied") may seem complicated, but they are actually very simple to make—they just take some time. But you can make some of the components, or the whole recipe, well ahead of time.

Note: See page 100 on how to pre-cook, store, and otherwise deal with stuffed pasta.

Per serving: Calories: 521, Protein: 28 g, Carbohydrate: 55 g, Fat: 21 g

Cannelloni

(can be soy-free)

Yield: 6 servings

Cannelloni are one of the most popular Italian dishes served in North America. In Northern Italy, they are often stuffed crepes (see page 107), covered with white sauce and baked. Cannelloni alla Napoletana, more familiar to most North Americans, are stuffed pasta tubes with a tomato sauce and cheese topping.

The following filling is a vegetarian version of the traditional meat and spinach filling, but you can use any of the fillings for crepes (pp. 107-08)—particularly the Spinach and "Cheese" Filling or the "Cheese" Filling—or ravioli filling (pp. 100-01). For some of the lighter vegetable fillings, you may prefer to use only the tomato sauce or the white sauce, not both.

This dish is a wonderful one for company because it can be made ahead of time and it never fails to please.

Note: Don't use no-boil shells. The results are not as good, and even slightly overbaking reduces the dish to mush.

Have ready:

2½ to 3 cups Marinara Sauce, p. 42, with a handful of fresh chopped basil added

1 recipe thick Dairy-Free White Sauce, p. 36

"Meat" and Spinach Filling:

1 pound fresh spinach, or 1 (10-ounce) package frozen chopped spinach

2 tablespoons extra-virgin olive oil

2 cups chopped onion

3 cloves garlic, minced

3 cups commercial "hamburger crumbles" (regular or Italian), or 3 cups ground seitan, pp. 178-79, or 3 cups frozen tofu, thawed, crumbled, and squeezed, and mixed with ⅓ cup light soy sauce, or 2¼ cups dry textured soy protein granules soaked in 1⅞ cups boiling water with ⅓ cup light soy sauce added

3 tablespoons chopped fresh oregano, or 1 tablespoon dried oregano

Salt and freshly ground black pepper, to taste

28 to 30 small canneloni shells (made without egg whites)

¼ to ½ cup Soymage Parmesan substitute, or soy-free alternative, p. 37

Prepare the fresh greens by steaming them over several inches of boiling water until wilted, about 3 minutes. Then drain, squeeze dry, and chop. If you are using frozen chopped spinach, thaw, then squeeze it dry.

To make the filling, heat the olive oil in a large nonstick skillet over medium-high heat. Add the onions and sauté until they begin to soften. Add the garlic and sauté a few minutes longer. Add the squeezed spinach and stir-fry for a few minutes. Add the hamburger substitute, oregano, salt, and pepper, and cook until the mixture is fairly dry. Set aside to cool.

Preheat the oven to 350°F.

Boil the cannelloni shells in a large pot of salted water according to the package directions. Drain and cool until you can handle them.

Fill the the cannelloni by holding a tube in one hand, covering the bottom with your fingers, and packing in the filling with your other hand. If you use a "cheese" filling, you can use a pastry bag with no tip to fill the tubes.

To bake, place the stuffed tubes in a shallow 9 x 13-inch baking pan with a little bit of the tomato sauce on the bottom. Cover them with the tomato sauce, then drizzle with the white sauce, and sprinkle with soy Parmesan or soy-free alternative. Bake for 30 minutes.

Per serving: Calories: 587, Protein: 41 g, Carbohydrate: 72 g, Fat: 15 g

Crepes
CRESPELLE VEGAN
(can be soy-free)

Yield: 12 crepes

¼ cup water

1 tablespoon powdered egg replacer

1 cup unbleached white flour or whole wheat pastry flour

¾ cup plus 1 tablespoon water

½ cup soymilk or rice milk, or ½ cup water plus 1 tablespoon soymilk powder

¼ cup chick-pea or full-fat soy flour

2 tablespoons nutritional yeast flakes

2 teaspoons unbleached sugar

½ teaspoon baking powder

Crepes have been made in Italy for centuries with many different types of flours. They are particularly popular in Tuscany. In Emilia Romagna and Piedmont, they are called cannelloni, or they are folded into triangles and called fazzoletti, after the folded black handerkerchiefs that older farm women still wear on their heads. In southern Italy they are often referred to as manicotti. Filled crepes that are cut into short lengths and baked are called bocconcini, which means "little mouthfuls." Crepe "cakes," or timbali, are crepes stacked with filling in between and cut into wedges.

Many delicious vegetables stuffings are popular. Use a filling as simple as steamed, chopped in-season vegetables held together with a thick white sauce, p. 36, or one of the fillings on pages 107-08.

Crepes can be made ahead and even frozen, and they make an elegant dinner dish for company or special occasions, such as Easter dinner.

These vegan crepes are nice and tender, thin but not fragile, roll well, and have a delicate flavor.

½ teaspoon salt
Pinch of white pepper
Pinch of freshly ground nutmeg

Mix the water and egg replacer in a blender until frothy. Add the remaining ingredients to the blender, and beat for one minute. The batter should be like heavy cream. This can be made ahead, but the batter does not require resting for 30 minutes, as many crepe batters do.

Crespelle are made like ordinary crepes. Heat an 8-inch nonstick skillet over medium-high heat, and wipe it lightly with oil before making each crepe. Use 3 tablespoons of batter per crepe, stirring the batter before you make each crepe. Roll and tilt the pan after you add the batter until it evenly covers the bottom. Cook for a few seconds, or until the top looks dry. Carefully loosen the crepe with a spatula, and flip it over. After a few seconds the other side should be dry. Fold into quarters or roll like a jelly roll. Place on a plate or leave them flat if you are going to stack them with filling. If you are going to use the crepes shortly, cover them with a clean tea towel.

Either fill the crepes and serve according to the specific directions in the recipe you're using, or let them cool and place in a plastic bag or rigid container with pieces of waxed paper in between each crepe. You can refrigerate them for up to 3 days or freeze them for future use. (Thaw thoroughly before filling.)

Per crepe: Calories: 55, Protein: 3 g, Carbohydrate: 10 g, Fat: 0 g

Dessert Crepes

Omit the pepper and use 1½ tablespoons sugar, 1 teaspoon vanilla, and ½ teaspoon pure orange or lemon extract. Roll around Cashew Pastry Cream, p. 219, or Tofu or Cashew Mascarpone, pp. 33 and 36, and top with sweetened fresh fruit.

Saffron Crepes

Add ¼ teaspoon Spanish saffron.

Stuffed Crepes

CRESPELLE RIPIENE

(can be soy-free)

Yield: 6 servings

Have ready:

1 recipe Crepes, p. 105 (12 crepes)

2 cups Marinara Sauce, pp. 42-43, or a medium Dairy-Free White Sauce, p. 36

Spinach and "Cheese" Filling:

2 onions, minced

1 tablespoon extra-virgin olive oil

2 pounds fresh, cleaned spinach or other greens, or 2 (10-ounce) packages chopped frozen spinach or other greens

1½ cups Tofu Ricotta, p. 32, or Almond Ricotta, p. 35

4 to 6 tablespoons Soymage Parmesan substitute, or soy-free alternative, p. 37

Salt, freshly ground pepper, and nutmeg, to taste

Sauté the onions in the olive oil in a nonstick skillet until they are soft and starting to brown, adding a tiny bit of water as needed to keep from sticking.

Meanwhile, place the fresh spinach in boiling water until it is completely wilted, then drain, squeeze dry, and chop. If using frozen spinach, thaw it thoroughly; you can quick-thaw it by placing the whole carton in the microwave for 5 minutes. Squeeze it as dry as possible.

Mix the spinach in a bowl with the cooked onions, ricotta, soy Parmesan, salt, pepper, and nutmeg. (It should be strongly seasoned.)

Preheat the oven to 425°F.

Place a generous amount of filling down the center of each crepe, and roll it up. Place the rolls in an oiled baking dish. (You can prepare the crepes up to this point several hours ahead of time.) Pour a little of

S
tom
a m
36,
Parı
soy-free alternative, p. 37. For a really special dish, layer white sauce over the tomato sauce.

Porcini Filling

Make the Mushroom Filling, but add about ½ ounce of dried porcini or boletus mushrooms which have soaked in ½ cup of hot water for 45 minutes, then are chopped. Strain the broth and use it instead of the wine.

Asparagus and Mushroom Filling

Use either the Mushroom or the Porcini Filling, and add 1 cup of cooked fresh asparagus cut into ½-inch pieces.

Fazzoletti

Spread 2 or 3 tablespoons filling over one half of the crepe, fold over the other half, then fold the whole thing in half to make a triangle. Stand the fazzoletti up in the oiled baking pan or casserole with their points sticking upwards. Dab a little margarine on the point of each fazzoletti. Bake about 20 minutes and serve the sauce on the side.

the sauce you are using over the crepes, sprinkle with soy Parmesan or soy-free alternative, and bake 20 minutes. Serve with more sauce on the side.

Per serving: Calories: 336, Protein: 18 g, Carbohydrate: 40 g, Fat: 11 g

"Cheese" Filling for Crepes

Mix together well 2½ cups Tofu Ricotta, p. 32, or Almond Ricotta, p. 35, ½ cup Soymage Parmesan substitute, or soy-free alternative, p. 37, ½ cup chopped fresh Italian parsley (or ¼ cup chopped Italian parsley and ¼ cup chopped fresh basil), and salt, freshly ground pepper, and nutmeg to taste. This recipe can be served with a light tomato sauce (pp. 42-43) or Dairy-Free White Sauce, p. 36, and Soymage Parmesan substitute, or soy-free alternative, p. 37.

"Meat" and Spinach Filling

Use the Canneloni Filling on page 104 and serve with a light tomato sauce, pp. 42-43, and Soymage Parmesan substitute, or soy-free alternative, p. 37. You can also drizzle some white sauce, p. 36, over the tomato sauce, if you wish.

Mushroom Filling

Note: Criminis are my choice for this recipe, but you can use fresh shiitakes, oyster mushrooms, chanterelles, or portobellos, if you like.

Heat 2 tablespoons extra-virgin olive oil or good-tasting dairy-free margarine in a large, nonstick skillet. Add 1 medium onion, minced, and sauté over medium-high heat until the onion softens and begins to color. Turn the heat to high, add ½ cup dry white wine, and let it evaporate. Add 1 pound chopped mushrooms and 1 teaspoon chopped fresh rosemary, if you like. Watch closely until the mushrooms have extruded their liquid and this liquid almost evaporates. Season to taste with salt and pepper, and add ¼ cup Dairy-Free White Sauce, p. 36, and ¼ cup Soymage Parmesan substitute, or soy-free alternative, p. 37, if desired.

Bocconcini

Preheat the oven to 375°F.

Make the "Cheese" Filling, p. 108, but omit the parsley or parsley and basil. With a very sharp knife, cut the ends off of each rolled crepe, then cut each crepe into 3 pieces. Rub a large baking dish with nondairy margarine, and arrange the bocconcini close together, standing up (with the filling showing). Bake 20 minutes and serve hot.

Timbalo di Crespelle

STACKED CREPE "CAKE"

(can be soy-free)

Yield: 6 servings

This type of timbalo is often served for special occasion dinners in Italy.

1 recipe Crepes, p. 105 (12 crepes)
1½ cups thick Dairy-Free White Sauce, p. 36
1½ cups Marinara Sauce or a variation, pp. 42-43
½ cup Soymage Parmesan substitute, or soy-free alternative, p. 37
1 recipe for any of the fillings on pp. 107-08

Preheat the oven to 350°F.

Place a crepe on the bottom of a well-oiled 2-quart souffle dish. Cover it with ⅛th of the filling. Sprinkle with a little soy Parmesan or soy-free alternative. Top with a crepe and cover that with ⅓ of the white sauce. Cover with another crepe, another ⅛ of the filling, and some soy Parmesan or soy-free alternative. Cover with another crepe and spread with ⅓ of the tomato sauce. Repeat the layers, ending with tomato sauce. Sprinkle with the remaining soy Parmesan or soy-free alternative. Bake for 30 to 40 minutes. Let stand 10 minutes before cutting into wedges like a cake.

Per serving: Calories: 500, Protein: 29 g, Carbohydrate: 45 g, Fat: 21 g

Pasticcio con Cucuzzeddi

SICILIAN ZUCCHINI AND "MEAT" LAYERED WITH PASTA

(can be soy-free)

Yield: 6 to 8 servings

1 pound lasagne noodles (do not use the "no-boil" kind)
1½ pounds zucchini, sliced ½ inch thick
2 tablespoons extra-virgin olive oil
1 large onion, minced
4 cloves garlic, minced

"Cucuzzeddi" is zucchini in the Sicilian dialect, and if you have a surplus in your garden, here is a delicious way to use it. The dish is somewhat like lasagne, but without the white sauce.

3 cups chopped reconstituted textured soy protein chunks, p. 174, chopped seitan veal, p. 180, or commercial vegetarian "hamburger crumbles"

2 pounds ripe plum tomatoes, chopped, or 1 (28-ounce) can plum tomatoes, chopped, or diced tomatoes, with juice

½ cup vegetarian broth

¼ cup chopped fresh basil

¼ cup chopped fresh Italian parsley

1 teaspoon salt

Freshly ground black pepper, to taste

1 cup Soymage Parmesan substitute, or soy-free alternative, p. 37

Boil the noodles in lots of boiling salted water until al dente. Rinse under cold running water, drain, and lay out flat.

Brush or spray the zucchini slices with extra-virgin olive oil, and lay them on cookie sheets. Broil 3 to 4 inches from the heat until they begin to brown. Turn over and broil until soft in the middle and brown. Set aside.

In a large, nonstick skillet, heat the 2 tablespoons olive oil over medium-high heat. Add the onion and garlic, and sauté until the onion starts to soften. Add the soy protein, seitan, or "hamburger crumbles," the tomatoes, broth, basil, parsley, salt, and pepper. Simmer this for about 30 minutes. Taste for seasoning.

Microwave Option: Place the mixture in a microwave-safe bowl, and cook on high for 10 minutes.

Preheat the oven to 350°F.

Oil a 9 x 13-inch baking pan. Layer ⅓ of the noodles, ⅓ of the sauce, half the zucchini, and ⅓ cup of the soy Parmesan or soy-free alternative. Repeat this layering, then top with the last ⅓ of the noodles, ⅓ of the sauce, and remaining soy Parmesan. Bake for 30 minutes, and let rest for 10 minutes before cutting.

Per serving: Calories: 297, Protein: 22 g, Carbohydrate: 38 g, Fat: 7 g

Baked Macaroni and Tomatoes
MACARONI E POMODORO AL FORNO
(can be soy-free)

Yield: 6 servings

1 tablespoon extra-virgin olive oil

1 small onion, minced

1 small green bell pepper, seeded and chopped

1 clove garlic, minced

2 pounds ripe plum tomatoes, chopped, or 1 (28-ounce) can diced tomatoes or Italian plum tomatoes, chopped, with juice

⅞ cup water

1 teaspoon salt

1 teaspoon dried oregano

1 teaspoon dried thyme

12 ounces penne rigate (or any tubular pasta—elbow macaroni, rigatoni, etc.)

½ recipe cold, thick Dairy-Free White Sauce, p. 36 (1 cup)

¼ cup Soymage Parmesan substitute, or soy-free alternative, p. 37

This is another of my husband Brian's recipes. Originally, the topping was mozzarella cheese, but a combination of thick white sauce and soy Parmesan makes a delicious complement to the juicy, tomatoey macaroni it covers. This is one of our favorite weeknight dishes.

In a heavy medium pot, heat the olive oil. Add the onion, green pepper, and garlic, and sauté over medium heat until the onion softens. Add the tomatoes, water, salt, oregano, and thyme. Bring to a boil, then reduce the heat, cover, and simmer for 1 to 2 hours, stirring occasionally.

About 45 minutes before serving time, preheat the oven to 400°F. Boil the pasta in a large pot of salted water until al dente. Drain and mix with the tomato sauce. Place in an oiled 9 x 13-inch pan or 12-inch round casserole. Dot spoonfuls of the cold white sauce on top of the macaroni, and sprinkle with the soy Parmesan or soy-free alternative. Bake for 15 minutes and serve immediately.

Per serving: Calories: 213, Protein: 8 g, Carbohydrate: 26 g, Fat: 8 g

If you must use a commercial sauce for lasagne, try to purchase one from a deli that you know makes quality products, or at least add some fresh herbs, sautéed onions, and/or mushrooms, etc., to the best-quality canned or bottled sauce you can find. For a "meaty" sauce, add ground, store-bought seitan (made without ginger) or commercial vegetarian hamburger replacement to the sauce. I make double or triple quantities of ragù and freeze some of it in the right quantities for lasagne (5 to 6 cups). Then I can make it without much effort whenever I want to.

I have developed a succulent vegetarian version of the traditional Lasagne al Forno Bolognese, made with a rich ragù, thick white sauce, and thin, plain or spinach homemade pasta, plus some more modern variations. Italians are experimenting with lighter vegetable lasagne, so feel free to play with this dish! Celiacs and those with *wheat allergies* can now find good-quality rice lasagne noodles, and you can make *tomato-free* lasagne using a mushroom ragù, p. 44, as the sauce, if you like.

Lasagne

Lasagne is one of the best known and well-loved Italian dishes in North America. Unfortunately, it is often a travesty of the real thing, made with sour cottage cheese and inferior commercial tomato sauce.

The cheese- and meat-laden lasagne that most North Americans know and love is actually a version of Lasagne di Carnivale, a once-a-year feast dish of southern Italy which incorporated sausage, fried meatballs, three cheeses, and hard-boiled eggs—all of the foods most people were too poor to eat on an everyday basis and which were forbidden during Lent.

Most of the northern Italian lasagne are made with layers of meat sauce (ragù), thick white sauce, thin sheets of pasta, and perhaps some Parmesan cheese—not with tomato sauce with some hamburger added, ricotta, mozzarella, and Parmesan cheeses, and thick, commercial lasagne noodles, as it usually is on our continent.

The best lasagne are made with homemade pasta. Although I know it won't always be possible to make your own pasta for lasagne (and I do enjoy lasagne made with commercial dry noodles), try making it with your own homemade noodles—I think you'll agree that it melts in your mouth! When you do use commercial dry noodles, I suggest that you cook them first. I have tried recipes using uncooked noodles, but I don't think the results are very good. Cooking the noodles does not take much effort, and it takes twice as long to bake the dish using raw noodles. If you disagree with me and want to use uncooked noodles anyway, add 1⅓ cups water to the sauce for each ½ pound dried noodles used, cover the dish tightly, and bake twice as long as the recipe directs.

Lasagne Al Forno Bolognese

(can be soy-free)

Yield: 8 servings

1 recipe Vegan Homemade Pasta, p. 77, the basic or spinach version

1 recipe Ragù alla Bolognese, p. 45 (5 to 6 cups)

1½ recipes thick Dairy-Free White Sauce, p. 36 (3 cups)

Optional: **½ to 1 cup Soymage Parmesan substitute, or soy-free alternative, p. 37***

*If you don't use soy Parmesan or a soy-free alternative, top the dish with about ½ cup fresh bread crumbs tossed with 1 tablespoon extra-virgin olive oil.

If the sauces aren't made yet, make them first. The white sauce can be cold. Make the pasta, rolling it as thinly as possible (second-to-last or last setting on the pasta roller) and cutting it into 3 x 4-inch rectangles. Cook for 1 minute *only* in lots of boiling, salted water. Drain and rinse under cold water, then lay out flat between layers of waxed paper.

Oil a shallow 9 x 13-inch baking pan. Preheat the oven to 350°F.

Spread a thin layer of ragù on the bottom of the pan. Cover that with a layer of noodles, touching. Spread a layer of ragù over that, and then a layer of white sauce, smoothing it out with the back of a spoon. Sprinkle with some of the soy Parmesan or soy-free alternative, if using. Repeat the layering until everything is used up, ending with a layer of white sauce and soy Parmesan, soy-free alternative, or bread crumbs. Bake for 30 minutes.

Let the dish rest for 10 to 15 minutes before cutting into squares.

Per serving: Calories: 372, Protein: 27 g, Carbohydrate: 35 g, Fat: 12 g

This is the traditional northern Italian lasagne, and what my husband invariably requests for his birthday dinner.

This recipe consists of three other recipes, all of which can be made ahead of time, either on different days or earlier the same day. The pasta dough can be made ahead of time, but should be rolled out and cooked just before assembling the dish, unless you cook the pasta sheets as directed and freeze or refrigerate them between layers of waxed paper (see page 100). Other convenient time-savers would be to use a ragù that you have made earlier and frozen and make the white sauce in the microwave.

Variations:

1) Substitute 15 to 18 dry wheat or rice lasagne noodles, cooked al dente, for the homemade pasta. Spinach or whole wheat noodles may be used.

2) Instead of Ragù alla Bolognese, use 1 recipe Ragù alla Napoletana, or 5 to 6 cups Brian's Wine-Free Mushroom Tomato Sauce, p. 44, with hamburger replacement added.

3) For a tomato-free lasagne, omit the Ragù alla Bolognese and use Roasted Mushroom Stew, p. 157, instead.

4) For a Vegetable Lasagne, omit the ragù and substitute one recipe Puttenaio (Prostitute's Stew, p. 155), omitting the potato and using another pepper instead.

5) For Spinach Lasagne, omit the ragù and use instead about 3 cups Marinara Sauce, p. 42, or any of its variations, except the creamy sauce, or use Brian's Wine-Free Mushroom Tomato Sauce, p. 44, without the meat substitute.

In addition to the white sauce and soy Parmesan or soy-free alternative, add a layer of 2 cups Tofu or Almond Ricotta, pp. 32 or 35, mixed with 3 packages of chopped frozen spinach, thawed and squeezed dry (or 3 pounds fresh spinach, cooked, squeezed dry, and chopped), 4 cloves garlic, crushed, ¼ teaspoon freshly grated nutmeg, and salt and freshly ground black pepper, to taste.

6) For Vegetable-Ricotta Lasagne, follow the recipe for Spinach Lasagne, but omit the spinach and add instead about 3 to 4 cups of any roasted, steamed, grilled, or sautéed vegetable, by itself or mixed. You can use mushrooms, bell peppers, broccoli, zucchini, eggplant, carrots, etc.

7) For southern Italian Lasagne di Carnivale, use 1 recipe Ragù alla Napoletana, p. 43, in the Lasagne al Forno recipe, instead of the Ragù alla Bolognese. Use the white sauce layer and the soy Parmesan or soy-free alternative, and add a layer of 2 cups Tofu or Almond Ricotta, pp. 32 or 35, with a sprinkling of freshly grated nutmeg, salt, and freshly ground pepper, to taste, and a layer of Italian "Meatballs" (Polpetti), p. 185.

This most closely resembles the type of lasagne most North Americans know and love.

Sicilian-Style Eggplant Timbale

TIMBALO ALLA SAN GIOVANNELLA

(can be soy-free)

Yield: 8 servings

2½ pounds eggplant, peeled and sliced ⅜ inch thick
Salt

Sauce:
1 tablespoon extra-virgin olive oil
1 medium onion, chopped
1 stalk celery, chopped
1 small carrot, peeled and chopped
1 clove garlic, minced
2 pounds ripe plum tomatoes, or 1 (28-ounce) can Italian tomatoes
  with their juice, run through a food mill or processed briefly in
  a food processor or blender
½ cup tomato paste
½ cup dry red wine (can be nonalcoholic)
1 tablespoon chopped fresh basil, or 1 teaspoon dried basil
1 tablespoon chopped fresh oregano, or 1 teaspoon dried oregano
1 teaspoon salt
Freshly ground pepper, to taste
Optional: 2 cups crumbled commercial or cooked, homemade
  hamburger replacement, p. 175, or ground seitan, p. 179

1 pound penne rigate

Olive oil for brushing
1 tablespoon chopped fresh oregano, or 1 teaspoon dried oregano
  for topping
Optional: ¼ cup soy Parmesan, or soy-free alternative, p. 37

Sprinkle the eggplant generously with salt, and place on clean tea
towels or stand up in a colander to drain for about half an hour.

This is an impressive and delicious company dish. It takes a little more time than you might ordinarily spend on a meal (about an hour to prepare and half an hour of baking), but it's not at all difficult. Grilling instead of frying the eggplant eliminates the greasiness.

Variations: Instead of the eggplant, you can line the bowl with parboiled Savoy cabbage leaves or sheets of cooked homemade pasta dough, p. 77. Cover the filling with more of the same.

A very elegant timbalo can be made by lining the greased bowl, which has been coated with fine bread crumbs, with cold Yellow Risotto (use about 3 cups rice, or 1½ times the basic recipe on page 135). Line the bowl with two-thirds of the risotto, and cover the filling with the rest. Sprinkle the top with more bread crumbs. Bake at 400°F if using the risotto.

While the eggplant drains, make the sauce. Heat the olive oil in a medium heavy pot, and sauté the onion, celery, carrot, and garlic in the oil over medium-high heat until they begin to soften. Add the remaining sauce ingredients, and bring to a boil. (If you are using dried herbs, add them at this point; if you are using fresh herbs, add them towards the end of cooking.) Turn the heat down to a simmer, cover, and cook about 30 minutes.

Put a large pot of water on to boil for the pasta, and turn on your oven broiler. Rinse the eggplant under running water, and pat it dry with a clean tea towel. Place the slices on oiled cookie sheets, and brush the tops with a little olive oil. Broil the eggplant about 3 to 4 inches from the heat, watching it carefully until it begins to brown. Turn the slices over and broil on the other side. Immediately remove from the heat. Turn the oven to "bake," and set the temperature to 350°F.

Add salt to the pasta water, and boil the penne rapidly for 7 minutes (until *almost* al dente). Drain it and place it back in the pot with 2 cups of the sauce. Add salt and pepper to taste, the 1 tablespoon fresh oregano (or 1 teaspoon dried oregano), and optional soy Parmesan or soy-free alternative.

Oil a 2½-quart Pyrex or oven-safe ceramic bowl. Take the largest eggplant slices, and line the bowl with them, overlapping them slightly and letting them hang over the edge of the bowl. Line the bottom with some of the smaller pieces, and save a few for the top. Fill with the penne mixture, top with the remaining eggplant slices, and fold the overhanging eggplant over the the top. Press down gently. Bake for 25 minutes.

Remove from the oven and gently loosen the sides with a pie server. Place a serving platter over the top of the bowl, and invert it, but let it rest 10 minutes before removing the bowl.

Unmold and cut it into wedges; serve with the rest of the sauce on the side.

Per serving: Calories: 230, Protein: 15 g, Carbohydrate: 34 g, Fat: 2 g

This is a small collection of my personal favorites. There are so many delicious soups in every region of Italy that even the vegetarian ones alone could fill a large volume! Soups have always been the mainstay of Italian peasant cooking—filling, warming, comforting, easy to stretch, and a good way to use up leftovers or whatever is in good supply in the garden.

To differentiate among the many types of Italian soups, zuppe are thick soups that do not contain pasta or rice, are not creamed, and are generally ladled over toasted bread (such as onion soup). Minestre are vegetable soups which range from light and delicate to thick meals-in-a-bowl, often containing rice or pasta. Minestrine ("little soups") are thin broths with a some tiny pasta (pastina) cooked in them. Minestrone ("big soup") is thick vegetable soup which is cooked for several hours and served either with pesto, olive oil, or Parmesan cheese. Passati are puréed vegetable soups, usually thickened with potato.

Please consult pages 18-19 on the subject of vegetarian bouillon cubes, powders, and pastes. An excellent recipe for vegetarian broth is given here; you can find instructions for chick-pea broth on pages 119-20 and mushroom broth on pages 35-36. Remember that Italian broths are generally lighter than the English-style broths we're most accustomed to.

IX
Pasta in Broth and Soups
PASTE IN BRODO
ZUPPE E MINESTRE

"Since a dinner of minestrone satisfies both body and soul, and its cost is minimal, even to one who has no kitchen garden, little else is needed . . . to complete it."
—Angelo M. Pellegrini, *Lean Years, Happy Years* (Seattle: Madrona, 1983)

Vegetable Broth
BRODO VEGETALE
(soy-free)

Yield: about 3 quarts

1 tablespoon extra-virgin olive oil

2 large onions, or 4 leeks, coarsely chopped

4 carrots, scrubbed and chopped

2 large stalks celery with leaves, diced, or a handful of lovage, or about 1 cup chopped celeriac (no more or it will overwhelm the broth)

1 large handful Italian parsley and stalks

1 to 2 whole heads garlic, cloves separated and smashed with a knife (no need to peel)

Optional: **½ cup dry white wine (can be nonalcoholic)**

This makes an excellent basic broth or stock—inexpensive and you can control the amount of salt. You can make large quantities of it once a month, if you wish. Freeze it in one or 2-cup quantities, and/or in ice cube trays. (Pop the cubes out into plastic bags when they are solid.) The cubes contain about 2 tablespoons of broth, and they are handy when you need small amounts.

1 large bay leaf

½ teaspoon dried crumbled sage

½ teaspoon dried crumbled thyme

3 quarts water

Approximately 1 tablespoon salt (omit if you're going to reduce the broth a lot)

Freshly ground black or white pepper

In a large, heavy pot, heat the olive oil. Sauté the onions, carrots, celery, and garlic until the onions have softened and started to brown. If you want a darker stock, allow them to brown a bit more, adding a bit of water or white wine as you stir them to keep them from sticking.

If you wish to use wine, pour it in at this point and deglaze the pan by scraping up any brown bits of cooked vegetable. Add the parsley, herbs, and water, and bring to a boil. Cover and simmer for about 2 hours. Strain through a sieve, discarding the vegetables, then line the sieve with cheesecloth, and strain again. The broth will keep about a week in covered jars in the refrigerator. If you wish to keep it after a week, boil it again for a few minutes, bottle, and refrigerate or freeze.

Per cup: Calories: 35, Protein: 1 g, Carbohydrate: 5 g, Fat: 1 g

Reduced Broth

This is very useful for adding intense flavor, especially in place of fat. I often omit half the fat in a pasta sauce, and use reduced broth instead of the omitted fat. Cook the unsalted, strained broth down to about ⅓ of its original volume (i.e., cook 3 quarts broth down to 1 quart). Taste for salt after reducing. Keep refrigerated in a tightly covered container.

Jelled Broth

Adding agar to reduced broth gives it even more body, so that it coats foods the way melted fat does. To 2 cups of reduced broth, add ¾ teaspoon agar powder or 1½ tablespoons agar flakes dissolved in 2 tablespoons cold water, and simmer for 3 or 4 minutes. Keep refrigerated in a tightly covered container. The jell will melt when heated.

Amounts and types of vegetables don't have to be exact, but I like lots of onions, garlic, and carrots. For a "brown" stock, you can roast the vegetables at 400°F for 45 minutes. For variety, you can use the outside leaves of organic lettuce or any other vegetables *except* those from the cabbage family and beets. The strong flavors of cabbage and broccoli and color of beets will overwhelm the broth. Add any fresh herbs that you have in abundance and think would add a good flavor to the broth.

When the broth is finished, it should taste good enough to drink as a hot beverage. If it tastes a bit flat, and you've added enough salt, try adding about ¼ cup light miso, a tablespoon or two of tomato paste, some Marmite or other yeast extract, some soy sauce, a little nutritional yeast, some dried mushroom soaking water, and /or even a couple of commercial vegetarian broth cubes.

For a quickly made broth, pressure cook it for 20 to 30 minutes.

Italian Onion Soup

ZUPPA DI CIPOLLE

(can be soy-free)

Yield: 6 servings

Yes, you can make an excellent onion soup without beef stock. This recipe, spiked with marsala, is very easy and makes an excellent light supper.

1¼ pounds onions, sliced very thinly
1 tablespoon extra-virgin olive oil
1 tablespoon unbleached sugar or maple syrup
1 teaspoon salt
8 cups hot water
6 vegetarian bouillon cubes (or enough for 6 cups water)
4 teaspoons Marmite, yeast extract, or dark miso
2 teaspoons soy sauce, or soy-free alternative, p. 170
⅔ cup marsala, dry sherry, madeira, or Sauterne
Freshly ground white pepper, to taste
6 thick slices rustic Italian bread, toasted
Soymage Parmesan substitute, or soy-free alternative, p. 37

In a large, heavy pot, heat the oil over medium heat. Add the onions and sauté until they become tender and start to brown, stirring often and adding a little water from time to time if they start to stick.

Add the sugar and salt, and stir briefly. Add the water, bouillon, Marmite or miso, and soy sauce. Cover and simmer for 30 minutes. Add the wine and simmer uncovered for about 5 minutes. Taste for seasoning and add white pepper to taste.

Place a piece of toast in each soup bowl, and ladle the soup over it. Sprinkle liberally with soy Parmesan, and serve hot.

Per serving: Calories: 223, Protein: 8 g, Carbohydrate: 31 g, Fat: 3 g

Chick-pea or White Bean Broth

When you are cooking chick-peas or white beans (cannellini), save the extra cooking broth. Chick-pea broth is golden and jells when it is cold, very much like homemade chicken broth, and cannellini broth is light-colored and slightly thickened. Not only can they be used as part of the broth in soups, but you can use them instead of part (or all) of the oil in salad dressings, to cut down on calories and fat, and instead of part of the oil in pesto and in pasta dishes. I keep some of each frozen in cubes and always have some chick-pea broth in a jar in the refrigerator. It keeps about a week, or longer if you boil it every few days.

You can use the broth from pressure-cooked beans, but I have found that the broth from pressure-cooked chick-peas doesn't jell as well as beans that are cooked conventionally.

Soak the beans or chick-peas overnight, if possible. Pour off the soaking water, and cover with fresh water. Bring to a boil, adding any flavorings you wish, then turn down the heat, cover, and simmer for 1½ to 4½ hours for chick-peas, about for cannellini, depending on the age of the beans and how well they've been soaked.

One caution—don't use these bean broths to reduce for Reduced or Jelled Broth, p. 118. They get very viscous and sweet when reduced. Vegetable broth , p. 117, is the choice for reduction.

This thick, spicy soup (which is unlike any other split-pea soup you've ever encountered, I guarantee) was a favorite when my children were young.

Sicilian-Style Split Pea Soup
MINESTRA DI PISELLI ALLA SICILIANA
(can be soy-free)

Yield: 6 to 8 servings

2 tablespoons extra-virgin olive oil

1 large onion, chopped

2 carrots, chopped

2 stalks celery, chopped

3 cloves garlic, minced

1 cup dried split peas

2 pounds ripe plum tomatoes, chopped, or 1 (28-ounce) can diced tomatoes

5 cups vegetarian broth

¼ cup chopped fresh Italian parsley

1 bay leaf

1 small dried red hot chile, crumbled

¼ teaspoon dried thyme

¼ teaspoon basil

¼ teaspoon freshly ground black pepper

3 to 4 ounces small shell pasta (conchigliette) or small elbow macaroni

Salt, to taste

1 teaspoon roasted sesame oil

Heat the olive oil in a large, heavy pot. Sauté the onion, carrots, celery, and garlic in the oil until the onions have softened. Add the broth, split peas, tomatoes, herbs, and spices, and bring to a boil. Cover, turn down the heat, and simmer about 1½ hours, or until the peas are soft.

Any time while the soup is simmering, cook the pasta in boiling salted water until almost done. Drain it and add to the soup when the peas are soft. Taste for salt and stir in the sesame oil. Serve hot.

Per serving: Calories: 180, Protein: 7 g, Carbohydrate: 26 g, Fat: 5 g

Squash Soup

PASSATO DI ZUCCA

(can be soy-free)

Yield: 6 to 8 servings

1 medium butternut or Hubbard squash (about 1½ pounds)
2 large orange sweet potatoes (about 1 pound)
2 tablespoons nondairy margarine
2 medium onions, sliced
6 to 7 cups vegetarian broth or chick-pea broth, pp. 119-20
Salt and freshly ground pepper, to taste
Pinch of freshly ground nutmeg
4 slices Italian bread, with the crusts cut off
Soymage Parmesan substitute, or soy-free alternative, p. 37

Cut the squash in half with a cleaver or large knife, scrape out the seeds, and divide each half into about 4 pieces. (They don't have to be exactly equal.) Cut the sweet potatoes into about 6 equal pieces each.

You can pressure-cook the squash and sweet potatoes together in a steam-basket for 6 minutes at high pressure (15 pounds). Release the pressure under running water. When the vegetables are cool enough to handle, peel off the sweet potato skins, and scoop the soft flesh out of the squash skins.

Microwave Option: You can also microwave the squash pieces in a large microwave casserole. Add about ¼ cup of water, cover with the lid or a Pyrex pie plate, and cook on high about 10 minutes. If they aren't all soft, remove the cooked ones and cook the rest for about 2 minutes more, or until soft. Scoop the soft flesh out of the peel, and set aside. Peel the sweet potatoes and cut into 1-inch pieces. Place in a Pyrex pie dish with 2 tablespoons water, cover with a plate, and cook on high for about 5 minutes.

While the squash and sweet potatoes are cooking, melt the margarine in a heavy-bottomed soup pot, and add the onions. Sauté over medium heat until they are soft and translucent—don't allow them to brown. Add a little water, as necessary, to keep them from sticking. Add the cooked squash, sweet potato, and broth, and bring to a boil.

In North America we are used to winter squash cooked with maple syrup or brown sugar, but the pairing of sweet squash with savory broth and cheese is also delightful. This soup is perfect for a cold winter day.

A "meaty" squash such as butternut or a blue-gray Hubbard, combined with orange sweet potato, is the closest we can get to the Italian "pumpkin" or zucca.

If you cook the squash and sweet potato in a pressure cooker, this soup is very quick to make. A microwave takes somewhat longer, due to the quantity. You can steam small chunks of sweet potato conventionally in 12 to 15 minutes, but it's very time-consuming to peel and cut a winter squash into 1-inch pieces, so I've left out this alternative. If you have a sufficient quantity of leftover baked squash and sweet potato, you can use that instead.

Turn down the heat, cover, and let simmer for 5 minutes.

The Italian way to make a passato (something that is "passed through" a sieve) is to run it through a rotary food mill (mouli). If you don't have one of those, you can purée it briefly in a food processor or blender. (Be sure to leave the center plastic part of the blender lid or food processor open so that hot steam doesn't build up and shoot out—cover the opening loosely with a folded tea towel.). You can also process it right in the pot with a hand blender, but don't purée it to a frothy cream. A passato should have some texture and not be frothy.

Pour it back into the pot, and keep it warm over low heat. Add salt and pepper to taste and a pinch of nutmeg.

Toast the bread and cut it into ½-inch cubes. Serve the soup with a sprinkling of the croutons and some soy Parmesan or soy-free alternative.

Per serving: Calories: 174, Protein: 4 g, Carbohydrate: 31 g, Fat: 3 g

Minestrone Alla Milanese
THICK MILANESE VEGETABLE SOUP
(can be soy-free)

Yield: 6 to 8 servings

2 tablespoons extra-virgin olive oil
Optional: 1 teaspoon roasted sesame oil
3 medium onions, minced
4 medium carrots, peeled and shredded or minced
2 stalks celery, finely diced
1 medium potato, peeled and shredded
½ pound Savoy cabbage, finely shredded (You can replace some of the cabbage with other greens, if you like.)

Optional: 1 or 2 medium zucchini, finely diced

Optional: 4 ounces small, whole green beans (fresh or frozen), trimmed and diced

8 cups light vegetarian broth

2 bay leaves

1 teaspoon crumbled sage leaves

1 to 2 cups diced fresh or canned tomatoes

Optional: 1 cup soaked borlotti, cranberry, romano, or pinto beans, or 1 (14- to 16-ounce) can cooked beans, rinsed and drained

½ cup arborio rice

2 to 4 tablespoons minced fresh Italian parsley

1 cup fresh shelled or frozen baby peas (petite pois)

2 tablespoons minced fresh basil, or 1 tablespoon frozen basil paste

Salt and freshly ground pepper, to taste

Optional: Soymage Parmesan substitute, or soy-free alternative, p. 37

Milanese minestrone is different from other minestrones by virtue of the fact that the vegetables are finely chopped and rice is used instead of pasta. In some versions peas replace beans, but other versions contain both peas and beans. I find this minestrone much lighter than most, even though it is thick with vegetables.

If you prefer, omit the rice and substitute either 2 large diced, peeled potatoes *or* ½ cup small pasta (whole grain is fine), such as small elbow macaroni; little tubes, like ditali (or ditalini), coralli, or tubettini; rice- or seed-shaped orzo (similar types are called riso, rosamarina, seme di mela, or seme di melone); annellini (little rings); conchigliette (little shells); or farfalline (little butterflies).

In a large soup pot with a heavy bottom, heat the oil. Sauté the onion over medium heat until it begins to soften. Add the other vegetables one at a time, sautéing for a few minutes after each addition and adding a little bit of water, broth, or dry white wine as needed to prevent sticking.

Add the broth, sage, bay leaves, tomatoes, and optional beans. Bring to a boil, then reduce the heat and simmer for 45 minutes to 1½ hours (or until the beans are cooked). Add the rice, parsley, and peas, and cook for 15 minutes more. Add salt and pepper to taste, and stir in the basil. If the soup is too thick for your liking, add a bit more broth. Cook a few minutes more, then serve immediately with optional soy Parmesan or soy-free alternative or drizzle with extra-virgin olive oil or pesto, pp. 49-5 .

Per serving: Calories: 256, Protein: 9 g, Carbohydrate: 43 g, Fat: 5 g

Pasta with Chick-Peas

PASTA COI CECI

(can be soy-free)

Yield: 6 servings

This very simple dish, inspired by one from Abruzzi and Molise, is one of my very favorite winter comfort foods. I am constantly amazed by how such common foods can yield such wonderful flavor when combined by an Italian hand in the kitchen.

8 cups flavorful vegetarian broth (can be chick-pea broth, pp. 119-20, with some vegetarian bouillon cubes added for flavor, if necessary)

2½ to 3 cups cooked or canned chick-peas, drained

2 or 3 carrots, diced

8 ounces shell pasta (conchiglie or conchigliette)

3 cloves garlic, minced

1 tablespoon extra-virgin olive oil

Optional: **1 to 2 handfuls chopped greens, any kind**

Topping:

Extra-virgin olive oil

Dried hot red pepper flakes

Bring the broth to a boil in a large pot. Add the chick-peas, carrots, and pasta, and turn down to a simmer.

In a small skillet, sauté the garlic over medium heat in the 1 tablespoon olive oil until it just begins to turn beige—don't let it get golden or brown. Add this to the soup (along with greens, if you are using them).

When the carrots and pasta are tender, the soup is ready. If it's too thick for your taste, add a bit more broth.

Ladle the soup into bowls, and pass extra-virgin olive oil and red pepper flakes for each diner to add as desired.

Per serving: Calories: 218, Protein: 9 g, Carbohydrate: 34 g, Fat: 3 g

My Homestyle Lentil Soup
MINESTRA DI LENTICCHIE CASALINGA
(can be soy-free)

Yield: 8 servings

2 tablespoons extra-virgin olive oil

2 medium onions, chopped

2 stalks celery, chopped

Optional: 2 carrots, chopped

2 cloves garlic, minced

8 cups light vegetarian broth or water

1½ cups dried brown lentils, rinsed and sorted

2 pounds ripe plum tomatoes, chopped, or 1 (28-ounce) can diced
   tomatoes

½ cup dry red wine

2 bay leaves

½ teaspoon dried basil

½ teaspoon dried thyme

Salt and pepper, to taste

Optional: 1 to 2 vegetarian bouillon cubes

½ cup orzo pasta (seme di melone) or other tiny pasta

Salt and freshly ground pepper, to taste

Optional: 1 cup chopped cooked greens, or 1 (10-ounce) package
   frozen chopped spinach, thawed and squeezed dry

Roasted sesame oil

Soymage Parmesan substitute, or soy-free alternative , p. 37

In a large soup pot with a heavy bottom, heat the olive oil over medium-high heat, then sauté the onions until they begin to soften. Add the celery, optional carrots, and garlic, and sauté a few minutes more. Add the broth or water, lentils, tomatoes, red wine, and herbs. Bring to a boil, then turn down the heat, cover, and simmer for about 1½ hours. Add salt and pepper to taste along with bouillon cubes, if the flavor is lacking. Add the orzo and optional greens, if using, and cook 15 minutes more. Serve with soy Parmesan or alternative and a drizzle of

Lentil soup has been one of my favorites since childhood—my mother used to make her version several times a month, and we never tired of it. Italian lentil soups are generally very simple, but there are as many versions as there are cooks. I like to add a little red wine, some herbs, and seme di melone (melon seed pasta, better known as orzo) to make a very hearty soup which needs only crusty bread (and perhaps a salad) to make a meal.

For an unusual flavor, use French sorrel (sometimes known as "sour grass") as the greens in this soup.

Baked Lentils with "Cotechino Sausage"

Prepare the Lentil Stew variation on the next page.

Make up one batch of Vegetarian "Cotechino" Sausage, either soy-based, p. 177, or seitan, p. 183, and brown in a little oil in a nonstick skillet.

Preheat the oven to 400°F. Place the lentils in a large casserole, and top with the sausages. Bake for about 20 minutes, and serve with crusty bread.

roasted sesame oil, if you like. This gives a flavor similar to that of pancetta fat, which goes well with lentils.

Per serving: Calories: 247, Protein: 10 g, Carbohydrate: 36 g, Fat: 3 g

Lentil Stew *(Lenticchie in Umido)*

Use only 6 cups broth or water, and use 2 cups lentils. Use the optional carrots and omit the pasta and optional greens.

Pasta E Fagioli

PASTA AND BEAN BROTH

(soy-free)

Yield: 6 servings

This could really qualify as a stew, rather than a soup, but because it is literally pasta in broth, I've included it in this chapter. Pasta e fagioli (often called pasta fazool in American-Italian) is an Italian peasant dish with lots of scope for variation—there are probably thousands of versions. Some recipes instruct you to purée the beans, but I prefer them whole. Other versions include chopped onion, a bit of hot pepper, thyme, rosemary, and/or oregano. Other vegetables, such as green beans, can be added, and you can use pasta such as shells (conchiglie), "wagon wheels" (ruote), or elbow macaroni instead of the ones I've suggested. Whichever way, it's delicious and easy.

1 carrot, chopped

2 stalks celery, chopped

3 or 4 cloves garlic, minced or crushed

2 (15- or 16-ounce) cans white kidney cannellini, red kidney, small red, pinto, or romano beans or chick-peas, drained (3 to 4 cups cooked)

2 cups or more vegetarian broth

1 pound ripe plum tomatoes, chopped, or 1 (14-ounce) can diced tomatoes

2 tablespoons chopped fresh Italian parsley

1 teaspoon dried marjoram

1 pound pasta, such as farfalle (bows), penne, or ziti

Chopped parsley for garnish

Optional: Soymage Parmesan substitute, or soy-free alternative, p. 37

Put on a large pot of salted water to boil for the pasta.

In a large nonstick or lightly oiled pot, steam-fry the carrot, celery, and garlic in their juices for 3 or 4 minutes. Add the beans, broth, parsley, and marjoram. Cover and simmer over low heat for 5 minutes.

Meanwhile, cook the pasta in the boiling water until al dente. Drain the pasta and add to the pot with the vegetables. Taste for seasoning.

Serve in bowls with a sprinkle of parsley and soy Parmesan and crusty bread on the side.

Per serving: Calories: 293, Protein: 14 g, Carbohydrate: 56 g, Fat: 1 g

Cream of Cabbage Soup
PASSATO DI CAVOLO
(can be soy-free)

Yield: 4 servings

1½ pounds Savoy cabbage
4 cups vegetarian broth
1 onion, chopped
2 cloves garlic, minced
1 to 2 tablespoons good-tasting nondairy margarine
⅔ cup extra-firm *silken* tofu
⅔ cup nondairy milk
⅓ cup Soymage Parmesan substitute, or soy-free alternative, p. 37
Salt and freshly ground pepper, to taste
Extra-virgin olive oil for topping

Slice the cabbage very thinly, and cover with the broth in a medium pot. Cover with a lid and bring to a boil, then reduce the heat and simmer until the cabbage is tender.

Drain off the broth and set aside. Run the cabbage through a food mill (mouli) or food processor until it is coarsely ground. Set aside.

Melt the margarine in the pot the cabbage was cooked in over medium-high heat. Add the onion and garlic, and sauté until the onion softens. Add the ground cabbage and stir for a minute or two. Add about 3 cups of the broth.

Process the tofu and nondairy milk in a blender until it is very smooth. Add this to the soup along with the soy Parmesan. If the soup is too thick for you, add a little more of the reserved broth. Add salt and pepper to taste, and drizzle a little extra-virgin olive oil over each serving.

Per serving: Calories: 163, Protein: 11 g, Carbohydrate: 12 g, Fat: 7 g

Our local Italian restaurant, Pasta Art, in Courtenay, B.C., gave us a taste of this once, and we loved it. Of course, theirs was made with cream, butter, and dairy Parmesan cheese, but it wasn't too difficult to make a rich-tasting vegan version, and it is now one of our favorites.

This can be made soy-free by using Easy Cashew Creme for Cooking, p. 40, instead of the tofu creme and by using the soy-free Parmesan alternative on page 37.

X
Cornmeal and Rice Dishes
POLENTA, RISOTTI E RISO

"Recipe: the best of ingredients, as fresh as they can be found, and within the bounds of skill, preserve their identity in the preparation."
—Luigi Barzini in the introduction to *The Cooking of Italy*

Italians do have alternatives to bread and pasta—polenta, which is made from corn, and risotto, a creamy rice dish, are the most popular. There are other rice dishes similar to baked pilafs or paellas (especially in Sicily, where the Spanish and Moorish influence is strong), as well as rice balls stuffed with a variety of fillings and cooked to a crispy golden brown on the outside. (See page 141 for rice timbali and molded, filled rice casseroles.)

Polenta is one of those peasant dishes which hardly anyone not of Italian ancestry knew existed a few years ago, but which is "trendy" now. It's a great dish for those allergic to wheat and makes for a delicious change of pace.

Risotto has also become trendy in recent years, especially as Italian rice has become more readily available. Unlike Oriental-style steamed rice that many of us are used to, risotto is traditionally cooked by adding hot liquid and stirring until it evaporates, then adding more, until the rice is just tender and has a creamy "sauce" surrounding each grain. With a good vegetable broth, Soymage Parmesan substitute, good wine, and an array of fresh vegetables and herbs, vegetarian risotti can rival any of the rich meat and seafood versions.

Many home cooks are discouraged from making polenta and risotto because traditional methods for cooking them require standing at the stove, stirring for 20 minutes or more—something most people are not willing to do very often, if at all. Fortunately (because these foods are worth eating on a regular basis), modern methods allow us to cook these dishes with very little time and effort, and with sensational results.

Polenta

Polenta is the Italian name for savory cornmeal mush. It sounds mundane, but it's a perfect foil for spicy sauces or mushroom stews. It can be creamy and soft when served fresh, or dense and firm when allowed to cool, then is sliced and baked, grilled, or browned in a skillet. It's a great change from potatoes, pasta, bread, or rice, especially in the wintertime.

Polenta harkens back to the Roman "puls" or "pulmentum," a porridge made from farro, a kind of spelt. When necessary, it was also made from chestnut flour, millet, acorns, buckwheat, and even oats. It was a staple of plebian Romans and of soldiers, in particular. When corn came from the Americas, the northern Italians took to it readily and made their polenta from the new golden grain. It is still primarily a northern dish and southern Italians are wont to call their northern neighbors (in a more or less derogatory fashion) "mangiapolenta" or "polenta eaters."

New ways to cook polenta: There's really no need to stand and stir polenta for an hour or more, as was done in the past by Italian housewives. Instead of using the coarse-ground, long-cooking polenta, use ordinary, inexpensive yellow cornmeal and a double boiler, pressure cooker, or microwave to make polenta effortlessly and quickly enough for everyday meals. (Don't bother with the readymade polenta sold in tubes—it isn't worth the money!)

Serve fresh polenta with Soymage Parmesan substitute (or soy-free alternative, p. 37) and herbs for a primo or first course, or as a main dish topped with the following: chunky spaghetti sauce or ragù, pp. 42-51; roasted or sautéed mushroom mixtures (my favorite, especially in the fall, when the chanterelles are up); vegetarian Italian sausage in tomato sauce; roasted vegetables, p. 73; or a stew (see chapters XII and XIII). Smooth it over thick vegetable mixtures or stews in a casserole, and bake it. Or press it with the back of a spoon into an oiled pie pan, and let it cool, to bake as a "crust" for thick, savory vegetable or stew mixtures.

Make an impressive molded polenta (timbalo) by making firm polenta (see pages 130-32), then scraping it into a well-oiled mold, such as you might use for a jellied salad. For timbalini, or individual molds, spoon the freshly cooked polenta into small, oiled pudding molds, wide cups, or custard cups. Let stand 5 to 10 minutes to firm up, then invert onto a serving dish and serve right away, or reheat later, uncovered, in a microwave for 10 minutes. Slice it either with a sharp knife or with taut string, as the Italians do. Sauce it as suggested previously.

Firm, sliced polenta can be browned in a nonstick pan or pan-fried in a little olive oil, or you can bake, broil, or grill it to be served for dinner with any topping you might use for potatoes, pasta, or rice. You can even use thin slices as a substitute for lasagne noodles.

For an appetizer, grill polenta slices and top with Pesto, pp. 49-51, sautéed mushrooms or greens and garlic, Raw Tomato Sauce with Black Olives, p. 86, and other toppings, as you would bruschetta.

See page 98 for polenta gnocchi.

Basic Double-Boiler or Pressure Cooker Polenta

For a soft, creamy polenta, use the larger amount of liquid listed below. For a firm or molded polenta, use the lesser amount. For a savory polenta, use a flavorful vegetarian broth and optional herbs, etc.

Taste the polenta when you think it's done, and make sure that it doesn't have an unpleasant, bitter taste. If it does, let it cook a little longer.

Use yellow cornmeal for more color and nutrition. (Interestingly enough, Venetians prefer white cornmeal, however.) For a richer polenta, you may stir in a good-tasting nondairy margarine and/or Soymage Parmesan substitute, or soy-free alternative, p. 37, to taste after cooking or use all or part nondairy milk instead of water or broth.

Servings	Cornmeal	*Cold* Water or Broth	Salt
4	1 cup	2 cups to 4 cups	¼ tsp
6	1+½ cup	3 cups to 6 cups	½ tsp
8	2 cups	4 cups to 8 cups	¾ tsp

Whichever way you are cooking the polenta, mix the cornmeal with the *cold* water or broth, and salt. (Don't try to stir hot water into dry cornmeal, or it will clump up.) Use the lesser amount of water if you want a firm or molded polenta; use the greater amount for a creamy, fresh polenta. (Soft creamy polenta will still firm up when it's cold, though.)

For the Double-Boiler Method, mix the cornmeal and water in the top of a double boiler. Add water to the bottom of the double boiler, and bring to a boil. Place the top of the double boiler over high heat, and bring to a boil quickly, stirring almost constantly with a whisk or wooden spoon to prevent sticking and clumping. As soon as it boils, set it *immediately* in the bottom part of the double boiler, over the simmering water. Let it simmer for 20 minutes, partially covered, and stir it now and then, until the mush is creamy and smooth (for soft polenta) or very thick and not gritty anymore (for firm polenta).

Serve immediately or pour into a well-oiled mold, loaf pan, or flat baking pan. Let set 5 to 10 minutes for a hot mold, or chill (even for several days), if you want to slice it. You can quick-chill it by spreading it no more than ½ inch thick in a flat pan or muffin tins and placing it in the freezer for a few minutes.

For the Pressure-Cooker Method, mix the polenta, cold water or broth, and salt in a heat-proof or stainless steel bowl or casserole that will fit into your pressure cooker. Cover with foil. Fold a long piece of heavy foil 2 inches wide, and use that to lift the casserole/bowl in and out of the cooker. Place the casserole/bowl on a rack over 1 to 2 inches of water in the bottom for your cooker. Close the cooker and bring to 15 pounds pressure over high heat, then turn the heat down just enough to maintain this pressure, and cook 10 minutes. Remove from the heat and let rest 5 minutes, then quick-release the pressure under cold running water. Stir the polenta and prepare for serving as for the double boiler method.

Basic Microwave Polenta

(soy-free)

Yield: 4 to 6 servings

Use the smaller amount of cornmeal for soft polenta and the larger amount for firm or molded polenta. For a richer polenta, you may add some good-tasting nondairy margarine and/or Soymage Parmesan substitute, or soy-free alternate, p. 37, to taste.

Servings	*Cold* Water or Broth	Cornmeal	Salt
4 to 6	4 cups	¾ to 1¼ cups	½ tsp

Whisk the ingredients together in a large microwave-safe bowl or casserole. Cover and cook on high for 5 minutes. Whisk the polenta. Cover and cook on high 3 minutes. Whisk again. Cover and cook again for 3 minutes more. Let stand 1 minute. Taste the polenta and make sure that it doesn't have an unpleasant, bitter taste. If it does, let it cook a little longer.

Serve immediately or pour into a well-oiled mold, loaf pan, or flat baking pan. Let set 5 to 10 minutes for a hot mold, or chill (even for several days), if you want to slice it. You can quick-chill it by spreading it no more than ½-inch thick in a flat pan or muffin tins

Polenta Layered with Sauce (*al Sugo*)

For a hearty casserole dish, layer ½-inch thick slices of firm polenta with Ragù alla Napoletana, p. 43, or Ragù alla Bolognese, p. 45. Sprinkle each layer of sauce with Soymage Parmesan substitute, or soy-free alternative, p. 37, and drizzle with a medium Dairy-Free White Sauce, p. 36, if you wish. You should have two layers of polenta and two layers of sauce. Bake at 450°F for 20 minutes, then let stand 10 minutes before serving.

Savory Polenta

When the polenta is almost cooked, stir in dried or fresh herbs; drained, chopped sun-dried tomatoes in oil or roasted red peppers; a bit of soy bacon bits, chopped veggie ham, veggie Canadian or "back" bacon, crumbled vegetarian Italian sausage, or Italian-style hamburger replacement; minced Italian parsley; chopped garlic; sautéed onions; chopped cooked greens, such as kale; cooked red kidney or romano beans; freshly ground pepper or dried chile flakes; and/or Soymage Parmesan substitute, or soy-free alternative, p. 37.

and placing it in the freezer for a few minutes.

To brown firm polenta slices without frying in oil:

Either grill or broil polenta slices 3 to 4 inches from the heat source until speckled with browned spots, brown them over high to medium-high heat in a nonstick skillet, or place them on a lightly oiled or nonstick cookie sheet, and bake them at 450°F for 10 to 15 minutes.

Polenta Vegetable Pie

Make two ½-inch-thick layers of polenta in round 8- to 10-inch pie or cake pans. When firm, layer the polenta with sautéed or roasted vegetables of your choice, seasoned with garlic, herbs, onions, etc. You can also add some soy Parmesan (or alternative), and/or Dairy-Free White Sauce to each layer, if you wish. Bake as for Polenta Layered with Sauce, p. 131.

Vegetarian Italian "Scrapple"

Try a combination of cooked greens, sautéed onions, celery, garlic, and cooked beans in the broth-flavored polenta. Allowed it to cool, then slice and pan-fry in a little olive oil.

Rice and Risotto

According to Anna del Conte's *Gastronomy of Italy*, the Romans used rice as a medicine, but did not grow it. Apparently, the Spanish first grew rice in Campania in the 15th century. The Moors and the Spanish also grew rice in Sicily and, despite the preference for pasta in that region, many delicious rice dishes survive in Sicily today.

Italy is now the biggest producer of rice in Europe (except for the former U.S.S.R.), and 60 percent of it is exported. Most of Italy's rice is grown in the Po Valley, in the northern regions of Piedmont, Lombardy, Emilia-Romagna, and the Veneto.

There are a few rice dishes sprinkled throughout this book, and I'll give you a few other rice dishes in this chapter. However, the most famous by far (with good reason!), and the one which I will concentrate on, is risotto.

Until the 19th century, rice was mainly eaten in soups in Italy. Risotto, as we know it, became popular in northern Italy at that time, introduced by the chef of the first king of Italy and further popularized by the great cooking writer Pellegrino Artusi.

Risotto begins with superfino rice sautéed in fat, usually along with some onion. Then hot broth (and sometimes wine) is stirred in a little at a time, and the rice is stirred until that broth is absorbed. This continues until the specified amount of broth is used up and the rice is tender, but still firm at the center—not mushy!

Traditionally, a heavy-gauge copper pot was used for risotto, but enameled cast-iron or heavy-bottomed stainless steel is just fine.

There is some difference of opinion among experts about the amount of time it takes to cook risotto. Some, like Carlo Middione, will tell you 16 to 18 minutes—no longer! Other cooks, like Marcella Hazan, instruct us to begin tasting after 20 minutes and possibly cook for 5 minutes longer. You must experiment to see how you like it best. Risotto should not be like a porridge. The rice grains should be separate and slightly chewy in the middle (but not hard) and creamy on the outside.

Some people like risotto quite soupy, and others (myself included) like it when it has more of a saucy coating. If my recipes aren't "wet" enough for you, feel free to add a little more broth—about ¼ cup more for each cup of rice. "Soupy" risotto can be unappetizing for people who have never experienced this dish before.

Parmesan cheese and butter (a combination called "mantecare") were always whipped in at the end of cooking, but many modern cooks dispense with adding more fat. In any case, you can add the soy Parmesan and stir the rice for one to three minutes to get a creamy consistency. In some recipes, a jellied broth or nondairy cream is whipped in at the end.

Almost any other ingredient can be added to the risotto—vegetables, particularly, in any combination—and new risotti are being invented every day. I start with the basic yellow risotto (risotto giallo) and add whatever vegetables, herbs, meat alternates, wines, vegetable juices, etc., take my fancy. The resulting dish is substantial, creamy, elegant, savory, and like nothing else in the world. Risotto is traditionally served on its own, in a large, heated soup plate.

Besides the classic method, I am going to give you three excellent modern methods for making delicious risotto without the continual stirring and surveillance, plus a clever, partially made-ahead method. If you don't believe that such a thing is possible, please try each method—I believe you will be convinced, *and* you will eat risotto far more often! Please try the classic method first, however—or at least read the recipe, as it will give you a good sense of how the dish comes together. Risotto not only makes an elegant first course or primo for company, but also a wonderful main dish (or one-dish meal, when it's full of vegetables) for lunch, dinner, or supper.

The ingredients for a risotto are important. You must use a medium-grain rice. Italian-grown superfino arborio is the most easily obtainable—most large supermarkets carry it now. There is a newer hybrid called carnaroli that you may be able to find in large urban areas, and vialone nano (which is preferred by Venetians) or the Roma variety may be available in specialty shops. I personally do not care for risotto made with brown rice, although I have seen recipes for it. The risotti I made with it tasted heavy and muddy. I think brown rice is much better in pilafs and other rice preparations that are drier.

An excellent vegetarian broth is also a necessity. Make your own, p. 117, or see pages 18-19 for notes on broth cubes, powders, and pastes.

I have cut down considerably on the fat in my risotto recipes, but you will still need a little extra-virgin olive oil and/or good-quality, good-tasting nondairy margarine.

I use Soymage Parmesan substitute, which I think is quite delicious, but, if you can't eat soy, you can use the soy-free alternative on page 37 or leave it out.

Saffron is added to many recipes for risotto. Use real Spanish saffron, which can be purchased in little vials or boxes for under $5 or $6. Since you only use a tiny bit at a time, this will last you quite a while. This is much preferable to the cheaper "American saffron," which is not the real thing.

Risotto should be eaten right away. It doesn't sit or reheat well (except as patties or in arancini/rice balls). However, I'm going to dare to admit that I have microwaved a serving of leftover risotto for about 90 seconds with fairly good results. You can form leftover risotto into patties, or smooth it into a flat pan, chill, and cut it into rounds, squares, or triangles. Brown them in a little olive oil or on a nonstick skillet, or bake or grill like polenta (see page 132).

Classic Yellow Risotto

RISOTTO GIALLO CLASSICO

(can be soy-free)

Yield: 8 servings as an appetizer, 4 servings as a main dish

½ teaspoon Spanish saffron

6 cups hot vegetarian broth, or 5½ cups broth plus ½ cup dry white or red wine, dry white vermouth, marsala, or dry sherry

1 to 2 tablespoons extra-virgin olive oil or good-tasting nondairy margarine

1 small to large onion, minced (depending on how much you like)

Optional: **1 to 3 cloves garlic, minced**

2 cups superfino arborio rice (or other Italian superfino rice)

¼ cup Soymage Parmesan substitute, or soy-free alternative, p. 37

Salt and pepper, to taste

You should make risotto the classic way at least once before you try the faster modern methods, so that you know what the dish should be like. You can always read a book while you stir!

Soak the saffron in the hot broth.

Heat the oil or margarine in a medium, heavy-bottomed saucepan (preferably nonstick), and add the onion and optional garlic. Sauté until the onion begins to soften, adding a few drops of water if necessary to keep from sticking. Don't brown the onion or garlic.

Stir in the rice and sauté it for about 3 minutes, then add ½ cup of broth or wine. Stir over medium heat until the liquid almost evaporates. Add another ½ cup hot broth, and keep stirring! Continue stirring until the liquid is absorbed, adding ½ cup of broth at a time, until the rice is "al dente"—tender, but with a firm bite in the center. Some cooks say to start tasting after 15 minutes of cooking, others say after 20 minutes. Start with 15 minutes at first—you'll soon discover your own preference.

The rice should be creamy, but not runny. At this point, turn off the heat, add the soy Parmesan or alternative, and stir for one to three minutes. Serve very hot on a heated soup plate with a spoon and fork.

To partially cook risotto ahead of time (as restaurants sometimes do), cook the risotto for only 10 minutes, making sure that you have let the rice absorb all the liquid added to this point. Immediately spread the rice out on a jelly roll pan (cookie sheet with sides). Let it cool. You can keep it at room temperature (don't refrigerate it) for several hours. When you are ready to serve it, bring the rest of the broth to a boil in a saucepan. In your original risotto cooking pot, mix the rice with a little of the broth over medium heat. When the rice heats up, start adding more hot broth, ¼ cup at a time, cooking for 6 to 10 more minutes, or until al dente to your liking.

Per appetizer serving: Calories: 150, Protein: 4 g, Carbohydrate: 24 g, Fat: 2 g

Easy Stove-Top Yellow Risotto
RISOTTO GIALLO FACILE
(can be soy-free)

Yield: 8 servings as an appetizer, 4 servings as a main course

½ teaspoon Spanish saffron

6 cups hot vegetarian broth, or 5½ cups hot vegetarian broth plus ½ cup dry white or red wine, dry vermouth, dry marsala, or dry sherry

1 to 2 tablespoons extra-virgin olive oil or good-tasting nondairy margarine

1 small to large onion, minced (depending on how much you like)

Optional: 1 to 3 cloves garlic, minced

2 cups superfino arborio rice (or other Italian superfino rice)

¼ cup Soymage Parmesan substitute, or soy-free alternative, p. 37

Salt and pepper, to taste

Soak the saffron in the hot broth.

Heat the oil or margarine in a medium, heavy-bottomed saucepan (preferably nonstick), and add the onion and optional garlic. Sauté until the onion begins to soften, adding a few drops of water if necessary to keep from sticking. Don't brown the onion or garlic.

Stir in the rice and sauté it for about 3 minutes, then add the remain-

This is a departure from the classic stove-top method of stirring the liquid in a little at a time (which takes 20 to 25 minutes and a lot of attention). So it isn't quite as creamy. But it's still deliciously rich-tasting. This method saves a lot of effort.

This recipe can be halved, but you should not double it.

ing ingredients, except the soy Parmesan, salt, and pepper. Make sure the broth is hot when you add it to the rice. Bring it to a boil, then turn down the heat to medium, uncover, and simmer 15 to 20 minutes, or until the rice is al dente to your liking. Stir now and then. Remove from the heat and stir in soy Parmesan for one to three minutes. Serve very hot on heated soup plates with spoons and forks.

Per appetizer serving: Calories: 150, Protein: 4 g, Carbohydrate: 24 g, Fat: 2 g

Pressure Cooked Yellow Risotto

RISOTTO GIALLO A LA PENTOLA

(can be soy-free)

Yield: 8 servings as an appetizer, 4 servings as a main course

½ teaspoon Spanish saffron

5½ cups hot vegetarian broth, or 5 cups hot vegetarian broth plus ½ cup dry white or red wine, dry vermouth, dry marsala, or dry sherry

1 onion, minced (small to large, depending on how much you like)

Optional: 1 to 3 cloves garlic, minced

1 to 2 tablespoons extra-virgin olive oil or good-tasting nondairy margarine

2½ cups superfino arborio rice or other Italian superfino rice

¼ cup Soymage Parmesan substitute, or soy-free alternative, p. 37

Salt and pepper, to taste

Soak the saffron in the broth.

In the pressure cooker, sauté the onion (and optional garlic) in the oil or margarine over medium-high heat until the onion starts to soften (don't let it brown). Add the rice and sauté for about three minutes. Add the liquid and place the cover on your cooker, sealing it properly according to the manufacturer's instructions. Let it come up to pressure, then reduce the heat immediately, keeping it just high enough to keep the pressure up. Set your timer from this point for 8 minutes. When the 8 minutes are up, transfer the pot to a sink, and

You need one of the "new generation" pressure cookers (with a stationary pressure regulator instead of a "jiggler") to make this properly, but what a revelation when you try it! I tried it as soon as I opened my new Lagostina pressure cooker, and now we have perfect risotto in 8 minutes as often as we like! It took much longer in my old pressure cooker, and also tended to stick dangerously—the new cookers have a double layer of stainless steel on the bottom to prevent scorching. The new generation of Italian cooks takes advantage of this method too.

Note: This recipe can be halved, and it can also be doubled successfully if you have a large cooker. (This is the only method that allows you to successfully cook 2 to 2½ pounds of rice at a time for risotto.)

"If anything could convince the true cook, or even the ardent eater, that the microwave oven is a tool worth having, it would be that it makes risotto divinely, effortlessly, and relatively rapidly while the cook talks to the guests. From being a once-a-year treat, it can go to being an everyday delight."

And:

"The very idiosyncrasy of cooking that makes the microwave oven generally unacceptable for the cooking of floury dishes makes risotto work well. Starch absorbs liquid slowly in the microwave oven, and it also absorbs too much. That is exactly what you want the rice to do in a risotto."

—Barbara Kafka, one of America's most renowned food writers and for many years a columnist for *Gourmet* magazine, in her book *Microwave Gourmet* (New York: William Morrow, 1987)

This is the exception to the rule that it isn't really a time-saver to cook rice in a microwave oven. With this method, you can have creamy, savory risotto in under half an hour, with no stirring. It's actually no faster than the easy stovetop method described on

bring the pressure down quickly under running water. Open the pot and return it to the stove, placing it over medium heat.

Add salt and pepper to taste and the soy Parmesan or alternative. Stir for one to three minutes, until the consistency is to your liking. Serve very hot on heated soup plates with spoons and forks.

Per appetizer serving: Calories: 168, Protein: 5 g, Carbohydrate: 29 g, Fat: 2 g

Microwave Yellow Risotto
RISOTTO GIALLO A LA MICROWAVE
(can be soy-free)

Yield: 4 servings as an appetizer, 2 servings as a main dish

¼ teaspoon Spanish saffron

3 cups lukewarm vegetarian broth, or 2¾ cups lukewarm vegetarian broth plus ¼ cup dry white or red wine, dry vermouth, dry marsala, or dry sherry

1 tablespoon extra-virgin olive oil or good-tasting nondairy margarine

1 small onion, minced

Optional: 1 to 2 cloves garlic, minced

1 cup superfino arborio rice or other Italian superfino rice

2 tablespoons Soymage Parmesan substitute, or soy-free alternative, p. 37

Salt and pepper, to taste

Soak the saffron in the broth.

In a medium- to large-sized microwave-safe casserole, place the oil, onion, and garlic. Cover and cook on high for 3 minutes. Add the rice, and cook uncovered on high 3 minutes, then add the liquid.

Stir well and cook uncovered on high for 14 to 15 minutes. Taste the rice to see if it is done—you may need to cook it for another minute or so. Add salt and pepper to taste. Add the soy Parmesan or alternative, stirring for one to three minutes. Serve very hot on heated soup plates with spoons and forks. You can also double the recipe, using a large casserole. Cook the onions 4½ minutes and the rice 4½ minutes. Use boiling hot broth. After adding the liquid, cook on high for 9 minutes. Stir. Cook 9 minutes more, then proceed as above.

Per appetizer serving: Calories: 164, Protein: 5 g, Carbohydrate: 26 g, Fat: 3 g

Other Ideas for Risotto

• Use freshly extracted juices instead of all or some of the broth. Carrot and celery are obvious choices, but try other vegetable juices. You can add appropriate vegetables, if you wish.

• If you want a hearty one-dish meal, add some type of protein—slices of pan-fried Breast of Tofu, p. 170; leftover "scaloppine," pp. 186-88, with most of the sauce drained off; sliced canned Chinese vegetarian roast duck (mun chai'ya), rinsed and browned in a little olive oil; canned vegetarian scallops, browned in garlic and olive oil (add lots of Italian parsley); cubes of smoked tofu; cooked red kidney beans, baby limas, fresh favas, etc.; a handful of pine nuts; sliced seitan, pp. 178-80; some chopped vegetarian Canadian or "back" bacon; even a little leftover vegetarian burger, sausage, or meatballs of any sort.

• Add 2 or more tablespoons of chopped fresh herbs—basil, sage, rosemary, marjoram, etc.—or a pinch of dried red pepper flakes.

• Vegetables that you can add at the beginning of cooking (sautéing for about 10 minutes with the onions) are: carrots; thinly sliced, trimmed fresh artichokes, see page 66; diced bell peppers; caramelized onions, p. 73; soaked dried mushrooms, pp. 35-36; green onions; zucchini; fresh mushrooms; chopped leaks; chopped celery; sliced fennel; and peeled, chopped winter squash.

• Vegetables to add at the end of cooking time are: grilled eggplant cubes; steamed broccoli; steamed spinach; roasted vegetables of any sort, p. 73; chopped radicchio, perhaps with a bit of diced vegetarian Canadian or "back" bacon added; roasted garlic, p. 72; soaked, chopped dried tomatoes, or chopped, drained sun-dried tomatoes in oil; chopped pitted Italian olives; cooked asparagus; chopped fresh basil; chopped roasted red peppers; cooked squeezed-dry greens of any sort; Savoy cabbage; and zest of lemon (omit the saffron).

• Vegetables to add half-way through the cooking time are: crisp-tender steamed green beans; chopped, soaked dried tomato; chopped, peeled ripe plum tomato (and basil); fresh or thawed frozen petit pois (baby peas).

• Invent your own combinations of vegetables, herbs, juices, and other foods with risotto—a summer combo, perhaps with nasturtium blossoms added at the end; an autumn one with roasted root vegetables. Sauté longer-cooking vegetables with the onions, and cook with the risotto. Add tender or precooked vegetables in the middle or toward the end of cooking.

page 136, but requires less attention. Another advantage is that you can cook it right in the serving dish, so you have no dirty pot!

Note: This method was tested using a 1.5 cubic foot, 900 watt microwave. You may have to adjust the timing slightly if you have a different size or different wattage microwave.

Milanese Rice

(Risotta alla Milanese)

Traditionally this is a saffron risotto with beef marrow added, which adds a glistening, rich coating to the rice. Instead of the marrow, stir in ½ cup of Jelled Broth, p. 118, and about 2 tablespoons minced Italian parsley along with the soy Parmesan, salt, and pepper, just before serving. This is so rich-tasting that your guests will think they are eating something very indulgent!

Golden Stuffed Rice Balls
ARANCINI DI RISO
(can be soy-free)

Yield: 10 orange-sized balls

½ recipe Yellow Risotto, pp. 135-37 (Classic, Easy Stove-Top, or Pressure-Cooker Methods), chilled,
or 1 recipe Microwave Yellow Risotto, chilled
2 tablespoons Soymage Parmesan substitute, or soy-free alternative, p. 37

Filling:
⅔ cup cold, thick, "meaty" spaghetti sauce, such as Brian's Wine-Free Mushroom Tomato Sauce, p. 44, with hamburger replacement added
⅓ cup thawed frozen petit pois (baby peas)

1 to 1½ cups fine fresh bread crumbs

Mix the risotto with the soy Parmesan, set aside, then combine the cold sauce with the peas for the filling.

For each ball, measure out ¼ cup risotto and another 1 tablespoon, kept separate. Place the ¼ cup risotto in the palm of one hand, and flatten it slightly. Place 1 tablespoon of the filling in the center of the risotto. Close up your hand to make the rice enclose the filling, using the extra 1 tablespoon rice to cover the gap at the top. Form the rice firmly into a ball. (You can flatten this slightly, if you prefer.)

Dredge the balls in the bread crumbs until completely coated. Place the balls on a greased cookie sheet, and refrigerate to firm up while you heat the oven to 350°F.

Spray the balls with a fine mist of olive oil from a pump sprayer (like an Eco-Pump or Donvier Spray pump, p. 28). Bake 15 minutes, then turn over and bake 15 minutes longer, or until golden.

"Arancini" means oranges, referring to the golden color of these crispy rice balls, I suppose. They are a popular Sicilian dish. Since they can be a bit complicated to make, I only make them when I have leftover Yellow Risotto and leftover "meaty" spaghetti sauce on hand. (You can double the recipes on purpose when you are making them and then have these the next day.)

Rice Croquettes
(*Crochetti di Riso*)
Form leftover, cold basic yellow risotto (or any other type of risotto that isn't too chunky) into small balls, cones, logs, etc., and coat with fine fresh bread crumbs. Fry in hot oil until golden, or oven-bake as for Stuffed Rice Balls, p. 140. Serve hot with any simple tomato sauce, pp. 42-43, Ragù ala Napoletana, p. 43, or Brian's Mushroom Tomato Sauce, p. 44.

These croquettes are excellent when made with a spinach risotto or any risotto made with finely shredded greens.

These can be eaten "as is" or as a snack, or served with a tomato sauce.

Per rice ball: Calories: 84, Protein: 3 g, Carbohydrate: 13 g, Fat: 1 g

Suppli

Suppli "al telefono" are rice balls filled with mozzarella cheese and ham. The melted cheese strings out into "telephone wires" when bitten into—hence the name! These vegan suppli will not form "wires," but taste delectable.

Make the same as for Stuffed Rice Balls, except divide the rice into 14 equal-sized portions (a little under ¼ cup each), and use ½ cup thick, cold Dairy-Free White Sauce, p. 36, mixed with 2 tablespoons minced vegetarian Canadian or "back" bacon as the filling. Form and bake the balls as you would Stuffed Rice Balls, using about 1½ teaspoons filling per ball.

Note: Instead of the vegetarian Canadian or "back" bacon, you can use minced, soaked dried tomatoes, p. 23, sun-dried tomatoes in oil (drain well), or minced, soaked dried porcini or boletus mushrooms, pp. 35-36.

Molded Risotto (Timbalo) or Risotto Timbalini

For the timbalo, press the freshly cooked risotto firmly into an oiled ring mold. Immediately invert on a heated platter, and unmold. Fill the center with "scaloppine" (see recipes on pages 186-89).

For a Baked Timbalo di Risotto, make 1½ times the basic yellow risotto recipe (use 3 cups rice), and let it get cold. Press two-thirds of it into the bottom and sides of an oiled, 10-inch oven-proof bowl or deep, rounded casserole which has been coated with fine bread crumbs. Fill the cavity with something "meaty"—an Italian stew, p. 191; Oven-Broiled Breast of Tofu, or Seitan Chicken with Vegetables, pp. 170-72; a ragù, pp. 43-46, with "meatballs" or Italian "sausage," pp. 177 and 183, or a commercial vegetarian version; leftover vegetarian scaloppine, pp. 186-89; even a thick bean or lentil dish or vegetable stew (see chapter XII). Just make sure that it is quite thick. Cover the top with the rest of the basic risotto, sprinkle with more bread crumbs, and bake at 400°F for about 30 minutes. Let rest 15 minutes, then unmold onto a plate, and cut into wedges to serve.

For the Timbalini, press the freshly cooked risotto into small, oiled pudding molds, wide cups, or custard cups. Unmold and serve with "scaloppine." For a more elegant presentation, line the molds with thin grilled eggplant slices before adding the risotto.

Dishes

"Baked Omelets,"
Savory "Cakes,"
Tarts, Gratins, and
Other Vegetable
Casseroles

PANE, FRITTATE,
TORTE, TORTINI E
CASSERUOLE

"A classic example of
Ligurian culinary ingenu-
ity, it [a frittata, tortino, or
polpettone] is basically a
way of turning vegetables
into a main dish, or at least
a hearty appetizer, by
adding little more than
miscellaneous odds and
ends . . ."

Colman Andrews
Flavors of the Riviera
(New York: Bantam
Books, 1996)

Frittate are Italian omelets, which are thick and firm—more akin to the Spanish tortilla or Persian kuku than to soft, folded French omelets. They are usually full of vegetables and often contain potatoes or leftover pasta, as well. The traditional way to cook a frittata is in a skillet on top of the stove, but this simple tofu mixture works better in the oven.

Frittate are usually served at room temperature, and they make an excellent merenda (between-meal snack), either eaten out of hand or on a piece of crusty bread—great picnic food too! Although Italians do not eat eggs for breakfast, frittate are wonderful make-ahead brunch fare.

I'm giving you the basic vegan frittata batter and some of my favorite ways to use it, but feel free to substitute your own favorite vegetables and herbs. This egg-free version has excellent flavor, texture, and even an egg-like color. (The batter looks very pale, but turns a darker yellow when cooked).

Tortini (savory cakes) or polpettone (large croquette in Liguria) are similar to frittate, but are usually thicker and are always baked. They often have cooked rice or bread crumbs in them, instead of potatoes or pasta, and usually have bread crumbs sprinkled on top and lining the pan. Sometimes tortini or torte are more like a French vegetable gratin—vegetables held together with a white sauce or cheese.

I'm also including a section of vegetable casseroles. Some of these recipes may be called "tortino," but they are held together with something other than the tofu mixture used in my frittate recipes.

Basic Frittata

Yield: two 10-inch frittate

Batter:

1 pound medium-firm tofu

6 tablespoons unbleached white flour, or ¼ cup brown rice flour

¼ cup nutritional yeast flakes

1 tablespoon water, dry white wine, marsala, or dry sherry

1 teaspoon baking powder

½ teaspoon salt

½ teaspoon turmeric

¼ teaspoon white pepper

Additions:

2 tablespoons extra-virgin olive oil

1 large onion, thinly sliced (can substitute all or some with green
  onion or leek)

2 medium cooked potatoes, peeled and sliced, or 1 cup leftover
  cooked pasta (with or without sauce)

Freshly ground black pepper

2 tablespoons Soymage Parmesan substitute, or soy-free
  alternative, p. 37, for topping

Optional Additions: (1 to 2 cups total)

1 tablespoon to ⅔ cup chopped fresh herbs: can be Italian parsley
  or a mixture of parsley, basil, mint, sage, etc.

Chopped vegetarian ham, Canadian or "back" bacon, or
  pepperoni, or some cooked crumbled vegetarian Italian sausage
  (commercial or see pages 177 or 183)

Sliced black Italian olives

Chopped sun-dried tomato (in oil, or rehydrated)

Cooked, canned, or marinated artichoke hearts, thinly sliced

2 cloves garlic, minced

½ cup chopped cooked bitter greens, such as arugula, dandelion,
  endive, borage, etc.

Bell pepper, any or all colors, thinly sliced

Zucchini or other summer squash, thinly sliced

Asparagus, broccoli, cauliflower, mushrooms, greens, green
  beans, zucchini flowers, eggplant, etc., crisply cooked and cut
  in small pieces

Preheat the oven to 450°F.

Place 1 tablespoon olive oil in each of two 10-inch cast-iron skillets or
baking dishes, and place them in the oven while it heats up.

Blend all the ingredients for the batter in a food processor until very
smooth.

Add the onion and any vegetables that need to be sautéed to the hot
oil in the pans in the oven. Bake them for about 5 minutes, then add

them to the batter in a bowl, along with all other additions, and the potatoes, pasta, etc. Lower the oven temperature to 350°F.

Divide the mixture evenly between the two skillets, and spread evenly to the edges. Sprinkle with pepper and soy Parmesan. Bake for 30 minutes. Cool the skillets on racks for 10 minutes, then loosen the bottom of the frittatas and cut each into 6 pieces. Eat warm or at room temperature. Store leftovers in a covered container in the refrigerator. They make great sandwich fillers!

Per frittata (without additions): Calories: 297, Protein: 24 g, Carbohydrate: 26 g, Fat: 9 g

Common Vegetable Combinations for Frittate:

• Artichoke hearts, asparagus, parsley, a bit of lemon, dry white wine instead of water in the recipe

• Artichoke hearts, potatoes, roasted red pepper, vegetarian ham

• Asparagus and mushroom, with potato or spaghetti

• Browned or caramelized onions, with or without other vegetables

• Fried or grilled eggplant

• Green beans and potatoes

• Leeks and peas with fennel or mint

• Mushrooms and parsley, and substitute marsala wine for the water

• Potato and onion with a pinch of red pepper flakes

• Swiss chard with bread crumbs and marjoram

My favorite frittata is one made with onions, potato, red and green peppers, and artichoke hearts or zucchini, perhaps with some fresh basil and Italian parsley.

Ligurian Savory Cakes or Croquettes
(Tortini o Polpettone di Liguria)

Follow the Basic Frittata recipe, but use only one 10-inch cast-iron skillet or baking dish and 1 tablespoon of olive oil. You can use the potato or pasta in the batter, or you may substitute 1 to 2 cups cooked rice or 1 cup fresh bread crumbs.

Sprinkle the bottom of the pan and the top of the mixture with bread crumbs, and top with a sprinkling of pepper and soy Parmesan, as well. Smooth the whole recipe into the one pan, and bake for about 45 minutes. Cool on a rack to room temperature before cutting into wedges.

Tortini are often drizzled with a good extra-virgin olive oil before eating or can be served with a simple tomato sauce, pp. 42-43, vegetable sauce, or white sauce, p. 36.

You can use any of the flavoring suggestions for frittate, pp. 143-44. A very popular Ligurian tortino (called Torta di Riso e Spinaci or Torta Verde) can be made with 1 or 2 cups of leftover cooked rice, a 10-ounce box of frozen chopped spinach (thawed and squeezed dry), onion, and a pinch of nutmeg. Sometimes fresh herbs, such as mint, basil, marjoram, oregano, thyme, sage, rosemary, Italian parsley, and/or garlic are added.

Another Ligurian tortino is called Polpettone di Fagiolini, which means a large green bean croquette. No starchy base is used in this. Instead of the potatoes, rice, or pasta, use 2 pounds fresh or frozen small whole green beans. Trim them, cook 10 or 12 minutes, drain, and cut into 1-inch lengths. Mix about ⅓ cup soy Parmesan in the batter, in addition to what you sprinkle on top with the bread crumbs. Add a clove of chopped garlic, a bit of chopped Italian parsley, and fresh oregano or marjoram to the sautéed onions, as well.

Vegetable-Ricotta Gratin
TORTINO DI VERDURE
(can be soy-free)

Yield: 4 to 6 servings

This is a nice light summer casserole. You can vary the vegetables and even use cooked rice or pasta instead of the potatoes.

1 pound eggplant, sliced ¼ inch thick,
  or 1 pound mushrooms, sliced and sautéed,
  or 1 pound bell peppers, any color, seeded and roasted (can be
  roasted red peppers from a jar)
1 pound zucchini or any summer squash, sliced ¼ inch thick,
  or 1 pound fresh greens or broccoli, steamed, chopped, and
  squeezed dry
2 medium waxy potatoes,
  or 1½ to 2 cups cooked rice or small pasta
1 large onion, thinly sliced
1¼ cups Tofu Ricotta, p. 32, or Almond Ricotta, p. 35
¾ cup Marinara Sauce or a variation, pp. 42-43
½ cup fresh bread crumbs (whole wheat are fine)
¼ cup Soymage Parmesan substitute, or soy-free alternative, p. 37
2 tablespoons minced fresh basil
2 tablespoons minced fresh Italian parsley
Salt and freshly ground black pepper, to taste
1 tablespoon extra-virgin olive oil

Grill the eggplant and zucchini about 3 or 4 inches under the broiler

Small "Omelets" (Frittatine)

To make Frittatine, make the Basic Fritatta Batter, p. 142, adding ½ to 1 cup chopped fresh herbs and/or cooked, chopped greens, squeezed dry.

Preheat the oven to 400°F. Spread ¼ to ½ cup of the batter on oiled cookie sheets, making rounds as thin as possible without holes, about 8 inches across. Bake for 5 to 7 minutes, or until browned on the bottom. Then flip them over and cook another 5 to 7 minutes, or until golden brown on the other side.

Cool the omelets. To serve, stack or roll them with filling for spinach lasagne or canneloni, p. 114 or 104, sautéed mushrooms and vegetarian ham, or any filling you might use for crepes, pp. 107-08, and reheat briefly in a 350°F oven. Serve with a tomato sauce, pp. 42-51, or white sauce, p. 36. Frittatine can be used as sandwich fillers.

until they are slightly browned on each side and soft in the center. Set aside.

Boil the potatoes until they are just tender. Slice them thinly as soon as they are cool enough to handle.

Either steam-fry the onions in a nonstick pan until they are tender, or place them in a glass pie pan, cover with a plate, and microwave on high for about 4 minutes. Mix the bread crumbs with the basil and parsley.

Preheat the oven to 350°F, and oil a 10-inch casserole.

Mix the onions with ¼ of the ricotta, and spread in the bottom of the casserole. Top this with 1 tablespoon of the soy Parmesan and one quarter of the bread crumbs (about 3 tablespoons). Top this with all of the potato slices (or cooked rice or pasta, if you are using them instead).

Spread on ¼ cup ricotta, and sprinkle with 1 tablespoon soy Parmesan and about 3 tablespoons of the crumbs. Spread this with the marinara or tomato sauce. Top this with the grilled zucchini (or other squash or steamed greens), and spread with ¼ cup ricotta. Sprinkle with 1 tablespoon soy Parmesan and about 3 tablespoons crumbs. Top with the grilled eggplant (or roasted peppers or sautéed mushrooms). Spread with the last ½ cup "ricotta," the last 1 table-spoon of soy Parmesan, and the remaining bread crumbs. Drizzle with the olive oil, and bake 30 to 40 minutes. Serve hot or at room temperature.

Per serving: Calories: 232, Protein: 10 g, Carbohydrate: 29 g, Fat: 8 g

Eggplant Parmesan
MELANZANE ALL PARMAGIANA
(can be soy-free)

Yield: 6 servings

3 pounds eggplant, sliced ¼ inch thick
2 cups thick Dairy-Free White Sauce, p. 36
¾ cup toasted bread crumbs, p. 31
½ cup Soymage Parmesan substitute, or soy-free alternative, p. 37

Tomato Sauce:
½ medium onion, minced
2 cloves garlic, chopped
1 tablespoon extra-virgin olive oil
4 cups chopped fresh or canned, drained plum tomatoes
⅓ cup chopped fresh basil
Salt and freshly ground black pepper, to taste

Salt the eggplant and place it in a colander to drain while you make the white sauce. Prepare the bread crumbs and set aside.

To make the tomato sauce, sauté the onion and garlic in the olive oil in a heavy, medium pot until softened. Add the tomatoes and simmer for about 15 minutes. Add the basil and salt and pepper to taste. (Add a pinch of sugar if you are using canned tomatoes.) If you prefer a smooth sauce, run it through a food mill (mouli) or process it briefly in a food processor before adding the basil.

Rinse the eggplant and pat it dry. Brush it with olive oil, and broil it 3 or 4 inches from the heat on both sides until it is slightly browned and soft inside.

Preheat the oven to 325°F. Oil a 10-inch casserole. Lay half the eggplant on the bottom, and top with half the bread crumbs. Spread with half the tomato sauce, half the white sauce, and half the soy Parmesan (or alternative). Layer the remaining ingredients. Bake for 20 minutes, or until bubbly and browned on top.

Per serving: Calories: 233, Protein: 10 g, Carbohydrate: 28 g, Fat: 9 g

Despite the name, this dish appears to be Neapolitan or Sicilian in origin—and, of course, the southern Italians are masters of eggplant preparation.

You may have had very heavy versions of this dish—greasy, deep-fried eggplant layered in a heavy tomato sauce with two kinds of cheese. This light interpretation is much more appealing to modern tastes, with grilled eggplant, a light basil-tomato sauce, and white sauce with soy Parmesan providing a creamy contrast.

You can also make this dish with zucchini or a mixture of zucchini and eggplant.

Gratin of Broccoli or Cauliflower
BROCCOLI O CAVOLFIORE GRATINATI
(can be soy-free)

Yield: 4 servings

This makes a nice light supper dish.

1 large head broccoli or cauliflower
¾ to 1 cup thick Dairy-Free White Sauce, p. 36
2 tablespoons fresh bread crumbs
1 tablespoon Soymage Parmesan substitute, or soy-free alternate, p. 37
1 clove garlic, minced or crushed
2 tablespoons chopped fresh Italian parsley

Separate the broccoli or cauliflower into large florets. Peel the broccoli stalks and cut them into chunks. Steam or boil the vegetables just until crisp-tender.

Meanwhile, preheat the broiler of your oven.

Drain the vegetables, place them in an oiled casserole, and top with the white sauce. In a mini-chopper, food processor, or with a hand blender, grind the bread crumbs, soy Parmesan, garlic, and parsley together. Sprinkle this over the white sauce. Heat the dish under the broiler just long enough to turn the bread crumbs golden. Serve immediately.

Per serving: Calories: 90, Protein: 5 g, Carbohydrate: 8 g, Fat: 5 g

Baked Sliced Potatoes with Tomatoes
PATATE IN TEGAME
(can be soy-free)

Yield: 4 servings

1½ pounds potatoes, thinly sliced
2 to 4 cloves garlic, thinly sliced
¾ pound fresh, ripe plum tomatoes, thinly sliced, or 1 (14-ounce) can plum tomatoes or diced tomatoes, drained
2½ tablespoons extra-virgin olive oil

This delicious casserole can be served at any meal, including brunch, and makes a wonderful potluck offering. You can use almost any kind of potato (I like Yukon Golds) and either fresh or canned tomatoes. Traditional recipes call for more olive oil, but I find them a little greasy, so I have cut down the amount—add more if you wish.

¼ **cup Soymage Parmesan substitute, or soy-free alternate, p. 37**
Salt and freshly ground black pepper, to taste

Oil a 10-inch glass or ceramic baking dish or pie plate with olive oil. If you are using the canned tomatoes, break them up with your hands.

Preheat the oven to 350°F.

Layer ⅓ of the potatoes in the dish. Sprinkle with salt and pepper. Layer on ⅓ of the tomatoes, half of the garlic, and sprinkle on 1 tablespoon of the soy Parmesan. Drizzle with ½ tablespoon olive oil. Repeat the layering twice, then sprinkle the top with 2 tablespoons of soy Parmesan, and drizzle with 1 tablespoon olive oil. Cover the dish and bake for about 1 hour. Uncover the dish and bake 15 minutes more, or until the potatoes are tender and the top is golden. Serve hot.

Per serving: Calories: 260, Protein: 5 g, Carbohydrate: 38 g, Fat: 9 g

Potato Tortino
TORTINO DI PATATE
(can be soy-free)

Yield: 6 servings

2 pounds waxy potatoes
1 large onion, thinly sliced
2 to 4 tablespoons extra-virgin olive oil
¼ **cup vegetarian broth or nondairy milk**
½ **cup fine dry bread crumbs**
Salt and freshly ground black pepper, to taste
Optional:
You may add about 1 tablespoon Soymage Parmesan substitute, or soy-free alternative, p. 37, to each layer and on top. You may add also, instead of, or in addition to the soy Parmesan, about 1 cup of thick Dairy-Free White Sauce, p. 36, dividing it among the layers.

A potato tortino is made with thinly sliced pre-cooked waxy potatoes. It can be made simply with potatoes, sautéed onions, and bread crumbs, or a more elaborate version can be made by adding soy Parmesan, vegetarian bacon, ham, or sausage, tomatoes, mushrooms, sautéed greens, and/or Dairy-Free White Sauce.

Instead of or in addition to these, you may add (choose one):

- ½ pound fresh, ripe sliced plum tomatoes, or 1 cup canned tomatoes, drained and diced or chopped (add a clove of chopped garlic to the onions)
- 1 to 2 cups sautéed greens with garlic (pp. 74-75)
- 2 tablespoons chopped fresh rosemary and 1 ounce dried porcini or boletus mushrooms, soaked, pp. 35-36, drained, and chopped (Use reserved soaking water for liquid instead of broth or milk.)
- ½ pound any kind of fresh mushrooms, sliced and sautéed in a little extra-virgin olive oil (also use rosemary)

You may also opt to add (choose one):

- 6 thin slices commercial vegetarian Canadian or "back" bacon or ham (This takes the place of "speck," a northern Italian smoked ham.)
- about 1 cup crumbled, browned vegetarian Italian sausage, commercial or homemade soy version, p. 177, or seitan version, p. 183 (This goes well with greens.)

Peel the potatoes, if you wish, cut into even-sized chunks, and steam or boil until they are just tender, but still firm. When they can be handled easily, drain and slice the potatoes about ¼ inch thick.

Heat the olive oil in a large nonstick skillet over medium-high heat. Sauté the onions in the oil until they are soft and starting to brown.

Preheat the oven to 400°F.

Coat a 10-inch glass or ceramic casserole or pie pan with olive oil or nondairy margarine, and sprinkle it with some of the bread crumbs. Layer the potatoes and onions in the dish, adding salt and pepper between layers and any of the optional ingredients you may be using. End with potatoes, salt, and pepper. Pour the broth or milk over the dish, and top with the remaining bread crumbs (and soy Parmesan, if you wish). Bake 20 to 30 minutes, or until bubbly and golden on top. Serve hot.

Per serving without options: Calories: 231, Protein: 3 g, Carbohydrate: 39 g, Fat: 7 g

Ligurian Easter Pie
TORTA PASQUELINA
(can be soy-free)

Yield: 8 to 12 servings

Filling:

1 to 2 pounds Swiss chard (depending on how "green" you like your pie)

2½ cups Tofu Ricotta, p. 32, or Almond Ricotta, p. 35

1 tablespoon extra-virgin olive oil

3 or 4 fresh artichoke hearts (see pages 66-67 for trimming and cooking information), poached in vegetable broth for about 10 minutes, or until tender, then drained and sliced,
or ½ (10-ounce) package frozen, thawed artichoke hearts, drained and quartered,
or ½ (14-ounce) can artichokes in water

¼ pound fresh white or brown mushrooms, sliced

1 clove garlic, minced

½ cup Soymage Parmesan substitute, or soy-free alternative, p. 37

2 tablespoons flour

½ tablespoon chopped fresh marjoram

½ teaspoon salt

¼ teaspoon freshly ground pepper

¼ teaspoon freshly ground nutmeg

Phyllo Crust:

½ pound frozen phyllo pastry, thawed

¼ cup extra-virgin olive oil

Torta pasquelina is a world-famous specialty of the Genoa region, where my grandmother's family originated. The traditional pie (often eaten cold at family picnics on Easter Monday) was made with 33 layers of paper-thin dough (one layer for each year of Jesus's life), encasing a rich filling made from a ricotta-like cheese, Parmesan, Swiss chard, and herbs, with eggs broken into depressions in the filling.

Modern cooks now use frozen phyllo pastry, and this vegan filling is rich with artichokes and mushrooms.

You should make this pie either a day or two ahead or early in the morning so that it has time to cool thoroughly—it is most delicious at room temperature.

Wash and trim the chard. Steam for about 5 minutes, or until tender. Drain and squeeze it as dry as possible. Chop it coarsely and place in a large bowl along with the ricotta.

Preheat the oven to 325°F.

Heat the oil in a large nonstick skillet, and add the sliced or quartered artichoke hearts, mushrooms, and garlic. Sauté for a few minutes until the mushrooms brown and wilt a little. Add these vegetables to the bowl of chard and ricotta, along with the remaining filling ingredients. Mix thoroughly.

Coat a 9-inch springform pan with olive oil. With scissors, cut the large sheets of phyllo pastry in half to make about 18 to 20 rectangles. Trim half of them into 9-inch rounds, and set aside covered with a towel. Place one rectangular sheet in the pan, pressing the sheet gently against the sides and letting the 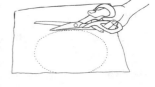 corners hang over the pan. Crisscross the remaining rectangles of phyllo over the first sheet so that all sides of the pan are covered with pastry, brushing each sheet with a little of the olive oil before placing it down (see illustration).

Fill the pastry case with the filling, smoothing the top. Layer the phyllo rounds on top of the filling, brushing each successive round with a little olive oil. Bring the overhanging edges of the bottom layer up and over the top. Brush generously with the remaining olive oil.

Place the pie in the oven, and bake for about 1 hour, or until the pastry is golden brown and crispy, and the filling has puffed up some in the middle. (Turn the heat down to 300°F if the pastry is browning too quickly.) Cool on a rack until the pan can be handled, then remove the outer ring of the pan, and place the torta on a serving platter. Cool thoroughly and serve at room temperature.

If made ahead, you can refrigerate the cooled pie for a day or two, then bring to room temperature before serving. Cut into wedges to serve.

Note: If you have no Swiss chard, you can substitute other greens, prepared the same way, or even one or two 10-ounce packages of frozen chopped spinach or other greens (thawed and squeezed dry), but the flavor will be different.

Per serving: Calories: 237, Protein: 10 g, Carbohydrate: 23 g, Fat: 11 g

Green Herb Tart *(Erbazzone)*

This is a sort of Italian Spanikopita. For the filling, use 2½ pounds greens (any kind—add some "bitter greens" for more flavor), and omit the mushrooms and artichokes. Add 2 to 3 chopped onions and 3 cloves chopped garlic, sautéed in the olive oil. Add 1 teaspoon roasted sesame oil. Omit the nutmeg and marjoram.

Do not cut the sheets of phyllo in half. Instead, drape them over a 14-inch pizza pan, overlapping, so that there is some overhang and the whole pan is evenly covered. Brush with olive oil as directed. Spoon the filling in the middle, and spread it out into a 10-inch circle. Bring the overhanging phyllo pastry up over the filling, and brush with oil. Bake at 350°F for about 30 to 35 minutes, or until crisp and golden brown.

Note: If you wish, you can bake these next three variations like 10-inch open-faced quiches, using Italian Sweet Pastry, p. 225, as the bottom crust, without using the sugar, lemon, and vanilla extracts. Bake at 375°F for about 35 minutes in this case.

Mushroom Tart *(Torta di Funghi)*

Omit the chard and artichoke hearts, and use 1 pound of fresh mushrooms (any kind) and 2 ounces of soaked porcini or boletus mushrooms (see pages 35-36), squeezed dry and chopped.

Artichoke Tart *(Torta di Carciofi)*

Omit the chard and mushrooms, and use either 15 to 18 fresh artichokes, trimmed and poached as directed on pages 66-67, the same number of frozen, thawed, drained artichoke hearts, or about three 14-ounce cans artichoke hearts in water, drained. Quarter or slice the artichokes.

Asparagus Tart *(Torta di Asparagi)*

Omit the chard, mushrooms, and artichokes, and add 1 pound fresh asparagus. Trim off any tough pieces, cook until crisp-tender, and cut into 1-inch pieces.

Torta Rustica
VEGETABLE TORTA IN A BREAD CRUST
(can be soy-free)

Yield: 10 servings

This torta is called "rustica" because it has a bread dough crust. Use the basic Ligurian Easter Pie filling, p. 151, (minus the mushrooms and artichokes) and add layers of whatever sounds good to you. Here are my suggestions. This is best served cold and makes an elegant picnic dish.

1 recipe Pizza dough, p. 199, risen twice

6 to 8 slices commercial vegetarian Canadian or "back" bacon or ham

1 pound eggplant, sliced and broiled (but not marinated) as for Marinated Grilled Eggplant, p. 71

2 medium (6- to 8-inch) zucchini, sliced and broiled (but not marinated) as for Marinated Grilled Zucchini, p. 71

2 large roasted red peppers, pp. 74-75, or from a jar

1 cup fresh basil leaves

1 recipe Filling for Ligurian Easter Pie, p. 151, using 2 pounds spinach or other greens, but omitting the mushrooms and artichokes

Extra-virgin olive oil

Preheat the oven to 350°F.

Oil a 9-inch springform pan well. Roll out ⅔ of the dough thinly enough to line the pan with some overhang. Layer half the Canadian bacon, ½ the eggplant, ½ the zucchini, ½ the roasted pepper, ½ the basil leaves, and top with half of the green torta filling. Repeat the layering. Roll out the remaining dough thinly, and cover the top of the torta with it. Fold the overhanging dough up over, and crimp the edges attractively to seal. Make several slits in the top of the dough, preferably in a nice design. Cover the whole thing with foil.

Bake for 1 hour. Raise the heat to 400°F. Remove the foil and brush with olive oil. Bake until the crust is golden brown. Place the torta on a rack, and cool for at least 2 hours. Refrigerate overnight before serving. Cut into wedges to serve.

Per serving: Calories: 310, Protein: 15 g, Carbohydrate: 42 g, Fat: 9 g

There is no need for Italian health department officials to exhort their citizens to eat their "daily 5 to 9" (the suggested amount of servings of fruits and vegetables), as ours in North America do. Vegetables are eaten in large quantities and are given high regard in Italy; they are used mostly in season, when they are fresh and ripe. Italians eagerly await the treats of each season's harvest to incorporate fresh vegetables into favorite soups, risotti, and pasta dishes, and to serve as antipasti, salads, side dishes, and often as main courses.

The diet of rural southern Italy is judged by experts to be one of the most healthful in the world, due in large part to its reliance on vegetables. It also happens to be one of the most delicious cuisines!

I think you'll find this small collection of vegetable and legume dishes very hearty and satisfying and, for the most part, open to experimentation and variation.

And don't forget that there are wonderful vegetable dishes in the chapters on appetizers and baked dishes that can also be served as main courses.

XII:
Vegetable and Bean Entrees & Stews
SECONDI DI VERDURE

"La cucina is more a state of mind than a codified roster of dishes."
—Andy Birsch,
Gourmet,
September 1994

Prostitute's Stew
PUTTENAIO
(soy-free)

Yield: 6 servings

1 tablespoon olive oil
1 large eggplant, cut into 1-inch chunks
1 large potato, peeled and cut into 1-inch chunks
1 small carrot, peeled and sliced
1 stick celery, diced
1 large zucchini, sliced
1 large green pepper, seeded and cut into 1-inch squares
1 medium onion, thinly sliced
2 cloves garlic, crushed
¼ cup vegetarian broth
2 pounds fresh, ripe tomatoes, thinly sliced,
   or 1 (28-ounce) can diced tomatoes and their juice
A small handful *each* of Italian parsley, and either rosemary, thyme, or basil, chopped

Don't ask—it's delicious anyway, sort of an Italian ratatouille with potatoes added. It can be served hot or cold, and leftovers make a delicious antipasto or side dish.

1 teaspoon salt

Freshly ground black pepper, to taste

Heat the oil in a large, heavy pot. Add the eggplant, potato, carrot, celery, zucchini, green pepper, onion, and garlic, and cook for about 5 minutes, stirring in the broth as needed to prevent it from sticking. Add the tomatoes (and juice, if using canned) and salt. Bring to a boil, then turn down, cover, and simmer 45 minutes. If there is still a lot of juice, remove the cover and cook down over high heat (watching carefully) until the juices are like a syrup. Add the fresh herbs, reduce the heat, cover, and simmer 15 minutes. Add the salt and the pepper to taste.

All you need is a good crusty bread to mop up the juices and perhaps a glass of good red wine!

Per serving: Calories: 135, Protein: 3 g, Carbohydrate: 25 g, Fat: 2 g

Ciambotta

SOUTHERN ITALIAN VEGETABLE STEW

(soy-free)

Yield: 4 servings

You might see this spelled "giambotta" or "cianfotta," but whichever way, it's delicious—deceptively so, because the ingredients are so simple. You can vary the vegetables and amounts according to what's in your garden or market. Serve with a good crusty bread to sop up the good juices.

½ pound eggplant, unpeeled and cut into 1-inch cubes

2 teaspoons salt

1 tablespoon extra-virgin olive oil

1 large onion, thinly sliced

5 large cloves garlic, minced

1 stalk celery, thinly sliced

A large handful of fresh basil, stems removed, chopped

1 pound ripe plum tomatoes, passed through a food mill or peeled and chopped finely in the food processor, or 1 (14-ounce) can Italian plum tomatoes, drained and chopped finely in the food processor

¾ pound new potatoes, or any waxy potato, scrubbed and cut into 1 x 2-inch pieces

½ teaspoon salt
½ pound zucchini, cut into ½-inch rounds
1 large or 2 small sweet red or yellow peppers, seeded and cut
 into ½-inch strips
Salt and freshly ground black pepper

Toss the eggplant cubes in a colander with the 2 teaspoons salt. Let it sit in the sink until it starts to "sweat" out the bitter juices. Rinse, drain, and pat the cubes dry, squeezing a little.

In a large pot, heat the oil and add the onion, garlic, and celery. Stir over high heat for about 5 minutes, adding a little water as necessary to prevent sticking and burning. Add the basil and stir for a few minutes, then add the tomatoes. When it comes to a simmer, add the eggplant, potatoes and the ½ teaspoon salt. Stir, bring to a boil, then turn down, cover, and simmer for 15 minutes. Add the zucchini and peppers, and simmer 15 minutes more, or until all of the vegetables are tender.

Add salt and pepper to taste, transfer to a warm serving bowl, and allow to stand 15 minutes before serving. Leftovers are delicious!

Per serving: Calories: 168, Protein: 3 g, Carbohydrate: 31 g, Fat: 2 g

Variations: You can use Yukon Gold potatoes instead of the waxy potatoes, if you wish. Instead of zucchini, you can use any summer squash, or try using cauliflower or fennel root. Instead of eggplant, you can use mushrooms.

Roasted Mushroom Stew
RAGÙ DI FUNGHI ARROSTO
(soy-free)

Yield: 6 to 8 servings

2 pounds mushrooms (see notes next page)
2 tablespoons extra-virgin olive oil or good-tasting nondairy
 margarine
8 cloves garlic, sliced, or ¼ cup chopped shallots
½ cup dry white wine (can be nonalcoholic), dry sherry, or
 marsala, or ¼ cup balsamic vinegar or brandy
1 cup vegetarian broth (plus up to 2 cups more, if you want
 more of a "gravy")

Mushroom ragù is a favored autumn dish all over Italy, served on polenta, crostini, pasta, or by itself with crusty bread. There are many ways to make it, but I like the oven method, because it produces a tasty, juicy stew without huge quantities of oil, and it virtually cooks itself. The seasonings can be varied according to your taste. The instructions look long, but that is only because of the various options—it's really a very simple dish to make, but hard to be exact about.

Mushrooms cooked this way, without flavoring, can be frozen too, if you happen to have a large quantity of wild mushrooms to contend with. We do this with chanterelles when we have a good picking year.

1 tablespoon chopped fresh thyme, or 1 teaspoon dried
1 tablespoon chopped fresh rosemary or sage, or 1 teaspoon dried
Salt and freshly ground black pepper, to taste
A handful of chopped fresh Italian parsley

Optional:
2 teaspoons roasted sesame oil
Chopped vegetarian Canadian or "back" bacon
½ to 1½ cups Easy Tofu Creme or Cashew Creme or Rice Creme, pages 39-40
1 to 2 tablespoons cornstarch dissolved in 2 tablespoons water, for thickening

Note: You can use any kind of mushroom—a mixture is nice. Chanterelles, fresh porcini (if you can afford them!), morels, fresh shiitake (discard stems), oyster mushrooms, along with cultivated crimini (brown button mushrooms), and the large portobellos, are all good. If all you have is cultivated white mushrooms, add 2 ounces dried porcini or boletus mushrooms, soaked (see pages 35-36) and chopped (save the liquid).

Preheat the oven to 450°F. Place the oil or margarine in a large, shallow baking pan, and place it in the oven while the oven heats up.

Leave any small mushrooms whole, and slice larger mushrooms into ¼- to ½-inch slices. When the oil is hot, add the mushrooms to the pan, and toss to coat them. Sprinkle them with a little salt, and add the garlic and herbs. If you are using the dried mushrooms, add them too. Other optional ingredients to add at this point would be the roasted sesame oil and vegetarian Canadian or "back" bacon. Let this roast for about 10 minutes, then turn them with a spatula and cook about 10 minutes more, or until the mushrooms are browned but not dry. If they seem to be drying out, add ¼ cup of broth (or mushroom soaking water) at a time.

After the 20 minutes of roasting, add the wine and let it bake until it almost evaporates, stirring up the brown bits on the bottom of the pan as you add it. Add the 1 cup vegetarian broth (and the dried mushroom soaking water, if using), and let that bake until it reduces by about half. Add the parsley.

At this point, you might like to use the stew as it is with the juices unthickened or with the creme added. (Reduce the juices to almost none if you are using this on crostini.) Or you can add more broth and thicken it with the dissolved cornstarch mixture; place the roasting pan over a burner over medium heat, and stir constantly until it thickens. You can add the creme to this version too, if you like. Whichever version you use, add salt and pepper to taste. Serve hot.

Per serving: Calories: 81, Protein: 2 g, Carbohydrate: 6 g, Fat: 4 g

Tuscan Beans with Tomato and Sage
FAGIOLI All' UCCELLETTO
(soy-free)

Yield: 6 servings

¼ cup extra-virgin olive oil

3 cloves garlic, chopped

5 fresh sage leaves

4 cups cooked cannellini (white kidney or Great Northern), beans, or 2½ (15 -ounce) cans beans, drained (You can use cranberry or pinto beans also.)

1 cup vegetarian broth

1 pound ripe plum tomatoes, chopped, or 1 (14-ounce) can diced tomatoes

Optional: **¼ teaspoon crushed red pepper flakes**

Salt and freshly ground pepper, to taste

In a medium pot or skillet, heat the olive oil. Sauté the garlic and sage until almost starting to brown. Add the beans, broth, and tomatoes, and simmer 15 to 25 minutes. Add salt and pepper, to taste. Serve with crusty bread.

Per serving: Calories: 236, Protein: 9 g, Carbohydrate: 28 g, Fat: 9 g

Tuscans are sometimes called "mangiafagioli," or "bean-eaters" by their fellow Italians because they love beans so much! And why not, when they taste this good?

Italian Baked Beans

Add 1 chopped onion and 1 cup diced celery to the garlic when sautéeing. Instead of the sage, use 2 tablespoons chopped parsley, ½ teaspoon dried crushed thyme (or ½ teaspoon fresh), and ¼ teaspoon dried basil (or 1 teaspoon chopped fresh). Pour the beans into a bean pot or deep casserole, and bake at 350°F for about one hour. Add some broth if the casserole gets too dry.

Cannellini Beans with Sautéed Kale

FAGIOLI CON CAVOLO RICCIO

(soy-free)

Yield: 6 to 8 servings

1½ pounds kale

3 tablespoons extra-virgin olive oil

2 large onions, thinly sliced

1 tablespoon roasted sesame oil

Salt and freshly ground pepper, to taste

About 3 cups cooked cannellini (white kidney or Great Northern) beans, or 2 (15-ounce) cans beans, drained (You can also use borlotti, romano, cranberry or pinto beans.)

Another simple dish with outstanding flavor, one of my favorites. A combination of olive and roasted sesame oils takes the place of pancetta (Italian bacon) in this recipe.

If you have no kale, use curly endive, escarole, turnip greens, rapini, or broccoli rabe instead.

Spicy Cannellini Beans

Add 3 cloves chopped garlic to the onions when sautéeing. To the kale, add ¼ teaspoon crushed red pepper flakes and 1 or 2 teaspoons dried oregano (or 1 to 2 tablespoons fresh, chopped). You can also add about ½ cup sliced red bell pepper for color, if you like.

Wash the kale well and drain it. Strip the greens off the tough stems (discard stems), and cut the leaves into ½-inch strips.

Heat the olive oil in a large nonstick skillet. Over medium-high heat, cook the onions until they are limp, then add the kale a little at a time, stirring until it wilts and turns brightly colored. Add the sesame oil, salt to taste, and plenty of freshly ground pepper.

Add the beans to the pan with the kale, and stir them around to heat thoroughly. You can also remove the kale to a warm serving dish and keep warm, stir in the beans in the skillet until they are hot, then serve alongside the kale. Either way, serve with crusty bread or spooned over soft polenta, pp. 130-32. A great winter meal!

Per serving: Calories: 221, Protein: 8 g, Carbohydrate: 28 g, Fat: 8 g

Puréed Beans with "Wild" Greens
LA CAPRIATA

Simply follow the recipe for Cannellini Beans with Sautéed Kale on the facing page, but purée the beans, seasoning them with a little extra-virgin olive oil, salt and freshly ground black pepper, and, perhaps, a little touch of red wine vinegar.

Use turnip greens, rapini, or other strong-tasting greens, chopped coarsely.

Omit the sesame oil and just use olive oil.

Spoon the bean purée onto a serving plate, and top with the sautéed greens. Serve with crostini, p. 54.

Beans in a Jug, Tuscan-Style
FAGLIOLI IN FIASCO
(soy-free)

Yield: 4 to 6 servings

2 cups dried cannellini (white kidney or Great Northern) beans
3 sage leaves
2 cloves garlic, coarsely chopped
1 tablespoon extra-virgin olive oil
Salt and freshly ground pepper, to taste
1 lemon, cut into wedges
More extra-virgin olive oil to drizzle on top

Soak the beans for about 8 hours, then drain.

Preheat the oven to 325°F. Place the soaked, drained beans in a 2- quart casserole, and pour in enough hot water to cover them by about ¼ inch. Add the sage leaves, garlic, and the 1 tablespoon olive oil. Partially cover and bake for about 1½ hours, or until the beans are very tender. Season to taste with salt and pepper, and serve warm or at room temperature with lemon wedges and olive oil to drizzle on top.

Per serving: Calories: 233, Protein: 13 g, Carbohydrate: 38 g, Fat: 3 g

La Capriata (or 'ncapriata in the Apulian dialect) is a marvellous and simple dish quite similar to Cannellini Beans with Sautéed Kale on the facing page, except that the beans are puréed. I have seen recipes for it using fava beans and cannellini beans; I've even used canned romano beans with great success. In any case, this dish dates back to the time of Greek rule and is enjoyed in Apulia, Calabria, and Basilicata even today, spread on toasted rustic Italian bread scraped with raw garlic cloves (see page 54). It's also an excellent antipasto dish or merende (snack).

This is one of the most simple and delicious bean dishes that I know of. Originally, the beans were baked in an empty Chianti bottle in a brick oven on baking day. (A casserole in a modern oven may not be as rustic, but the beans taste just as good!) They are often eaten cold but are delicious hot, as well. The beans are eaten with lemon juice and olive oil drizzled on top. Use leftovers as a delicious spread.

Giant Lima Beans, Peasant Style
FAGLIOLI DI SPAGNA ALLA CONTADINA
(soy-free)

Yield: 4 to 6 servings

I was never very fond of lima beans until I bought some of the giant ones (sometimes called "gigantes") and tried them in a Greek recipe. They really blend well with tomatoes, herbs, and a little hot pepper (a southern Italian touch).

This recipe is similar to the Greek one, but uses different herbs and has a crunchy topping. This is such a favorite that I often take it to potlucks.

**Beans with Rosemary
(Fagioli in Stufa)**
Follow the recipe for Beans in a Jug on page 161, but omit the sage and use 3 tablespoons chopped fresh rosemary instead. Season with salt and lots of freshly ground pepper. Omit the lemon and either pass roasted sesame oil to drizzle on top instead of more olive oil, or use half and half. Serve hot.

1 pound (3 cups) dried giant lima beans ("gigantes")
2 to 3 tablespoons extra virgin olive oil
3 onions, coarsely chopped or sliced
Optional: 1 carrot, chopped,
Optional: 1 celery stalk, chopped,
3 large green bell peppers, seeded and cut into strips (You can use red or yellow ones instead, or a mixture.)
2 pounds fresh plum tomatoes, chopped, or 1 (28-ounce) can diced tomatoes and their juice
2 cups water
4 cloves garlic, minced or crushed
2 teaspoons dried basil (or add 2 tablespoons minced fresh basil in the last 15 minutes of cooking, before adding the topping)
1½ teaspoons salt
Freshly ground black pepper, to taste
Optional: ¼ to ½ teaspoon red chile pepper flakes

Topping:
1 cup fresh bread crumbs
½ cup Soymage Parmesan substitute, soy-free alternative, p. 37, or minced hazelnuts (filberts) or walnuts
2 tablespoons minced fresh Italian parsley

Soak the beans overnight or for about 8 hours in plenty of cold water. When ready to cook, drain the water off and rinse the beans.

Preheat the oven to 350°F.

In a large, heavy skillet (preferably nonstick), heat the oil over medium-high heat. Sauté the onions (and optional carrot and celery) in the oil until they are translucent. Mix the beans and the sautéed vegetables in a large bean pot, medium Dutch oven, or small oval roasting pan with a lid. Pour the water into the skillet and scrape up any brown bits, then pour the water into the bean pot and add the peppers, tomatoes, garlic, basil, salt, pepper, and optional hot pepper. Cover and bake for about 2 hours, or until the beans are soft inside. Add a little more water if they get too dry. Add salt and pepper to taste.

During the last 15 minutes or so of cooking, mix the bread crumbs, nuts or soy Parmesan, and parsley, and sprinkle over the top.

Serve hot with crusty bread and steamed or sautéed greens.

Per serving: Calories: 308, Protein: 14 g, Carbohydrate: 43 g, Fat: 9 g

Crispy Eggplant Croquettes
POLPETTE DI MELANZANE
(can be soy-free)

Yield: 14 to 16 croquettes

1 medium eggplant, peeled and cut into 1-inch cubes
⅓ cup fresh bread crumbs
10 to 12 leaves fresh basil, sliced
¼ cup Soymage Parmesan substitute, or soy-free alternative, p. 37
2 large cloves garlic, crushed
½ teaspoon salt
Freshly ground black pepper, to taste
1½ cups "Cheesey" Bread Crumbs, p. 31

Place the cubes of eggplant in a colander, and sprinkle with salt. Let stand for about 30 minutes, then rinse and pat dry. (*Note:* You can omit this entire step if your eggplant is very fresh.)

Steam the eggplant cubes over boiling water for about 5 minutes, or until they are very tender. Drain and pat dry again.

Place the eggplant in the bowl of the food processor, and chop it quite finely, but don't reduce it to a purée. Add the remaining

Italians make polpette (meatballs) out of all sorts of vegetables, but the most popular ones are made with eggplant. Instead of the traditional deep-frying, I roll the balls in "cheesey" bread crumbs and bake them until they are golden and crispy. In small portions, these make a great antipasto dish. Serve with your favorite sauce.

Mushroom Croquettes (Polpette di Funghi)

Substitute about 1½ pounds fresh mushrooms for the eggplant. Slice and steam-fry them in a large, lightly oiled nonstick skillet until they are tender. Salt them while they are cooking to draw out the juices, then let the juices evaporate. Proceed with the recipe, using these instead of the steamed eggplant.

ingredients, *except* for the "Cheesey" Bread Crumbs. Process until well mixed. Place the mixture in a bowl, cover, and refrigerate for at least an hour.

Preheat the oven to 400°F. Roll the eggplant mixture into walnut-sized balls with wet fingers, then roll the balls in the bread crumbs, coating all over. Place the balls on lightly oiled, dark cookie sheets. If you have a pump-style oil sprayer (see page 28), you can spray a fine mist of olive oil over the balls before baking to produce a crisp crust.

Bake for about 5 minutes, or until the bottoms of the balls are golden brown, then turn them slightly. Repeat two more times, so that all four sides get browned, about 20 minutes total. Serve hot.

Per croquette: Calories: 32, Protein: 2 g, Carbohydrate: 5 g, Fat: 0 g

Baked Vegetable Casserole
TIELLA
(soy-free)

Yield: 4 to 6 servings

2½ tablespoons extra-virgin olive oil

2 large onions, thinly sliced

2 tablespoons minced garlic

½ pound mushrooms, thickly sliced (preferably shiitakes, or chanterelles, but brown domestics like crimini or portobellos will do just fine)

1 pound zucchini, sliced about ¼ inch thick

1 pound small waxy potatoes, parboiled 10 minutes

1 cup fresh or canned diced tomatoes with their juice

½ cup fresh basil leaves, rolled up and thinly sliced

Salt and freshly ground black pepper, to taste

½ cup fresh bread crumbs

Note: If you would like to add rice to this dish, parboil 1 cup of arborio rice in about 2 to 3 cups boiling salted water for 5 minutes, drain the rice, and place it on the bottom of the casserole before you start layering the vegetables.

The word "tiella" is related to the Spanish "paella," dating back to the times when the Spanish ruled southern Italy. A tiella is a baked, layered vegetable casserole from Abruzzo and Apulia—a delicious example of "cucina paesana." Tiella will always contain potatoes, onions, tomatoes, garlic, and olive oil. Zucchini, rice, celery, and sometimes wild mushrooms can be added.

No doubt this started out with raw vegetables layered together and cooked for many hours in the communal bake-oven after bread baking was finished so that the flavors melded. To speed up the cooking and intensify the flavors, I precook the vegetables. We also like this casserole with quite a bit of garlic in it. It mellows a lot with cooking, but it definitely adds something to the dish.

Heat 2 tablespoons of the olive oil in a large, heavy nonstick skillet. Add the onions and sauté over medium-high heat until they begin to get tender. Add one tablespoon of the minced garlic, and keep sautéeing until the onions begin to brown. Add the mushrooms and sauté 5 minutes more. Sprinkle with salt and pepper to taste. Set aside.

Place the zucchini slices on an oiled cookie sheet, and brush the tops lightly with oil. Broil 3 to 4 inches from the heat until they start to brown, then turn the slices over and brown the other side. Set aside.

Slice the potatoes thinly and set aside. Preheat the oven to 400°F.

Oil an oven-proof casserole that is 10 inches wide and 2 inches deep. Place half the onion-mushroom mixture in the bottom. Top with the potato slices, and sprinkle with ½ the chiffonaded basil and the second tablespoon of minced garlic, plus salt and pepper to taste. Cover this with the rest of the onion-mushroom mixture, the tomatoes, the remaining basil, and salt and pepper to taste. Sprinkle the bread crumbs over the top. Drizzle the last ½ tablespoon of olive oil over the top. Bake for 40 minutes and serve hot.

Per serving: Calories: 203, Protein: 4 g, Carbohydrate: 31 g, Fat: 7 g

Variations: You could add roasted bell peppers and use other herbs, such as oregano, marjoram, rosemary, or sage. Egg-plant can be substituted for the zucchini.

Stuffed Vegetables
VERDURE IMBOTTITI
(can be soy-free)

Yield: 4 servings

Stuffed vegetables are a favorite all around the Mediterranean, and there are many types of fillings—bread crumb, meat, fish, rice, and vegetable. The following stuffing is our favorite and combines all of these elements (vegetarian, of course!), including the use of miso in place of the ubiquitous anchovy.

We use this stuffing mixture in roasted peppers (any color), parboiled onions, eggplant, or zucchini (or other summer squash), and also in tomatoes and mushrooms. For a buffet dinner, you might like to multiply this stuffing recipe several times and present a tray of various stuffed vegetables. They are delicious hot or at room temperature

This recipe makes an excellent antipasto dish too.

Stuffing:

1 tablespoon extra-virgin olive oil

1 medium onion, minced

¼ cup chopped fresh Italian parsley

2 cloves garlic, minced

Any edible trimmings, pulp, or stems of the vegetables to be stuffed, chopped

½ cup cooked rice, any kind

½ cup fresh bread crumbs, preferably whole grain

½ cup vegetarian burger or sausage, commercial or homemade (pp. 175-77), crumbled,
   or ground seitan of any kind,
   or chopped sautéed mushrooms

2 tablespoons tomato paste

2 tablespoons vegetarian broth

2 tablespoons Soymage Parmesan substitute, or soy-free alternative, p. 37

1 tablespoon light soy or chick-pea miso

Salt and freshly ground pepper, to taste

Vegetable choices (select 1 or mix and match enough for 4 servings):

4 large bell peppers (any color), cut in half vertically and seeded

2 medium zucchini, cut in half lengthwise, with the middle hollowed out somewhat (save the hollowed-out bits)

2 medium-small eggplants or 4 Japanese eggplants, left whole

8 medium onions, peeled and left whole

16 large mushrooms, stemmed

4 large portobello mushrooms, stemmed (save stems)

8 medium firm, ripe unpeeled tomatoes (not plum or Italian)

To prepare the stuffing, heat the oil over high heat in a large, heavy nonstick skillet. Add the onion, garlic, parsley, and any trimmings, etc., that you are using. Sauté until the onions are soft and any liquid has evaporated. Add salt and pepper to taste. Add the remaining stuffing ingredients, and stir well. Set aside.

Preheat the oven to 350°F to 400°F. (See the end of the recipe for specific times according to the vegetables you will be stuffing.)

If using peppers, you can grill them or simply place them on an oiled cookie sheet, brush or spray with olive oil, and place under the broiler, about 3 to 4 inches from the heat source. Broil the outsides until they are blistered and slightly charred, and the insides are a bit juicy. Place them inside a plastic or paper bag for a few minutes, then peel the skins off under cold running water.

If using zucchini (or other summer squash), boil or steam for about 5 to 10 minutes, or until tender inside but still firm on the outside. Drain well. *Treat eggplants the same as for zucchini,* but leave them whole, just cutting off the top stem. After boiling, cut them in half lengthwise and scoop out hollows in the pulp, leaving a lining of "flesh" inside the skin. Save the pulp for the filling.

If using onions, boil them for about 10 minutes, cool under cold running water, and cut a slice from the top end. Remove most of the insides, leaving about a ¾-inch shell. *If using tomatoes,* cut a slice from the top and scoop out all but the firm outer shell.

If using mushrooms (either kind), choose firm, unbroken ones. They need only be stemmed and cleaned.

When your vegetables are prepared, fill them with the stuffing and place them, stuffing-side-up in an oiled pan, fairly close together. You can bake them as-is, or sprinkle the tops with soy Parmesan, bread crumbs (plain, Seasoned, or "Cheesey," see pages 31-32), or olive oil, or spread a little tomato sauce (commercial, or see pp. 41-52) over the tops. A little bit of water, vegetable cooking water, vegetarian broth, or wine should be poured around the vegetables to keep them from scorching. With the mushrooms and eggplant, this should only be a few tablespoons.

Bake the peppers and eggplant at 400°F for about 15 minutes; the zucchini at 350°F for about 30 minutes; the onions at 375°F for about 30 minutes; the mushrooms at 375°F for about 20 minutes; and the tomatoes at 350°F for 15 to 20 minutes.

Serve hot, either plain, drizzled with olive oil, or topped with a hot tomato sauce, pages 42-51; or at room temperature, plain or drizzled with olive oil.

Per serving: Calories: 154, Protein: 5 g, Carbohydrate: 22 g, Fat: 5 g

Stuffed Eggplant Rolls

INVOLATINE DI MELANZANE

(can be soy-free)

Yield: 4 servings

1 large eggplant (about 1½ pounds), cut lengthwise into 12 thin slices

Stuffing for Stuffed Vegetables, p. 166, or Spinach and "Cheese" Filling for Crepes, p. 107, or "Cheese" Filling for Crepes, p. 108

2 cups Marinara Sauce, p. 42, or one of its variations

2 tablespoons Soymage Parmesan substitute, or soy-free alternative, p. 37

This is a variation on a rather simple antipasto dish (see page 71). In this main dish, the filling is more substantial and makes a great company dish.

Sprinkle the eggplant slices with salt, and place in a colander to drain for 30 minutes. Rinse and pat dry. Place on two oiled cookie sheets, and brush or spray with olive oil. Place 3 to 4 inches from the broiler heat source, and broil until they are begin to brown on top. Turn them over, brush or spray with oil again, and broil until the other side begins to brown and the middle is softened. Turn the oven to 350°F.

Let the eggplant slices cool enough to handle. Spread some of the desired filling about ¼ inch thick over one side of each eggplant slice, then roll it up, starting at the narrow end. Place the rolls seam-side-down in an oiled casserole. Cover with the Marinara Sauce, and sprinkle with the soy Parmesan. Bake for about 45 minutes, and serve hot.

Per serving: Calories: 366, Protein: 20 g, Carbohydrate: 38 g, Fat: 14 g

Italians have not been great meat-eaters in the recent past, but advertising, American influence, and greater prosperity have given meat a larger place in the menu for many Italians.

Italian scaloppine dishes (thin "scallops" of meat, usually veal, quickly cooked with a simple sauce), stews, ground meat and sausage recipes, and some chicken dishes cooked with wine and vegetables are fairly easy to convert to vegetarian dishes. Why would we want to? Well, for many reasons. Some vegetarians miss the "chew" of meat or prefer to have an easily recognizable protein main course. I think I just miss some of the delicious sauces that form when meat or poultry is cooked with wine, herbs, garlic, and vegetables. When vegetable proteins are cooked the same way, all you need to do is add more broth (and possibly a little more of the herbs, garlic, etc.), and you can convert many of your favorite recipes easily and deliciously. Meats exude broth but vegetable proteins absorb them, so I add about 1 cup of good-quality vegetarian broth to any recipe for about four people that I am converting. Use my recipes and suggestions as guides to "veganize" some of your family favorites and save the animals!

You can use the very versatile textured vegetable protein chunks or flavored seitan chunks for meat-style stews. These are more readily available in health food stores these days, or you can purchase them by mail order (see page 249). Marinated extra-firm tofu can be used for some chicken-style dishes, especially those with a crispy outer coating. Other chicken-style dishes are better with seitan chicken cutlets, p. 181.

Either the textured vegetable protein chunks or very thinly sliced homemade veal or turkey seitan cutlets, p. 189, can be used to make delectable scaloppine. Veal or pork seitan cutlets can be used in braised chop or cutlet recipes.

Wine is a vital part of many of these recipes. If you don't use alcohol, investigate some of the quality nonalcoholic wines on the market today (see page 247).

XIV
Meat-Free Entrees
SECONDI DI SOYA O GRANO

"Any personal innovations should stem from knowledge of the authentic traditional version."
—Giuliano Bugialli
Classic Techniques of Italian Cooking
(New York: Simon & Schuster, 1982)

Homemade Meat Alternatives

There are innumerable vegan meat substitutes on the market today, many of them very low in fat and very tasty. I urge you to try all of the varieties available in your area. If you prefer to use your favorite types in my recipes instead of my homemade ones, please go right ahead. But these recipes are very tasty, and you'll save quite a bit of money if you make your own. (Make large batches and freeze some.)

If you are allergic to soy, there are a few soy-free meat substitutes on the market, usually based on seitan (wheat gluten), but most seitan is flavored with soy sauce. Even the seitan or seitan-and-bulgur-wheat or -chick-pea mixes that you can make yourself call for soy sauce for flavor. You can use my Soy-Free Flavoring Sauce, at right, instead, if you'd like to try these. I have included a great selection of soy-free meat alternatives here—try them even if you aren't allergic to soy!

Soy-Free Flavoring Sauce

Yield: 1¾ cups

1 cup water, broth, or dried mushroom soaking liquid

2 tablespoons *each* Marmite (or other yeast extract) and salt, dissolved in ½ cup *hot* water, broth, or mushroom liquid

2 tablespoons soy-free gravy browner (like Kitchen Bouquet)

Mix together and store in a bottle in the refrigerator. This will keep several weeks refrigerated.

Low-Salt Soy-Free Flavoring Sauce: For certain recipes, less salt is needed. If I call for Low-Salt Soy-Free Flavoring Sauce, it is the same recipe, minus the salt. This doesn't keep as well as the salted variety.

Breast of Tofu or Tofu Chicken
POLLO DI SOYA

Yield: 32 slices (4 to 6 servings)

I always have some extra-firm tofu slices marinating in the following mixture. They will keep refrigerated in the marinade for up to two weeks, ready for a quick and delicious meal. They can be pan-fried plain on a nonstick skillet or coated with Seasoned Flour and shallow-fried to make a crispy "skin" that is delectable hot or cold. Serve them plain, in salads and sandwiches, or with any sauce used on chicken.

Instead of slices, you can marinate ½-inch cubes for using in kebabs, etc.

Marinade:

1½ cups water

¼ cup soy sauce

3 tablespoons nutritional yeast flakes

2 teaspoons crumbled dried sage leaves, or 2 tablespoons chopped fresh sage

½ teaspoon dried rosemary, or ½ tablespoon fresh rosemary

½ teaspoon dried thyme, or ½ tablespoon chopped fresh thyme

½ teaspoon onion powder

2 pounds extra-firm or pressed tofu

Prepare the marinade by mixing all of the ingredients together in a 5- or 6-cup rigid plastic container with a tight-fitting lid. Slice the tofu about ¼-inch thick, and place in the marinade so that it is fairly tightly packed and covered with liquid. Cover and refrigerate for up to two weeks, shaking daily.

To pan-fry plain, simply cook the slices over medium heat in a non-stick skillet until golden brown on both sides.

To make crispy slices, coat the slices with Seasoned Flour, p. 33. Heat about ¼ inch of olive oil or light-flavored cooking oil in a heavy-bottomed 10-inch skillet. When the oil is hot but not smoking, add the slices and cook over high heat (watching carefully) until golden brown and crispy on the bottom. Turn the slices over and cook the other side until golden and crispy. Drain thoroughly on paper towels or paper bags, patting to remove any excess oil.

Per serving: Calories: 162, Protein: 16 g, Carbohydrate: 6 g, Fat: 8 g

Cooking Note: Don't skimp on the oil when frying these (don't worry, they won't absorb much of it). If you don't use enough, the slices tend to burn on the bottom and not turn crispy. They should puff up somewhat while they are frying and then collapse as they cool.

Lemon-Rosemary Breast of Tofu
POLLO DI SOYA CON ROSMARINO E LIMONE
(can be soy-free)

Yield: 3 to 4 servings

12 slices Breast of Tofu (see facing page), that have been marinating for a few days, or 3 or 4 large Seitan Chicken cutlets, p. 181, well-drained
Fresh bread crumbs, p. 31
2 tablespoons extra-virgin olive oil

Marinade:
Juice of 1 lemon
2 cloves garlic, crushed
1 tablespoon extra-virgin olive oil
1 tablespoon chopped fresh rosemary
Freshly ground black pepper, to taste

At least 6 hours before cooking, mix the marinade ingredients together, and pour them over the Breast of Tofu slices or seitan cutlets in a shallow covered container. Cover and refrigerate until cooking time, shaking the container once in a while while marinating.

When ready to cook, coat the pieces with the bread crumbs. Heat

I adapted this recipe from a Tuscan one called Pollastrino al Mattone (chicken under a brick) because I love the combination of lemon, garlic, rosemary, and olive oil with breast of tofu in a crispy coating.

You need breast of tofu that has been marinating for several days (or, to make soy-free, use homemade Seitan Chicken on page 181). Marinate them in the lemon marinade for a few hours. This is actually a very easy recipe to make and cooks in a matter of minutes. We like it with plain rice and a salad.

Variations

- Coat the tofu slices with Seasoned Flour, p. 33, instead of bread crumbs. Pan-fry in about ¼ inch of olive oil, as directed under "Crispy Slices" in the Breast of Tofu recipe, p. 170. Drain well.
- Oven-fry the slices, using the method for Beefy Seitan in the sidebar on page 179. Use plain fresh bread crumbs.

This delicious recipe, which has since become a favorite for quick dinners, was developed first as a filling for bread (see Vegetarian Chicken in Bread, p. 207). It was so good and so quick and easy to make, we have made it many times since, with several variations.

the oil in a heavy 10-inch skillet until very hot over medium-high heat. Fry the pieces until crisp and golden on both sides. Drain on paper towels. Quickly wipe any oil out of the pan, and add any marinade that is left over. Cook it over high heat until it reduces somewhat. Serve this drizzled over the cutlets.

Per serving: Calories: 190, Protein: 8 g, Carbohydrate: 4 g, Fat: 14 g

"Chicken" and Vegetable Oven-Broiled "Stew"

POLLO DI SOYA (O SEITAN) CON VERDURE AL FORNO

(can be soy-free)

Yield: 6 to 8 servings

¾ to 1 pound Breast of Tofu, p. 170, or seitan chicken, p. 181, cut into ½-inch cubes

2 carrots, peeled and sliced either thinly on the diagonal or into thin "fingers"

2 large onions, cut into ¼-inch slices or wedges

6 to 8 ounces fresh mushrooms, thickly sliced or whole

2 stalks celery, diced

12 cloves garlic, peeled and sliced

2 tablespoons extra-virgin olive oil

2 teaspoons roasted sesame oil

1 cup Breast of Tofu marinade, seitan chicken cooking liquid, or vegetarian broth

Freshly ground black pepper, to taste

¼ cup chopped fresh Italian parsley

Optional:

Juice of two lemons or ½ cup dry white wine

Red or orange bell pepper, cut into chunks

Sliced fennel bulb

1 to 2 tablespoons chopped fresh herbs, such as rosemary, sage, thyme, or basil

1 cup Easy Tofu Creme or Easy Cashew or Rice Creme, pp. 39-40, mixed with 2 teaspoons cornstarch

Preheat the broiler of your oven.

Place the tofu or seitan, vegetables, garlic, oils, and ½ cup of marinade or broth in a large, shallow baking pan or two 9 x 13-inch baking pans. Place the pan(s) 3 to 4 inches from the broiler flame, and broil for about 10 minutes, or until the top is starting to brown and scorch a little and the juices are evaporating. Add the rest of the broth (and optional lemon juice or wine, if using), stir the mixture, and place under the broiler again. When the top begins to brown and scorch again, add the parsley and any optional herbs, stir, and continue broiling until the carrots are crisp-tender, the tofu or seitan browned, and there are just enough pan juices to moisten everything nicely. You probably won't need salt because of the saltiness of the marinade or broth, but taste it for salt and liberally grind fresh black pepper over it.

If you like, stir in the creme and broil until it has thickened a little, stirring the mixture well.

Serve with crusty bread, simple herb focaccia, piadine, polenta, baked potatoes, plain rice, or broad eggless noodles.

Per serving: Calories: 138, Protein: 7 g, Carbohydrate: 9 g, Fat: 8 g

About Textured Soy Protein

Textured soy protein (or textured vegetable protein, as it is sometimes called) is a low-fat, inexpensive dry product, used as a meat substitute. It is *not* the same thing as "hydrolyzed plant protein" or "soy isolate," and contains no MSG or other additives. It is made from soy flour which is cooked under pressure, then extruded to make different sizes and shapes.

It has the advantage of being chewier and lower in fat than tofu and can take the place of frozen tofu in many recipes. Even if you object to the use of meat alternates on a regular basis, it makes a great transitional food for people who are accustomed to eating meat and, despite the best of motives and intentions, miss those familiar flavors and textures. I have had great success in serving textured soy protein dishes to nonvegetarians. Textured soy protein chunks have such a meaty texture that, when cooked in a flavorful mixture, I have had anxious vegetarians ask me if I'm sure their food includes no meat!

Textured soy protein will keep for a long time, has no cholesterol, almost no fat and sodium, and is an excellent source of protein and fiber. Organic varieties are available. It is easily rehydrated for use in soups, stews, casseroles, and sauces. In fact, if your mixture is very "brothy," you can just add the textured soy protein in its dry form, and it will absorb the flavorful broth.

The most readily available types are the granules and the chunks; see Mail Order Sources on page 249 if your health food store does not carry them. The granules can be used for burgers, sausage, balls, loaves, and in spaghetti sauces and meat-style stuffings for vegetables. (See the index for recipes.) The chunks make wonderful stews and scaloppine, which are usually very thin scallops of meat, quickly sautéed and served in a flavorful sauce. I reconstitute large amounts of the chunks and keep 2-cup containers of them and their cooking broth in the freezer. Then I can quickly thaw them out and make an elegant, but quick and easy, dish for dinner at the last minute.

The granules are quickly rehydrated by mixing an almost equal amount of very hot or boiling liquid with them, covering, and letting stand for 5 minutes or so. Water is fine if the granules are to be added to a spicy mixture, but you can use tomato juice or a flavorful broth, or just add 1 or 2 tablespoons light soy sauce or a teaspoon of yeast extract to the hot water. The general rule is ⅞ cup liquid to each cup of textured soy protein granules. This yields about 1⅓ cups.

Reconstituted textured soy protein granules and ground seitan, pp. 174 and 179, can be used almost interchangeably in many recipes. The sidebar to the left will give you the approximate yields for dry to reconstituted textured soy protein granules and its equivalent in ground seitan. When I'm substituting for meat in a recipe, I figure that 1 pound of meat is equal to about 2 cups of reconstituted granules or chunks or ground seitan in volume. By weight, ½ pound seitan is equal to about a pound of meat.

• ¾ cup dry textured soy protein granules plus ½ cup + 1 Tablespoon liquid
= 1 cup reconstituted textured soy protein or ground seitan
or ½ pound frozen tofu

• 1½ cups dry textured soy protein granules plus 1¼ cups liquid
= 2 cups reconstituted textured soy protein or ground seitan
or 1 pound frozen tofu

• 2¼ cups dry textured soy protein granules plus 1⅞ cups liquid
= 3 cups reconstituted textured soy protein or ground seitan
or 1½ pounds frozen tofu

The chunks take a little longer to reconstitute, but have an amazingly meat-like texture and a pleasant, mild flavor. Besides stews and scaloppine dishes, the chunks can be deep-fried or oven-fried. (Coat with Seasoned Flour and bake at 400°F for about 10 minutes per side).

Reconstitute the chunks by cooking 1½ cups dry chunks in 3 cups water with 3 tablespoons soy sauce, 3 tablespoons ketchup or tomato paste, and 1 tablespoon nutritional yeast flakes for 15 to 30 minutes, depending upon how tender you like them. Cool and store in the cooking broth. (I usually make 4 or more times this amount and freeze it in 2-cup portions.) Drain the chunks before using them, and pat them dry before coating with flour, frying, or marinating.

Note: If you make seitan, you can also reconstitute textured soy protein chunks in leftover seitan cooking broth of any flavor (see pages 178 and 180-81).

Vegetarian Burger

Yield: 8 patties, 24 to 26 meatballs (polpetti), or the equivalent of about 1 pound ground beef

1 cup dry textured soy protein granules

1 tablespoon tomato paste

1 tablespoon yeast extract (such as Marmite)

1 teaspoon salt

1 teaspoon gravy browner (such as Kitchen Bouquet) or vegetarian Worcestershire sauce

⅞ cup very hot dried mushroom soaking water, pp. 35-36, or vegetable broth

¼ pound medium-firm tofu, mashed

½ small onion, grated

2 cloves garlic, crushed

1 teaspoon dried marjoram, or 1 tablespoon chopped fresh marjoram

½ teaspoon dried thyme, or 1½ teaspoons chopped fresh thyme

Freshly ground black pepper, to taste

½ cup pure gluten powder (vital wheat gluten)

Polpetti should be cooked ahead of time if being added to a sauce, because they firm up considerably when cooled. This prevents them from falling apart in the sauce.

Patties can also be cooked ahead of time and frozen, then crumbled into dishes instead of ground beef. (It's preferable to use plain ground seitan, page 179, or a commercial hamburger replacement "crumble" in sauces.)

Mix the hot mushroom water with the tomato paste, yeast extract, salt, and gravy browner in a small bowl. Stir in the textured soy protein granules, and allow to soak for about 5 minutes. Add the tofu and seasonings.

The gluten powder should not be added until the mixture is cool (otherwise, it creates "strings"). To speed this up, you can spread the mixture out on a plate and place it in the freezer for a few minutes.

When the mixture is cool, add the gluten powder and mix well with your hands. Press firmly into 8 thin patties or 24 to 26 firm balls, and either steam or microwave.

To steam: Steam on a plate or steaming basket (with little holes) over simmering water, covered, for 20 minutes.

To microwave: Steam half the recipe at one time in a microwave on a plastic microwave steamer in a covered bowl over about 1 cup water for 5 minutes; or simply microwave in a covered glass pie plate for 4½ minutes, then uncovered for 1½ minutes. Cover and let stand 2 minutes.

These can be browned right away or refrigerated or frozen for browning later, or for crumbling into dishes. To brown, use a non-stick skillet with a little olive oil, or brush all sides with a little olive oil and grill on both sides.

Per patty: Calories: 86, Protein: 14 g, Carbohydrate: 6 g, Fat: 1 g

Vegetarian Hot Italian Sausage
SALSICCIA

Yield: 10 patties, 14 to 20 links, or equivalent of 1 pound sausage

½ cup plus 2 tablespoons boiling dried mushroom soaking water, pp. 35-36, or vegetable broth

¼ cup dry red wine, or 2 tablespoons balsamic vinegar plus 2 tablespoons water

1 tablespoon tomato paste

1 cup dry textured soy protein granules
1 teaspoon roasted sesame oil
¼ pound medium-firm tofu, mashed

Seasoning Mixture:
1 tablespoon minced fresh garlic
1 to 1½ teaspoons fennel seeds, crushed
½ to 1 teaspoon red pepper flakes
1 teaspoon salt
½ teaspoon freshly ground black pepper
½ cup pure gluten powder (vital wheat gluten)

Mix the hot mushroom water or broth with the wine or vinegar, tomato paste, and sesame oil in a small bowl. Stir in the textured soy protein granules, and allow to soak for about 5 minutes. Add the tofu and seasonings.

The gluten powder should not be added until the mixture is cool (otherwise, it creates "strings"). To speed this up, you can spread the mixture out on a plate and place it in the freezer for a few minutes.

When the mixture is cool, add the gluten powder and mix well with your hands. Press firmly into 10 thin patties, or 14 to 20 firm links, and either steam or microwave.

To steam: Steam on a plate or steaming basket (with little holes) over simmering water, covered, for 20 minutes.

To microwave: Steam half the recipe at one time in the microwave on a plastic microwave steamer in a covered bowl over about 1 cup water for 5 minutes; or simply microwave in a covered glass pie plate for 4½ minutes, then uncovered for 1½ minutes. Cover and let stand 2 minutes.

These can be browned right away or refrigerated or frozen for browning later or for crumbling into dishes. To brown, use a non-stick skillet with a little olive oil, or brush all sides with a little olive oil and grill on both sides.

Per patty: Calories: 72, Protein: 11 g, Carbohydrate: 4 g, Fat: 1 g

Cotechino "Sausage" (to serve with beans and lentils)

Use dry white wine instead of red wine (can be nonalcoholic). For the seasoning mixture, omit the red pepper flakes and fennel seeds, and add ½ teaspoon unbleached sugar, ¼ teaspoon thyme, ¼ teaspoon ground bay leaf, and a large pinch *each* of sage, marjoram, oregano, cinnamon, allspice, ginger, and nutmeg, and a drop of vanilla. Press firmly into 14 links. When browning these, add a bit of roasted sesame oil to the olive oil.

Italian Sweet Fennel "Sausage"

For the seasoning mixture, omit the red pepper flakes and add 1 teaspoon dried oregano or 1 tablespoon fresh oregano and a pinch of allspice.

Beefy Seitan
MANZO DI SEITAN
(can be soy-free)

Yield: about 1½ pounds cooked (about 6 cups chopped or ground), 8 servings

Gluten Mixture
Dry Ingredients:
2 cups pure gluten powder (vital wheat gluten)
2 tablespoons nutritional yeast flakes
1 teaspoon onion powder
½ teaspoon garlic granules
Freshly ground black or white pepper, to taste

Liquid Ingredients:
1 cup cold water or dried mushroom soaking water
½ cup hot water mixed with 2 teaspoons Marmite or other yeast extract
2 tablespoons ketchup
2 tablespoons soy sauce or Soy-Free Flavoring sauce, p. 170, with or without salt
2 teaspoons Kitchen Bouquet or other gravy browner (soy-free, if desired)

Cooking Broth
4 cups water or dried mushroom soaking water
¼ cup ketchup
¼ cup soy sauce or Soy-Free Flavoring Sauce, p. 170, with or without salt
4 teaspoons Marmite or other yeast extract
4 teaspoons Kitchen Bouquet or other gravy browner (soy-free, if desired)

To make the gluten, mix the dry ingredients together in a large bowl. In a smaller bowl, whisk together the liquid ingredients.

Pour the liquid into the dry ingredients, and mix well until it forms a ball.

To make a roast, shape the mixture into a ball or loaf shape, and place in a roasting pan or Dutch oven with a cover large enough to allow the ball to double. Press the ball or loaf down to flatten a bit. Preheat the oven to 350°F. Mix the cooking broth ingredients, and pour them over the gluten. Bake uncovered for half an hour. Prick the roast all over with a fork, and turn it over, using two spatulas. Lower the heat to 300°F, cover, and bake 1 hour more. Cool and store in the cooking broth.

You can also cook the roast in a slow-cooker on high for 10 hours.

To simmer on the stove-top instead, bring the cooking broth to a boil in a large pot, and slip the gluten in. Immediately turn the heat down, and keep the broth at a low simmer. *Do not boil*—this makes the seitan spongy. Simmer for about 1½ to 2 hours. Cool and store in the broth.

To make cutlets or steaks, divide the uncooked gluten mixture into 12 pieces, and flatten them with your hands and/or a rolling pin as thinly as you can. (They will expand—you can slice them more thinly after cooking to use as "scaloppine," etc.) For stew chunks, cut into very small pieces. Cover and bake them in the cooking broth at 350°F for 30 minutes, then at 300°F for 30 minutes. Cool and store in the cooking broth. You can also cook the cutlets or stew chunks in a slow-cooker on high for about 6 hours or simmer on the stove-top for 1 hour.

Per serving: Calories: 162, Protein: 30 g, Carbohydrate: 9 g, Fat: 1 g

Seitan is the Japanese word for flavored, cooked wheat gluten, and it has been used as a meat substitute in the Far East for centuries. It is particularly handy for vegans who are allergic to soy, if you use my soy-free recipe. Most commercial seitan is flavored with soy sauce.

This recipe is excellent hot or sliced cold for sandwiches or ground as a burger substitute for sauces, etc. (soy-free hamburger replacement "crumbles"!). The stew chunks can be floured, browned in a bit of olive oil, and used in your favorite beef stew recipe. Or oven-fry them by coating them with Seasoned Flour, p. 33, and bake at 400°F for about 10 minutes per side, or until golden. Seitan freezes very well.

Ground Seitan

Use seitan made by any method. Cut into chunks and run them through a regular meat-grinder or a food processor. You can then freeze them in convenient amounts for later use.

Seitan Veal or Turkey

VITELLO OR TACCHINO DI SEITAN

(can be soy-free)

Yield: about 1½ pounds cooked seitan (about 6 cups chopped), 8 servings

4½ cups water

1 cup chopped onion, or 3 tablespoons dried onion

¼ cup nutritional yeast flakes

¼ cup ground dried Chinese mushrooms (grind in a dry blender)

2 tablespoons soy sauce or Soy-Free Flavoring Sauce (with or without salt), p. 170

2 teaspoons Kitchen Bouquet or other gravy browner (soy-free, if desired)

2 teaspoons salt

½ teaspoon dried thyme, or ½ tablespoon chopped fresh thyme

½ teaspoon dried rosemary, or ½ tablespoon chopped fresh rosemary

¼ teaspoon dried sage, or 1 teaspoon chopped fresh sage

Make the gluten mixture as directed in Beefy Seitan on page 178, but use this cooking broth.

Per serving: Calories: 170, Protein: 32 g, Carbohydrate: 9 g, Fat: 1 g

This recipe makes excellent "scaloppine," if you make the cutlets and then slice them into even thinner scallops. For stews you can flour the stew chunks and brown them in olive oil or oven-fry them as directed in the recipe for Beefy Seitan (see sidebar, p. 179).

Seitan Pork

CARNE DI MAIALE DI SEITAN

(can be soy-free)

Yield: about 1½ pounds cooked seitan (about 6 cups chopped), 8 servings

4½ cups water

2 to 4 vegetarian broth cubes, depending on the brand—enough for 4 cups broth (soy-free, if necessary)

1 cup chopped onions, or 3 tablespoons dried onions

This recipe also makes excellent stew and scaloppine. (See above.)

¼ cup ground dried Chinese mushrooms (grind in dry blender)

2 tablespoons ketchup

2 bay leaves

½ to 1 teaspoon white pepper

1 teaspoon dried crumbled sage, or 1 tablespoon chopped fresh
   sage

½ teaspoon paprika

Make the Gluten Mixture as in the recipe for Beefy Seitan, but use this cooking broth.

Per serving: Calories: 170, Protein: 31 g, Carbohydrate: 10 g, Fat: 1 g

Seitan Chicken
POLLO DI SEITAN
(can be soy-free)

Yield: about 1½ pounds cooked seitan (about 6 cups chopped), 8 servings

4½ cups water

¾ cup low-salt soy sauce or salt-free Soy-Free Flavoring Sauce,
   p. 170

½ cup chopped onions, or 1½ tablespoons dried onions

2 tablespoons dried crumbled sage, or ⅓ cup chopped fresh
   sage

1½ teaspoons each dried rosemary and thyme, or 1½
   tablespoons each chopped fresh rosemary and thyme

Optional: ½ teaspoon salt if using salt-free Soy-Free Flavoring
   Sauce

Seitan chicken cutlets or chunks can be used in many sauced recipes. Brown them in olive oil or oven-fry as directed for Beefy Seitan in the sidebar on page 179.

Follow the directions for the gluten mixture in the recipe for Beefy Seitan on page 178, but use 1¾ cups pure gluten powder and ¼ cup chick-pea flour instead of 2 cups pure gluten powder. For the liquid ingredients, use 1½ cups water plus 2 tablespoons chicken-style vegetarian broth powder. Use this cooking broth.

Per serving: Calories: 155, Protein: 28 g, Carbohydrate: 10 g, Fat: 1 g

Seitan Burger

(can be soy-free)

Yield: 8 patties, 24 to 26 "meatballs" (polpetti), or equivalent to about 1 pound ground beef

As with the textured soy protein burger, these firm up considerably after cooking and cooling, so they should be prepared ahead of time if being added to a sauce.

You can make a large quantity of cooked patties ahead of time, freeze them, and then crumble them into dishes that call for cooked hamburger. Use plain ground seitan in sauces, however.

½ recipe Beefy Seitan (about 3 cups diced), squeezed well
   (Make sure the seitan is cool before you use it in this recipe.)
½ small onion, grated
2 teaspoons tomato paste
1 teaspoon Marmite or other yeast extract
1 teaspoon marjoram, or 1 tablespoon chopped fresh marjoram
2 cloves garlic, crushed
½ teaspoon salt
½ teaspoon dried thyme, or 1½ teaspoons chopped fresh thyme
¼ cup pure gluten powder (vital wheat gluten), or high-gluten
   unbleached or whole wheat flour

Grind the seitan in a food grinder or food processor until like ground meat. Add the onion, tomato paste, Marmite, marjoram, garlic, salt, and thyme, and mix well. Add the gluten powder or flour, and mix well with your hands.

Press firmly into 8 patties or 24 to 26 firm "meatballs." If using pure gluten powder, cover and steam on a plate or steaming basket over simmering water for 20 minutes. Or steam half the recipe at a time in a microwave using a plastic microwave steamer in a covered bowl over about 1 cup water for 5 minutes.

These can be refrigerated or frozen and browned later, if you wish. Brown them over medium heat in a nonstick skillet with a little olive oil, or brush with a little olive oil and grill.

If using wheat flour, omit the steaming and simply brown the patties or balls slowly on all sides in a nonstick skillet with a little olive oil over medium heat.

Per patty: Calories: 102, Protein: 19 g, Carbohydrate: 5 g, Fat: 0 g

Hot Italian Seitan Sausage
(can be soy-free)

Yield: 10 patties, 14 to 20 links, or equivalent of about 1 pound
sausage

**½ recipe Seitan Pork (about 3 cups diced), p. 180, or Seitan Veal,
p. 180, squeezed well (Make sure the seitan is cool before
you use it.)**

**2 tablespoons dry red wine (can be nonalcoholic),
or 1 tablespoon balsamic vinegar**

1 teaspoon roasted sesame oil

Seasoning Mixture:
1 tablespoon minced garlic
1 teaspoon crushed fennel seed
½ teaspoon salt
½ teaspoon red pepper flakes
Freshly ground black pepper, to taste

**¼ cup pure gluten powder (vital wheat gluten), or high-gluten
unbleached or whole wheat flour**

Grind the seitan in a food grinder or food processor until like ground
meat. Add the wine or vinegar, garlic, sesame oil, and seasoning mixture. Add the gluten powder or flour, and mix well with your hands.

Press firmly into 10 thin patties or 14 to 20 links. If using pure
gluten powder, cover and steam on a plate or steaming basket over
simmering water for 20 minutes, or steam half the recipe at a time
in a microwave using a plastic microwave steamer in a covered
bowl over about 1 cup water for 5 minutes.

If using wheat flour, omit the steaming and simply brown the patties
or balls slowly on all sides in a nonstick skillet with a little olive oil
over medium heat.These can be refrigerated or frozen and browned
later, if you wish. Brown them over medium heat in a nonstick skillet with a little olive oil, or brush with a little olive oil and grill.

Per patty: Calories: 87, Protein: 15 g, Carbohydrate: 4 g, Fat: 1 g

This is an absolutely fabulous recipe for "meat loaf," and you can use it plain or with a variety of stuffings. I make it with my homemade textured soy protein-based burger and Italian sausage, but you can make it with commercial vegetarian hamburger replacer and Italian "sausage" links, crumbled (about 4 cups of each, packed). *You can also make it soy-free* by using my homemade Seitan Burger, p. 182, mixed with homemade Italian Sweet Fennel "Sausage," made with seitan instead of textured soy granules.

Leftovers are wonderful for sandwiches, so don't be afraid to make this much. They can be frozen too.

Note: If you have room around the edges of the pan, you can roast some potato wedges and other cut vegetables, such as carrots, celery, fennel, etc., along with the loaf.

Stuffing Suggestions

• Vegetarian "deli slices," such as "pepperoni," "ham" or Canadian or "back" bacon, overlapped on top of the "meat loaf" mixture, sprinkled with a few capers, and topped with 3 pounds, or 3 (10 - ounce) packages frozen spinach that has been thawed, cooked, chopped, and squeezed dry.

Italian "Meat Loaf" and Stuffed "Meat Loaf"
POLPETTONE AND POLPETTONE RIPIENO
(can be soy-free)

Yield: 8 to 10 servings

"Meat loaf" Mixture:

Double recipe Vegetarian Burger, p. 175, or Seitan Burger, p. 182

Double recipe Vegetarian Italian Sweet Fennel Sausage, p. 177, or Hot Italian Seitan Sausage (Sweet Fennel variation), p. 183

⅔ cup Soymage Parmesan substitute, or soy-free alternative, p. 37

2 teaspoons crumbled dried rosemary, or 2 tablespoons chopped fresh rosemary

1 teaspoon freshly ground black pepper

About 1 cup vegetable broth or dry red wine (can be nonalcoholic), or a mixture

(See the optional stuffing suggestions in the sidebars.)

Preheat the oven to 350°F.

To make the plain meat loaf, mix the uncooked burger and sausage recipes together well with your hands, and form into a long, oval loaf. Place in a medium-sized, well-oiled covered roasting pan or oval casserole. Pour ½ cup of the broth around the loaf, cover, and bake for 1¼ hours. Check the loaf and add more broth if it's getting too dry. Uncover the loaf for the last 15 minutes of cooking. To serve, loosen with a spatula and then use two spatulas to lift the loaf onto a serving platter.

To make stuffed "meat loaf," mix the "meat loaf" mixture as instructed above. Pat the mixture into a 10 x 15-inch rectangle (with no holes) on a sheet of waxed paper coated with olive oil. (If you place the paper on an upside-down cookie sheet to start with, you can just slide the finished roll into the roasting pan instead of having to lift it and perhaps breaking it in the transfer.) Spread your stuffing ingredients to within an inch of the long edges and all the way to the end of the short edges. Using the oiled waxed paper as a guide, but not rolling it up with the loaf, gently roll the loaf like a jelly roll, starting with the long edge facing you. Pinch the seam to seal it, and then carefully slide the loaf into the well-oiled pan, as instructed previously. Bake and serve the same as for the plain meat loaf.

Serve with a light tomato sauce, such as those on pages 42-43.

Per serving: Calories: 280, Protein: 38 g, Carbohydrate: 17 g, Fat: 5 g

Italian "Meatballs"

POLPETTI

(can be soy-free)

Yield: 48 to 52 "meatballs"

1 recipe Vegetarian Burger (uncooked), p. 182

1 recipe Vegetarian Italian Sweet Fennel Sausage (uncooked), p. 177

⅓ cup Soymage Parmesan substitute, or soy-free alternate, p. 37

1 teaspoon dried crumbled rosemary, or 1 tablespoon chopped fresh rosemary

½ teaspoon freshly ground black pepper

Extra-virgin olive oil

Mix all of the ingredients together well with your hands. Press firmly into 48 to 52 balls.

Cover and steam on a plate or steaming basket (with little holes) over simmering water for 20 minutes. You can also steam half the recipe at one time in a microwave on a plastic microwave steamer in a covered bowl over about 1 cup water for 5 minutes. Or simply microwave in a covered glass pie plate for 4½ minutes, then uncovered for 1½ minutes. Cover and let stand 2 minutes.

After the balls have been steamed, they can be browned right away or refrigerated or frozen for browning later. To brown, use a non-stick skillet with a little olive oil.

Per "meatball": Calories: 25, Protein: 3 g, Carbohydrate: 2 g, Fat: 0 g

Stuffing Suggestions

• Lay roasted red peppers over the "meat loaf" mixture before rolling up.

• Any leftover tasty vegetables, chopped well.

• 1 cup dried tomatoes, soaked, drained, and chopped, mixed with about 1¼ packed cups fresh basil, chopped, and ¼ cup of Soymage Parmesan substitute moistened with 2 tablespoons wine of your choice.

Spaghetti and meatballs is an American-Italian invention, and you can certainly use this recipe for it if you like. But in Italy, meatballs, or polpetti, are eaten by themselves, with pan juices or with a light tomato sauce, pages 42-43, as a main dish or second course

For a soy-free version, substitute 1 recipe Seitan Burger, p. 182, and 1 recipe Italian Sweet Fennel "Sausage" (made with seitan instead of textured soy granules) instead of the soy Vegetarian Burger and Italian Sausage.

If you don't have time to make your own, use 2 cups each commercial vegetarian hamburger replacement and Italian "sausage" instead of the homemade variety.

Vegetarian Scaloppine

Scaloppine is the term used for very thin Italian-style cutlets (or scallops or medallions). They are usually made of veal, but in these modern times sometimes pork or turkey are used. For a vegetarian delicacy, textured soy protein chunks work very well in this quick dish with a savory sauce. The chunks can be reconstituted and flavored in large amounts, then frozen in 2- to 3-cup containers for later use. This is one of the most successful vegetarian dishes to serve to carnivores, by the way.

For a soy-free version, very thinly sliced seitan cutlets are equally delicious, and the cutlets are also marvelous in Italian recipes for "costolette" (veal or pork cutlets) and as substitutes for chicken pieces. Use my Seitan Veal or Turkey, p. 180, and prepare the same way as the soy chunks in these following scaloppine recipes.

Scaloppine can be finished in a number of ways, and no doubt you will make up a few of your own variations once you get the hang of it. You can use lemon juice, "cream," tomatoes, herbs, mushrooms, many different wines, etc. Vegetables such as sweet peppers or artichokes may be added, or olives, miso (in place of anchovies), a tiny bit of chopped vegetarian Canadian or "back" bacon, etc.

In Italy you would probably eat this type of dish with crusty bread, but North Americans might prefer plain rice, orzo, or eggless broad noodles.

Notes: When using reconstituted textured soy chunks in scaloppine, drain them well and pat dry before coating with seasoned flour, so they won't absorb too much of this mix.

Scaloppine with Rosemary, Lemon, and Olives

SCALOPPINE DI SOYA CON ROSMARINO, LIMONE E OLIVE

(can be soy-free)

Yield: 4 servings

2 to 3 cups reconstituted flavored textured soy protein chunks, p. 175,
  or 4 Seitan Veal or Turkey Cutlets, p. 180, cut in half
  crosswise and then horizontally to make "scallops"

¼ cup Seasoned Flour, p. 33

1 to 2 tablespoons extra-virgin olive oil

3 cloves garlic, minced

1 tablespoon minced fresh rosemary, or 1 teaspoon dried
  rosemary

Scaloppine Alla Calabrese

Use this recipe, but omit the rosemary, olives, lemon juice, and zest. Add 1 cup sliced mushrooms and 2 green bell peppers, thinly sliced, when sautéeing the garlic. Sauté until the mushrooms are tender.

½ cup dry white wine (can be nonalcoholic)

1 cup vegetarian broth

1 cup diced ripe plum tomatoes, or 1 (14-ounce) can diced
tomatoes, drained

16 black calamata olives, pitted

Grated zest of 1 lemon (preferably organic)

1 to 2 tablespoons fresh lemon juice

Salt and freshly ground pepper

Dredge the chunks (or "scallops") in the flour. In a heavy nonstick skillet, heat the olive oil over medium-high heat. Brown the chunks (or "scallops") in the hot oil. Add the garlic and rosemary, and stir-fry for a minute. Add the wine and stir until it thickens a bit.

Now add the broth, tomatoes, olives, and lemon zest. Keep stirring over high heat until a nice sauce forms. Add the lemon juice and salt and pepper to taste. Serve immediately.

Per serving: Calories: 183, Protein: 10 g, Carbohydrate: 13 g, Fat: 7 g

Scaloppine Alla Marsala

(can be soy-free)

Yield: 4 servings

This is one of the more traditional scaloppine dishes.

2 to 3 cups reconstituted flavored textured soy protein chunks,
p. 175,

or 4 Seitan Veal or Turkey Cutlets, p. 180, sliced in half
crosswise and then horizontally to make "scallops"

¼ cup Seasoned Flour, p. 33

Variations: Add 1 cup of sliced mushrooms (any kind) and/or 1 cup sliced sweet bell pepper while browning the scaloppine. You could also add a little garlic and/or some fresh herbs, such as basil, sage, or rosemary.

Other additions could be sun-dried tomatoes in oil; sautéed leeks; or sliced artichoke hearts.

Scaloppine All'Uccelletto

Use a mixture of olive oil and margarine. Use dry white wine or white vermouth in place of marsala.

For "Pollo con Rosamarina," this can also be made with seitan chicken cutlets, p. 181, or Breast of Tofu, p. 170. In this case, omit the bay leaf and add 1 tablespoon minced fresh rosemary (or 1 teaspoon dried) and 2 cloves garlic, chopped.

Scaloppine in Lemon Sauce

Make the same as for Scaloppine alla Marsala, but omit the wine and use the juice of 2 lemons. Add 2 garlic cloves, chopped, and sprinkle the finished dish with chopped parsley.

For "Pollo Oreganato," use seitan chicken cutlets, p. 181, or Breast of Tofu, p. 170. Add 2 tablespoons chopped fresh oregano, or 2 teaspoons dried.

2 tablespoons good-tasting nondairy margarine or extra-virgin olive oil
½ cup marsala (or you can use a good sherry or madeira)
1 cup vegetarian broth
1 bay leaf
Salt and freshly ground pepper
Lemon wedges

Dredge the chunks or "scallops" in the flour. In a heavy nonstick skillet heat the margarine or olive oil over medium-high heat. Brown the chunks or "scallops" in the hot fat.

Add the marsala, broth, and bay leaf, cover, and simmer over medium-low heat for about 5 minutes, adding a little water as needed to keep from sticking. You should have a nice sauce, not too thin. If it's taking too long to reduce the sauce, uncover the pan and raise the heat a little, but watch it carefully. Sprinkle with salt and pepper to taste. Serve with lemon wedges to squeeze over the scaloppine.

Per serving: Calories: 253, Protein: 15 g, Carbohydrate: 19 g, Fat: 5 g

Vegetarian Veal Parmesan *("Vitello" alla Parmigiana)*

I never liked the Americanized versions of this recipe, drowning in bad tomato sauce and cheese. This is a more authentic version.

Prepare the textured soy protein chunks or seitan as for Scaloppine alla Marsala, but don't slice the seitan into thinner pieces—leave in cutlets. Add a clove of garlic and a cup of sliced mushrooms. If you have no marsala, sherry, or madeira, you can use dry white vermouth, dry white or rosé wine, or even half dry white and half dry red wine (can be nonalcoholic).

Cook over medium-high heat, uncovered, until the liquid reduces to a nice sauce. Sprinkle the top of the finished dish with ¼ cup Soymage Parmesan substitute, or soy-free alternative, p. 37, and run it quickly under the broiler just to brown the top before serving. This can also be made with seitan chicken cutlets, p. 181, or Breast of Tofu, p. 170.

Seitan Veal Cutlets, Milan-Style
"COSTOLETTE DI VITELLO" ALLA MILANESE
(can be soy-free)

Yield: 6 servings

This is a very simple, but delicious way of preparing seitan veal cutlets.

6 Seitan Veal or Turkey cutlets, p. 180
Flour
½ cup soymilk or nut milk, mixed with 1 teaspoon lemon juice or vinegar
1 cup finely ground fresh bread crumbs
½ cup Soymage Parmesan substitute, or soy-free alternative, p. 37
¼ cup good-tasting nondairy margarine
Lemon wedges

Dredge the cutlets in the flour, then dip in the curdled soymilk. Mix the bread crumbs and soy Parmesan in a flat soup dish or plate, and coat the cutlets all over.

Heat the margarine in a large, heavy nonstick frying pan over medium heat. Cook the cutlets until both sides are golden brown. Drain on paper and serve with the lemon wedges to squeeze over the cutlets.

Per serving: Calories: 222, Protein: 25 g, Carbohydrate: 9 g, Fat: 9 g

Seitan Pork Chops in Red Wine
"COSTOLETTE DI MAIALE" Al VINO ROSSO
(can be soy-free)

Yield: 6 servings

This is a conversion of an old family favorite—so easy and so good!

6 Seitan Pork cutlets, p. 180
½ cup Seasoned Flour, p. 33
3 tablespoons extra-virgin olive oil
2 cloves garlic, minced
4 sage leaves
½ cup dry red wine

Scaloppine Alla Crema

In the Scaloppine Alla Marsala, pp. 187-88, use dry white wine or white vermouth or ⅓ cup brandy or cognac instead of wine. To finish the dish, add ½ to 1 cup Easy Tofu Creme, p. 39, or Easy Cashew or Rice Creme, p. 40. Stir over medium heat until the sauce thickens. Taste for seasoning.

If you like, add one onion, chopped and sautéed until translucent; or add ¼ pound of mushrooms, sliced (any kind), and/or 1 or 2 bell peppers (red, yellow, orange, or green), sliced, when you finish browning the seitan.

1 cup vegetarian broth

1 tablespoon tomato paste

Salt and freshly ground black pepper

Dredge the cutlets in the seasoned flour, and brown them in the hot olive oil in a large skillet over medium-high heat. Add the garlic and sage leaves, then stir in the wine and the broth mixed with the tomato paste. Cover and simmer over low heat for about 30 minutes, adding a bit of water if need to keep from sticking. Add salt and pepper to taste.

Per serving: Calories: 217, Protein: 21 g, Carbohydrate: 12 g, Fat: 7 g

Seitan Alla Cacciatore

(can be soy-free)

Yield: 4 servings

4 to 6 Seitan Chicken cutlets, cut in half, p. 181

¼ to ½ cup Seasoned Flour, p. 33

1 to 2 tablespoons extra-virgin olive oil

Cacciatore Sauce:

1 tablespoon extra-virgin olive oil

1 cup fresh mushrooms (can be any kind), sliced

1 medium onion, sliced

2 cloves garlic, minced or crushed

1 cup vegetarian broth mixed with 2 tablespoons tomato paste

¾ cup dry or medium white wine (can be nonalcoholic), marsala, dry sherry, madeira, or dry white vermouth

1 teaspoon dried rosemary, or 1 tablespoon fresh rosemary

Salt and freshly ground pepper, to taste

Notes: If you don't want to make the seitan chicken cutlets, you can use either of the following:

• 16 pieces of plain, pan-fried Breast of Tofu, p. 170, which is then dredged in Seasoned Flour and browned in the oil as directed for the seitan

• 2 to 3 cups reconstituted textured soy protein chunks, p. 175, drained and dredged in the seasoned flour and browned in olive oil as for the seitan.

Chicken cacciatore is one of the better-known Italian-American dishes. "Alla cacciatora" literally means "cooking in the hunter's way," and the dish can consist of many types of meat, poultry, or game, sautéed first and then cooked slowly with onions, mushrooms, herbs, and wine. Tomato is often added, but not as the primary ingredient, as it usually is in American recipes.

Celery and carrots are often added, or olives, anchovies, sweet peppers, and even a bit of hot pepper in some areas. The following recipe is one that I used to make with chicken, in the days before I became a vegetarian. It's a northern Italian version, quite simple, but extremely tasty. When using vegetable proteins, I add some broth, because these foods absorb rather than exude liquids like meats do.

In a large nonstick skillet, heat the 1 to 2 tablespoons olive oil over medium-high heat. Dredge the cutlets in the Seasoned Flour, and brown them on both sides in the oil. Set aside.

Prepare the sauce by adding the 1 tablespoon olive oil to the same pan. Over medium-high heat, sauté the mushrooms, onion, garlic, and rosemary until the onion is tender. Add the cutlets, wine, and broth mixed with the tomato paste. Cover and cook for about 45 minutes, adding a little water if needed to keep a sauce-like consistency. Add salt and pepper to taste.

In Italy you would most likely eat this with crusty bread, but North Americans like it with plain pasta—a eggless broad noodle is good.

Per serving: Calories: 345, Protein: 32 g, Carbohydrate: 21 g, Fat: 9 g

Stufado

BASIC ITALIAN STEW

(can be soy-free)

Yield: 4 servings

1½ cups dry textured soy protein chunks, reconstituted as instructed on p. 175
Flour
1 tablespoon extra-virgin olive oil
1 teaspoon roasted sesame oil
1 large onion, chopped
16 mushrooms, sliced
1 cup chopped celery with tops
½ carrot, peeled and chopped
2 stalks Italian parsley, chopped
2 cloves garlic, chopped
1 pound ripe plum tomatoes, chopped, or 1 (14-ounce) can plum or diced tomatoes, with their juice
4 carrots, peeled and cut into "fingers"
2 cups water

"Stufa" means stove in Italian—thus the name "stufado" for a mixture cooked for many hours on the stove. Stew is also affectionately referred to as "stufatino," or it can be known as "spezzatino."

The meat is cooked "in umido" (in liquid) for many hours, with wine, vegetables, and a soffritto of onion, garlic, carrot, celery, and parsley. Textured soy protein chunks are perfect in stews, *but if you are allergic to soy,* use 2 to 3 cups seitan stew chunks, p. 179, any flavor.

Vegetable protein foods do not need long cooking to tenderize, but a couple of hours melds the flavors together nicely.

Stews can be served with mashed potatoes,

crusty bread, or polenta, pp. 130-32.

This stew recipe can be altered to suit your taste. You can use a dry white wine or white vermouth instead of the red wine. You can add a little more Marmite (yeast extract) for a "beefier" flavor. You can substitute sage or oregano for the rosemary. You can eliminate the tomatoes and add another cup of broth, and then perhaps finish the dish with a little "cream," pages 39-40.

For a little extra tang or spice, you can add a few capers, a dash of lemon juice or balsamic vinegar, black calamata olives, or a sprinkle of hot pepper flakes at the end. Other vegetables, such as baby onions (cipollini), fennel, strips of bell peppers (any color), or soaked porcini or boletus mushrooms, pp. 35-36, could also be added.

½ cup dry red wine

1 vegetarian broth cube (enough for 1 cup broth)

2 teaspoons lite soy sauce, or soy-free alternative, p. 170

1½ teaspoons Marmite (yeast extract)

1 teaspoon dried thyme

½ teaspoon dried rosemary

A bay leaf

Pinch unbleached sugar

Salt and freshly ground pepper

Minced fresh Italian parsley

Dredge the chunks of textured soy protein (or seitan, if preferred) in flour. Heat the oil in a heavy pot or Dutch oven over medium-high heat. Brown the chunks in the oil. Remove and set aside. Add the onion to the pot, and steam-fry, adding a little water as necessary to keep from sticking, until the onions start to soften. Add the mushrooms, celery, ½ carrot, parsley, and garlic. Steam-fry until the vegetables start to soften.

Add the chunks, tomatoes, carrots, water, wine, bouillon cube, soy sauce, Marmite, herbs, and sugar. Simmer for about 2 hours. Add salt and pepper to taste, and sprinkle with Italian parsley.

Per serving: Calories: 236, Protein: 14 g, Carbohydrate: 27 g, Fat: 5 g

When Italian children ask their mothers "What's for lunch?," they may be answered with a swift "Pane e companatico"—the Italian equivalent of my late husband's Irish grandmother's "Bread and with-it." No Italian would serve a meal without bread, and it is never wasted in Italy. It is treated with reverence and often blessed both before baking or eating.

Italians eat about half a pound of bread a day, more even than other Europeans, and wouldn't we, if our bread were as good as theirs? The situation is improving in North America, and all cities and many towns boast good European-style bakeries with fresh crusty breads (not to be confused with what most supermarket bakeries consider a crusty bread). This type of bread needs to be purchased daily. If you don't have such an establishment nearby, I urge you to try your hand at baking it.

Each region has its favorite breads, with local variations in neighboring towns and villages. Consequently, it is nearly impossible to document all of the breads in Italy.

Indeed, whole books can and have been written on Italian breads and pizza—I can't really do the subject justice within the confines of these pages. However, I would like to offer you my two most basic and often-used Italian bread doughs (one with a starter and one without), plus my favorite pizza/focaccia dough (which can also be used for stuffed breads, bread "pies," etc.), and a flatbread dough. These are tried and true recipes for the home baker, I assure you. I'll also offer you some tips on making the doughs in a food processor, heavy-duty mixer, or bread machine. (We don't bake these doughs in a bread machine, however, just mix the dough.) Sticky Italian bread doughs are much easier for novices to make using these machines.

Whole grain breads (pane integrale) have become popular in Italy only in the last ten or fifteen years. "Brown" breads were considered the food of poverty, and anyone who could ate white bread. However, modern bakers are using whole wheat flours and bran (formerly fed only to animals) in some breads.

I like a combination of whole wheat and unbleached white flours in many of these breads—all whole wheat can be excessively heavy in a bread with no fat. I also prefer pizza dough made with unbleached flour or no more than half whole wheat. One hundred percent whole wheat pizza dough is usually a great disappointment, and I have had some truly dreadful examples served to me. You can successfully add a handful of bran to a white pizza dough if you

XIV
Bread, Rolls, Pizza, Hearth Breads, and Stuffed Breads

PANE, PANINI, PIZZE, FOCACCE, E PANE RIPIENE

"Senza il pane, tutto diventa orfano" —Without bread, everyone is an orphan. (Italian folk saying)

If you would like more information on making Italian breads and flat breads, I refer you to *The Italian Baker* by Carol Field (New York: Harper & Row, 1985); *The Il Fornaio Baking Book* by Franco Galli (San Francisco: Chronicle Books, 1993); and *Italian Pizza and Hearth Breads* by Elizabeth Romer (New York: Clarkson N. Potter, 1987). These I have found to be the most practical, helpful, and informative books on the subject, and Field and Romer's books have some fascinating historical notes as well.

wish, or just eat your breakfast cereal with bran and flaxseed and eat your pizza with fiber and antioxidant-rich vegetable toppings and a big salad on the side.

Do not cut down the salt in these breads. Salt plays an important role in controlling the activity of the yeast in breads. If you're worried about salt, cut it out of other foods. You won't get much in a slice or two of bread.

Special equipment

A reliable oven is your most important piece of equipment. I have a convection oven in my electric stove which has a fan that blows the heat around evenly and makes an evenly browned crust, but this is not necessary if you are vigilant.

Many books on Italian bread baking recommend baking stones, and these are great because they give a good, even crust similar to what you would get in a brick oven. But each one holds only one loaf of bread or one pizza, and they are not cheap. A less expensive alternative is to purchase slightly chipped unglazed tiles from a tile store and line your oven rack with these (make sure the rack is strong enough to hold the weight). Heat baking stones or tiles in the oven while the oven comes up to temperature.

If you are baking bread or pizza on a baking stone or tiles, you will need something to lift the bread and slide it onto the hot clay surface. Most of us don't have a baking peel (thin paddle) around the house, so you can rise the bread on well-floured baking parchment or cookie sheets with no rim or lip on them, so that they can slide off.

A plant mister for squirting water on the bread is handy, and you'll need a new razor blade for slashing the tops of the loaves. You'll need good-sized bowls for rising; ceramic ones are nice, but those cheap stainless steel ones that you can buy in supermarkets do just fine. A dough scraper for cleaning your board and cutting dough is helpful, and I also like to have a kitchen scale for weighing dough and ingredients.

As I mentioned above, Italian doughs are sticky, so you'll find it easier to knead with either the help of a heavy-duty mixer with a dough hook, a good food processor, or a bread machine. If you have one of those old-fashioned hand-crank dough-kneaders, you can use that. Otherwise, you'll need a really heavy wooden spoon (almost like a small paddle) and a lot of muscle (or a strong partner to spell you at beating and kneading the dough).

Basic Italian Crusty Bread Without a Starter

PANE ITALIANO
(soy-free)

Yield: 2 loaves or 12 to 16 panini (rolls)

1 tablespoon regular baking yeast
2 cups very warm water
3 cups unbleached or whole wheat flour, or 2 ½ cups unbleached
white flour with ½ cup wheat bran
2 teaspoons salt
3 cups unbleached flour

In a large bowl or the bowl of a heavy-duty mixer, dissolve the yeast in the water for about 5 minutes. Stir in the first 3 cups of flour and the salt. Beat well, cover with plastic wrap, and let this "sponge" (batter) rise for 1 or 2 hours in a warm spot or overnight in the refrigerator.

Stir in the last 3 cups of flour a little at a time, adding only as much as necessary to make a kneadable dough. Knead the dough with the dough hook of a heavy-duty mixer or by hand on a lightly floured surface for about 10 minutes. Add a little more flour as needed, but be careful not to make the dough too dry—it should be moist and very pliable but not sticky.

Slam the dough down hard on the surface a few times after kneading to get rid of air bubbles. Place the dough in a large, lightly oiled bowl, cover well, and let rise at room temperature until doubled. Punch down if you like, and let it rise once again, but this isn't necessary.

Punch the dough down and divide it in half. Shape the dough into 2 long loaves, rounds, or braided loaves, or into 12 to 16 loaf-shaped rolls. Place on nonstick or lightly oiled cookie sheets sprinkled with cornmeal or semolina cereal. If you are baking on stones or tiles, place the dough on greased and well-floured flat cookie sheets with no lip or rim or on pieces of stiff cardboard covered with greased and well-floured baking parchment. Sprinkle the tops with flour, and

In some areas you can buy delicious crusty breads fresh from a bakery, but there is nothing like fresh breads from your own oven. This type of bread is actually a very simple one and easy to make. Just remember not to try and speed it up—it needs time to develop flavor and texture. It also needs a hot oven and some moisture at the beginning of the baking to develop "oven spring" (the last burst of rising) and to form a golden crust.

You will notice that this bread, like most European breads, contains no sweetener or oil. The yeast can feed off the natural sugars in the flour, so it needs no additional sugar. The lack of oil gives the bread a crisp crust and chewy texture, but without it the bread goes stale fast. If you aren't going to eat it within a day, freeze it. (The moist dough keeps this bread from being dry.)

The following dough recipes may be halved or doubled, but when doubling the recipe, do not double the amount of yeast.

Sandwiches

(Panini Imbottite)

The rolls in Italian sandwich bars are soft, but you can use panini made from either of the bread recipes in this book, or your favorite bakery panini, hard rolls, Kaiser buns, bridge rolls, etc.

You can add green lettuce, arugula, or radicchio to almost all fillings. Moisten the bread with extra-virgin olive oil, Italian Wine Vinegar Dressing (page 61), or Low-fat Mayonnaise, plain, Garlic, Basil, or Sun-Dried Tomato variations (pps. 29-30). A thin smear of light soy or chick-pea miso takes the place of the ubiquitous anchovy.

For the Filling:

Use raw, sautéed, pickled, or grilled vegetables; vegetarian pâté; commercial vegetarian cold cuts; salads; vegetable or bean dishes; fritatte; and/or meat alternates. You can also use Tofu or Almond Ricotta Salata (Chapter III).

Toasted sandwiches are also popular in sandwich bars. For these, a compact square white bread with the crust cut off is used, and it is made in a sandwich grill like a grilled cheese sandwich.

cover with slightly damp, clean tea towels, or place inside of large plastic bags. Let rise at room temperature until doubled.

Meanwhile, preheat the oven to 425°F (convection ovens should be at 400°F). If using tiles or baking stones, preheat them in the oven as well.

In order to generate steam in your oven, place a shallow pan of hot water in the bottom of the oven, or squirt the loaves and the walls of the oven 2 or 3 times in the first 10 to 15 minutes of baking with cold water from a plant mister. (Remove the pan of water after 15 minutes.)

Before baking, slash the tops of the loaves in several places with a razor blade. Slide the loaves or rolls onto the hot stones or tiles, or place the cookie sheets on the oven racks. Bake 30 to 35 minutes, or until the bread is a rich golden brown. Rolls will take less time and a convection oven will also probably take less time. Remove the bread from the pans when done, and cool on racks.

When the bread has cooled, you can wrap it in foil and freeze it, then reheat it wrapped in the foil at 350°F for 20 minutes.

To Make in a Food Processor

You can make this dough in a large food processor or in two batches in a medium food processor, following the directions given with your machine. Mix and rise the sponge in a bowl first. Process the final dough (knead) for 30 to 60 seconds. This dough recipe may be halved or doubled, but when doubling the recipe, do not double the amount of yeast.

To Make in a Bread Machine

Making sticky Italian bread doughs in a modern bread machine is a wonderful time-saver and certainly very clean (no messy hands or counter). But you must bake the bread in a regular or convection oven or you will be disappointed, even if you have a "crusty bread" or "French bread" selection on your machine.

If your bread machine makes large, 2-pound loaves, it can probably handle kneading the whole recipe. If it's one with a smaller capacity, you may have to knead half a recipe at a time.

Use cold water. Place the ingredients in the bread container in the order that is instructed for your machine. Select the dough cycle and let it go to work.

You can remove the dough from the machine after it has been kneaded and rise it in a bowl. If the container in your machine is big enough for the dough to double, let it rise through the entire dough cycle, then remove for the final rising and proceed with the recipe as instructed for making the dough with a food processor.

Per slice: Calories: 171, Protein: 5 g, Carbohydrate: 37 g, Fat: 0 g

Italian Bread Starter
BIGA
(soy-free)

Yield: about 4 cups

½ teaspoon regular baking yeast
1½ cups lukewarm water
About 4 cups unbleached white flour

In a large bowl or gallon jar, mix the yeast in the water. Let it stand about 10 to 15 minutes. Slowly stir in the flour with a wooden spoon. Beat it for 3 or 4 minutes. Cover well and let stand at cool room temperature for 6 to 24 hours. The starter should triple in volume and then fall, and should be sticky.

I have left starter in the refrigerator in a covered container for a couple of days and it was fine, but it is preferable to freeze it in 1- or 2-cup amounts, so that it doesn't sour.

Many, if not most, Italian breads begin with a starter. This is not the same as a sourdough. It's basically a sponge dough that is fermented for up to a day before making the actual bread dough. It gives strength to the dough, as well as better aroma, flavor, and texture to the finished bread. I usually freeze some of the starter for future baking. Just allow it to thaw to room temperature before using, or remove it from the freezer the night before the day you plan to bake.

"Slipper" Bread
CIABATTA
(soy-free)

Yield: 2 loaves or 36 panini (rolls)

1 teaspoon regular baking yeast
½ cup warm water
2 cups cold water
1 cup freshly risen or thawed frozen Italian Bread Starter, above
5 cups unbleached white flour

1 cup whole wheat flour, or use ½ cup more unbleached white flour and ½ cup wheat bran

1 tablespoon salt

Ciabatta (pronounced cha-báhta) means "slipper" in Italian, and the bread was originally called that because it had a flattish, oval shape. In North America the dough is often shaped into round loaves and rolls, as well. It's usually made as a white bread, but I like it with a little whole wheat flour added.

This is a very wet dough and, unless your arm is very strong (or you have some help), it is very difficult to make without a heavy-duty mixer, or bread machine. One of those old-fashioned hand-crank kneading machines would probably do it.

This recipe may be halved or doubled, but when doubling the recipe, do not double the amount of yeast.

Dissolve the yeast in the warm water for about 10 minutes. Add this to a large bowl or the bowl of a heavy-duty mixer with a dough hook, along with the cold water, starter, and 2 cups of the unbleached flour. Stir in the salt and gradually add the remaining flour. It will be a bit wet-looking for a bread dough. Knead it for 3 to 5 minutes, using a heavy wooden spoon if you are making it by hand. Cover and let it rest for 20 minutes. Knead it again for about 15 minutes, using a large wooden spoon or paddle with someone to spell you, if making by hand. To knead the dough in a bread machine, see the instructions for making Basic Italian Crusty Bread on page 195.

Place the dough in an oiled bowl with enough room to triple in size. Sprinkle the top with flour, and cover the bowl with wet towels or place inside a plastic bag. Let rise at room temperature until the dough has tripled in size (2½ to 4 hours, depending on the temperature).

Handling the dough as little as possible, divide the dough into two equal halves or 36 small pieces. To make traditional "slipper" shapes, press and pull the dough halves into rough rectangles about an inch thick, and "dimple" the dough all over with your fingertips. To make round loaves, tuck the sides of each piece of dough under with floured hands to make a rough round. Panini or rolls are shaped the same way. Place the loaves or rolls on greased, floured cookie sheets, or, if you are baking on stones or tiles, either on greased and well-floured flat cookie sheets with no lip or rim or on pieces of stiff cardboard covered with greased and well-floured baking parchment. Flour the tops of the bread liberally.

Either place the pans inside large plastic bags, or cover with slightly damp, clean tea towels. Rolls take about 30 minutes to rise at normal room temperature, loaves about 2 hours—they should double.

Preheat the oven to 450°F (400°F for a convection oven). If using tiles or baking stones, preheat them in the oven. In order to generate

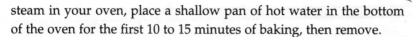

steam in your oven, place a shallow pan of hot water in the bottom of the oven for the first 10 to 15 minutes of baking, then remove.

Slide the loaves or rolls onto the hot stones or tiles, or place the cookie sheets on the oven racks. Bake panini about 25 minutes, loaves about 30 minutes, or until golden brown. (The baking time may be slightly less in a convection oven.)

Remove the bread from the pans, and cool on racks.

When the bread has cooled, you can freeze it wrapped in foil, then reheat it wrapped in the foil at 350°F for 20 minutes.

Per roll: Calories: 78, Protein: 3 g, Carbohydrate: 17 g, Fat: 0 g

Pizza Dough
PASTA PER PIZZA
(soy-free)

Yield: two 12 to 14-inch pizzas, or 5 smaller pizzette

Pizza is not often made in Italian homes because excellent, cheap pizza is available from pizzerias almost everywhere. But we can easily get a very good approximation of the real thing in our own homes.

This is my favorite pizza dough. I like to make it in the morning, let it rise once, and then refrigerate it until dinner. This seems to improve it—when baked, it gets all puffy around the edges like a brick oven pizza.

1¼ cups lukewarm water

½ tablespoon regular baking yeast

½ teaspoon unbleached sugar

3¼ cups unbleached white flour, or 3 cups unbleached white flour and ¼ cup wheat bran

1 tablespoon extra-virgin olive oil

½ tablespoon salt

Note: You can use up to 1½ cups whole wheat flour instead of an equal amount of white flour, if you wish, but I don't recommend any more.

In a medium bowl or the bowl of a heavy-duty mixer, mix the water, yeast, and sugar. Let stand until frothy. Add 2 cups of the flour, the oil, and salt, and stir well. Add the remaining flour and knead for 5 to 8 minutes. Place the dough in an oiled bowl, cover, and let rise in a warm spot for an hour.

Pizza

There is a North American myth that one hears or reads now and then that purports that pizza is actually an invention of Italian-Americans and that you can't get a good pizza in Italy. Perhaps you can't get an American-style pizza in Italy, with an indifferent, greasy crust, 20 toppings, half a pound of meat, and enough cheese to feed a family for a week, but that's because Italians don't like it that way!

Pizza is said by some Italian scholars to be a direct descendant of the flat bread baked by priestesses of Demeter (goddess of grain) in the Naples area. At any rate, the Greeks and Romans both ate flat breads with oil, vinegar, onions, and herbs for snacks. Writers from the 18th and 19th centuries observed that itinerant pizza sellers and pizzaioli with fixed stands sold their wares in the streets of Naples in affordable wedges—forerunners of our modern pizza-by-the-slice vendors! Even Italian queens, such as Maria Carolina (wife of King Fernando I) in the 1780s and Margherita (wife of Umberto I of Savoia) in the 1870s, loved pizza, and Margherita even had one named after her.

Pizza began to spread to other areas of Italy after World War II, when southern Italians ventured north to look for industrial jobs. And, of course, southern Italians who left Italy for new lives in North and South America and Great Britain brought pizza with them. Today, pizza is probably one of the most popular foods in the world!

Despite the proliferation of greasy, too-cheesey, excessively dressed fast-food American pizza (sometimes topped with such un-Italian items as pineapple), and far-out designer pizza sporting anything from hummus to Thai-style grilled duck, the classic Neapolitan pizza persists *because* it is so delicious and satisfying in its simplicity. You need a dough that can hold its own unadorned, excellent olive oil, fresh herbs, a smear of good tomato sauce, and perhaps a light topping of one, two, or three other tasty items

Punch the dough down and either use it right away, or cover it well with plastic wrap, and place it in the refrigerator until you are ready to bake.

To make the dough in a bread machine, follow the instructions for Basic Italian Crusty Bread, p. 195. This is a great convenience and makes wonderful pizza dough.

It would be great if we all had brick pizza ovens in our back patios, but most of us don't. I bake pizza very quickly in my electric stove's convection oven at 500°F, but experiment with your oven starting at 425°F. You want the dough to cook fast, but not dry out, and you want the topping to be juicy. If you want to use baking stones or ceramic tiles to bake your pizza on, heat them up in the oven as it comes up to temperature and slide the pizza onto the tiles from either oiled, well-floured flat cookie sheets (with no lip or rim) or baking parchment over stiff cardboard. Be aware, though, that toppings, sauce, and oil that may drip on the clay may be difficult to remove and may smell up the oven next time you bake. Otherwise, just use dark pizza pans or cookie sheets placed right on the oven racks.

When you are ready to bake, preheat the oven to between 425°F and 500°F, according to the type of oven you have. Punch down the dough and divide into two balls for 12-inch pizzas, or 5 balls for pizzette (small pizzas). On a well-floured board, roll the dough out to fit your pans or into five 4- to 6-inch pizzette, leaving a bit of a rim around the edge. Top your pizza as desired (see pages 201-03).

At 500°F in a convection oven, pizza will cook in about 8 minutes. At a lower temperature with no convection, it may take 15 minutes. The bottom of the crust should be crispy and golden, with perhaps a few scorched spots, and the top should be bubbly and slightly browned with a nice puffy edge. The crust should be chewy. Serve immediately, cutting into wedges with a sharp knife, a pizza cutter, or a pair of kitchen shears (my favorite). Pizza is considered a meal in itself in Italy, and Italians will eat a 10- to 12-inch pizza each. These pizzas are not as heavily covered with toppings as American pizza, so this is not as excessive as it sounds.

Topping the Pizza

An Italian pizza is *not* a receptacle for whatever leftovers are lurking in your refrigerator. Choose a few excellent ingredients, and don't overdo it.

Pizza is traditionally smeared with olive oil, and then tomato sauce, but I prefer to save the olive oil to drizzle on top when all the toppings are on. Without the usual American topping of mozzarella cheese, the pizza could be dry without a little olive oil on it. The olive oil also adds flavor, if it is a good one. *Don't omit the olive oil.* You can use as little as 1 tablespoon on a large pizza, and it really makes a juicy topping. You are saving a lot of fat by using no cheese, and the fat in olive oil is much more healthful than dairy fat.

Use about 1 cup of Pizza Sauce, p. 203, on a 12- to 14-inch pizza. Here are some traditional Italian pizzas which don't require cheese, except for a few that call for Parmesan. You can use Soymage Parmesan substitute, or soy-free alternative, p. 37. These will give you an idea of the simplicity of Italian pizza, so that you can create your own special combinations.

Per pizzette without toppings: Calories: 290, Protein: 8 g, Carbohydrate: 56 g, Fat: 4 g

(olives, sliced marinated artichoke hearts, onions, mushrooms, etc.). Cheese is used on some pizzas, but not all, and when used, it does not smother the other ingredients. For a vegan pizza, some toppings benefit from a sprinkle of soy Parmesan, but most need no cheese.

Pizza alla Napoletana
This is the most basic. Use 1 cup Pizza Sauce, p. 203, 3 cloves garlic, sliced, salt and freshly ground black pepper, and 1 to 2 tablespoons extra-virgin olive oil. You can add a scattering of chopped fresh oregano, marjoram, or basil, if you like. For Pizza alla Marinara, add about 1 tablespoon light soy or chick-pea miso (in place of anchovies), scattered over the pizza in little bits.

Pizza con Pomodoro Crudo e Basilico
Top the pizza with slices of fresh, ripe plum tomato, sprinkle with salt, and drizzle with 1 to 2 tablespoons extra-virgin olive oil. Just before serving, grind fresh black pepper on top, and arrange a few fresh basil leaves on top. You can drizzle with a little more oil, if you wish.

Pizza con "Salsicce" e Funghi
This is a heartier pizza. Use 1 cup Pizza Sauce, p. 203, 2 crumbled commercial or homemade vegetarian Italian sausages (soy-based, p. 177, or seitan, p. 183), ¾ to 1 cup thinly sliced mushrooms, 2 tablespoons Soymage

Parmesan substitute, or soy-free alternative, p. 37, and 1 to 2 tablespoons extra-virgin olive oil.

Pizza con Pepperoni (Pizza with Peppers)

Top with 1 small onion, thinly sliced, 1 large bell pepper (red, yellow, or orange), seeded and cut into strips, and a couple of large garlic cloves, thinly sliced, sautéed slowly in 2 tablespoons extra-virgin olive oil until soft, but not brown. A little fresh chopped oregano or marjoram is sprinkled on top, along with about 6 pitted black Italian olives, and salt and freshly ground black pepper to taste. You can also use roasted red peppers from a jar or homemade, pp. 74-75, or chopped oil-packed sun-dried tomatoes, instead of the sautéed peppers.

If all you have are green bell peppers, spread the pizza with 1 cup of Pizza Sauce, p. 203, cover with 1 small green pepper, seeded and cut into thin strips, 2 large cloves garlic, thinly sliced, 1 to 2 tablespoons extra-virgin olive oil, and salt and freshly ground black pepper to taste.

Pizza con Porcini

Spread the crust with 1 cup Pizza Sauce, p. 203. Have ready 1 ounce of dried porcini or boletus mushrooms, soaked, (see pages 35-36), drained, and chopped. Spread them over the sauce, sprinkle with chopped fresh Italian parsley, a couple of tablespoons of Soymage Parmesan substitute, or soy-free alternative, p. 37, and drizzle with 1 to 2 tablespoons of extra-virgin olive oil. If you like, add 1 slice of vegetarian Canadian or "back" bacon, chopped, or drizzle on 1 teaspoon of roasted sesame oil along with the olive oil.

Pizza con Funghi (Pizza with Mushrooms)

Top the dough with 1 cup Pizza Sauce, p. 203, and scatter the top with ¾ to 1 cup thinly sliced mushrooms of any kind (button, crimini, portobello, chanterelle, stemmed fresh shiitake, oyster, etc.). Top with about 6 fresh basil leaves, and drizzle the whole thing with 1 to 2 tablespoons extra-virgin olive oil. Sprinkle with salt and freshly ground black pepper. You can use chopped Italian parsley or sage leaves instead of the basil, if you wish, and/or add a couple of cloves of thinly sliced garlic.

Other Topping Alternatives

If you like, you could use some crumbled Tofu or Almond Ricotta Salata (pages 34-36) as the cheese on your pizza—just a little. It will melt a bit like goat cheese. You can add a sprinkle of hot red pepper flakes to a pizza, dot it with pesto, pp. 49-51, add some thin slices of marinated artichoke hearts, or vegetarian pepperoni or salami. Add other fresh herbs, such as thyme, sage, oregano, rosemary, or use capers, green olives as well as black, olive paste (olivada), a scattering of arugula or sautéed greens or rapini (I prefer this to broccoli on a pizza), grilled zucchini or eggplant slices, etc.—but don't put too many items on one pizza. You want to be able to really taste each component and not just have a "mishmash" of flavors.

Pizza is meant to be eaten very hot, straight from the oven. Italians don't keep leftover pizza and reheat it. I must admit that I do when we have some leftover—but I reheat it briefly in a toaster oven. Pizza gets distressingly soggy and tough when reheated in a microwave, no matter what you do.

Pizza Sauce
POLPA DI POMODORO
(soy-free)

Yield: 2 cups

2 tablespoons extra-virgin olive oil
4 cloves garlic, minced
2 pounds fresh ripe plum tomatoes, chopped,
   or 1 (28-ounce) can plum tomatoes, chopped, or diced tomatoes,
   with their juice
¼ teaspoon salt
Freshly ground black pepper, to taste

Even when made with canned tomatoes, this sauce has a fresh concentrated tomato flavor. It's easy as well as delicious, so don't bother buying over-salted commercial pizza sauce made with stale herbs anymore!

Note: Herbs and onions are added to the pizza, rather than the sauce.

Heat the olive oil in a heavy pot over medium heat. Add the garlic for just a minute, then add the tomatoes and their juice. Add the salt and pepper. Cook over medium heat, stirring now and then, uncovered, for about 10 minutes, or until it has cooked down to a thick, chunky pulp. (If you double or triple the recipe, it will take longer to cook down.) Taste for salt and pepper.

If you like your sauce chunky, leave it as is. I like to run mine through a rotary food mill (mouli), so that it's smooth. (I add back most of the seeds and bits of skin, because I like them and they add fiber.) You could use a hand-held blender or a regular blender or food processor, but don't let it get too frothy.

Uncooked Pizza Sauce

If you're in a hurry, just drain the canned tomatoes really well in a mesh strainer, and process them with the rest of the ingredients in a food processor.

Per ½ cup serving: Calories: 104, Protein: 1 g, Carbohydrate: 9 g, Fat: 7 g

Calzoni
FOLDED PIZZA
(can be soy-free)

Calzoni is a stuffed or folded pizza, a sort of large "pasty" or turnover. I've given you numerous filling options so that you can create your own filling. You can use virtually anything you would use in a pizza, but tomato sauce should be eaten with the baked calzoni, rather than baked into it. Don't make the filling too wet, or you'll have soggy calzoni.

Yield: 2 large calzoni (4 to 6 servings)

1 recipe Pizza dough, p. 199, risen
2 tablespoons extra-virgin olive oil
Salt and freshly ground black pepper, to taste

Filling Ingredients
(choose one):
1 to 2 cups thick cold Dairy-Free White Sauce, p. 36
1 to 2 cups Tofu Ricotta, p. 32, or Almond Ricotta, p. 35
1 cup Tofu Ricotta Salata, p. 34, or Almond Ricotta Salata, p. 36

(choose one, two, or three):
4 slices vegetarian Canadian or "back" bacon, ham, or pepperoni, chopped
1 cup cooked crumbled commercial or homemade vegetarian Italian sausage or regular vegetarian sausage, pp. 177 or 183
1 cup sautéed sliced onions
1 cup sliced marinated artichoke hearts
1 cup roasted red peppers (homemade, pp. 74-75, or from a jar)
1 cup sliced fresh, ripe tomatoes
1 to 2 cups grilled eggplant or zucchini strips
2 cups sautéed greens or broccoli
1 to 2 cups sautéed fresh mushrooms (any kind)

Optional Additions:
Chopped Italian parsley
Chopped garlic
Little bits of pesto, pp. 49-51
1 tablespoon light soy or chick-pea miso, in little bits (instead of anchovies)
Sprinkling of dried red chile flakes
Sliced pitted calamata olives

Soymage Parmesan substitute, or soy-free alternative, p. 37
Chopped fresh herbs, such as basil, sage, oregano, or marjoram

Preheat the oven to 425°F.

Divide the pizza dough in half, and roll each half out into a 12-inch circle. Place each circle on an oiled pizza pan, and spread one half of each circle with either Dairy-Free White Sauce or one of the ricottas. Add your choice of other ingredients, drizzle each calzoni with 1 tablespoon of olive oil, and add salt and pepper to taste. Leave a ½-inch edge around the filling, and don't fill it too full.

Fold the other half of the dough over the filling, and seal the edges well. Cut a couple of slits in the top of each calzoni, and brush the dough with olive oil. Bake immediately for about 20 minutes, or until golden. Serve hot with Pizza Sauce, p. 203, or more extra-virgin olive oil.

Per serving (with white sauce, "ham," onions, and artichokes):
Calories: 467, Protein: 14 g, Carbohydrate: 66 g, Fat: 15 g

Sicilian Bread Pie

IMPANATA

(can be soy-free)

Yield: 6 servings

Spinach Filling:
1 tablespoon extra-virgin olive oil
3 cloves garlic, chopped
2 pounds fresh spinach, chard, or beet greens, washed, chopped, steamed tender, and squeezed dry,
    or 2 (10-ounce) packages chopped spinach or other greens, thawed and squeezed dry
Optional:
¼ teaspoon dried red chile flakes
12 black olives, pitted and sliced
3 tablespoons chopped raisins, or 1 tablespoon capers
3 tablespoons toasted pine nuts

Sicilian stuffed breads make wonderful picnic or lunchbox food. When my children were in school, they welcomed almost any filling baked in a bread case—it was so much more exciting than a sandwich! I'm offering two of the more traditional stuffings, but feel free to experiment with other vegetables, or to use the fillings for tortas (Chapter XI), Stuffed Griddle Dumplings, p. 209, leftover vegetarian stews, and other vegetable dishes as fillings.

The spinach variety is sometimes called Torta del Venerdi Santo, or Good

Friday Pie—a traditional "magra" or Lenten dish—or simply Torta di Spinaci.

Serve these hot or cold in wedges. If you serve it hot, pass a simple tomato sauce (pp. 42-43 or 203) to spoon over it.

You can also make these into "scaccie" or stuffed rolls.

Note: If you use one whole recipe of pizza dough, you can make one of each kind.

¼ cup vegetarian broth
2 tablespoons light soy or chick-pea miso
Salt and freshly ground pepper, to taste

Broccoli Filling:
5 to 6 ounces fresh broccoli or rapini (or Chinese broccoli), steamed crisp-tender and chopped
1 tablespoon extra-virgin olive oil, plus 1 teaspoon roasted sesame oil
½ cup crumbled cooked vegetarian Italian sausage, homemade (pp. 177 and 183) or commercial
3 cloves garlic, chopped
Pinch dried red chile flakes
Salt and freshly ground pepper, to taste
Optional:
2 fresh, ripe tomatoes, sliced
2 tablespoons Soymage parmesan substitute, or soy-free alternative, p. 37
Nondairy milk for brushing

½ recipe Pizza dough, p. 199, risen

Spinach Filling: Heat the olive oil in a large nonstick skillet over high heat. Add the garlic and stir just until it starts to turn color. Add the spinach and any optionals. Mix the broth with the miso, and stir in until most of the liquid disappears. Add salt and pepper to taste. Set aside to cool—you can spread it on a plate and put it in the freezer to speed up the cooling.

Broccoli Filling: Heat the oil in a large nonstick skillet over high heat. Add the garlic and stir just until it starts to change color. Add the broccoli, sausage, chile flakes, and salt and pepper to taste. (Do not add the tomatoes or soy Parmesan at this point.) Set aside to cool.

Preheat the oven to 400°F.

To assemble, roll half of the dough out to fit a 9-inch oiled pie pan. Fill with whichever filling you are using. (If you are using the

Broccoli Filling, you can lay the tomato slices or sprinkle the soy Parmesan over the filling.) Roll out the rest of the dough to fit the top and seal the edges by crimping neatly.

Cut a few slits in the dough, brush with nondairy milk, and bake for 30 minutes. (There's no need to rise again before baking.)

Per serving (spinach filling): Calories: 188, Protein: 7 g, Carbohydrate: 30 g, Fat: 3 g

Per serving (broccoli filling): Calories: 167, Protein: 6 g, Carbohydrate: 26 g, Fat: 4 g

Vegetarian Chicken in Bread
POLLO DI SOYA O SEITAN IN PANE
(can be soy-free)

Yield: two 9-inch pies (8 to 12 servings)

1 recipe Pizza dough, p. 199, risen
1 recipe "Chicken" and Vegetable Oven-Broiled "Stew," p. 172
 (Do not use the optional creme.)
nondairy milk for brushing

Make the "stew" ahead of time, and let it cool.

Preheat the oven to 400°F.

Divide the dough into four equal pieces. Roll out two of the dough pieces into circles to fit the bottom and sides of two oiled 9-inch pie or cake pans. Divide the "stew" evenly between the two crusts. Roll the remaining dough to fit the tops of the pies, and seal the edges by crimping. Cut a few slits in the tops of the pies, and brush with nondairy milk. Bake immediately for about 30 minutes, or until golden brown.

Per serving: Calories: 241, Protein: 9 g, Carbohydrate: 35 g, Fat: 7 g

All stuffed breads make wonderful picnic food, and this recipe is no exception. But it's also a perfect luncheon dish for company. I devised it after seeing an Italian recipe for roast chicken stuffed with vegetables in a bread crust.

Piadine
(FLATBREAD FROM ROMAGNA)
(soy-free)

Yield: 12

3½ cups unbleached white flour
½ cup whole wheat flour
1½ teaspoons salt
¾ teaspoon baking powder
3 tablespoons extra-virgin olive oil
1 tablespoon roasted sesame oil
1¼ cups water

Piadine remind me very much of Mexican flour tortillas. They make a wonderful snack or light lunch when served in the traditional style with greens wilted in olive oil and garlic. A spread of Tofu or Almond Ricotta, or some Ricotta Salata (either soy or almond—see pages 32-36) with some fresh tomatoes, radishes, olives, and/or arugula and a sprinkle of good olive oil would also be good, as would a bean spread or pâté. Spread the filling on one half of the piadina, fold over the other half, and cut into two wedges, or sandwich the filling between two piadine and cut into quarters.

I've substituted olive oil with a touch of sesame oil for the traditional lard, and I use a little whole wheat flour to duplicate the coarser white flour of earlier times in the countryside.

Piadine are cooked over clay bakestones called testi, but a cast-iron skillet makes a perfectly good substitute.

If making by hand, mix the flours, salt, and baking powder in a medium bowl. Add the oils and mix with your fingertips until like fine crumbs. Add the water and knead on a floured surface for about 5 minutes, then place back in the bowl, cover, and let the dough rest for 20 minutes or so.

If making in a food processor, mix the flours, salt, and baking powder in the processor bowl, then add the oils and pulse until well mixed. With the motor running, add the water through the opening, and process for about 30 seconds. Let the dough rest for about 20 minutes.

On a floured surface, divide the dough into 12 equal pieces, and roll them into balls. Keep them covered while you work. Roll out each ball into a flat circle about ⅛-inch thick. Cover them with clean tea towels or plastic wrap while you heat the pan.

Heat the largest cast-iron skillet you have over medium-high heat until it's hot enough to make a drop of water dance and then disappear a second later. Place one piadina in the pan, and press down with the spatula. Cook for about 45 to 60 seconds, then flip it over; the cooked side should have faint scorch marks. If not, cook a few seconds longer. Cook the other side until it is speckled too. I like to place the hot piadine in a paper bag—that way they stay warm and flexible. To heat later, keep them wrapped tightly in foil, then reheat in a 325°F oven for 10 to 15 minutes.

Per piadine: Calories: 173, Protein: 4 g, Carbohydrate: 28 g, Fat: 5 g

Stuffed "Griddle Dumplings"
CONSUM
(soy-free)

Yield: 12

1 pound Swiss chard, beet greens, spinach, or savoy cabbage, or a mixture
1 pound bitter greens, such as arugula, radicchio, rapini (or Chinese broccoli), mustard or turnip greens, sorrel, young dandelion greens, curly endive, etc.
1 recipe Piadine dough, p. 208
2 to 4 tablespoons extra-virgin olive oil
1 tablespoon chopped garlic
Salt and freshly ground pepper, to taste

This traditional "griddle dumpling" from Romagna is actually a stuffed piadine (flatbread), similar to a calzone, but stuffed with greens. If you fry the stuffed breads in oil, they are called "cassoni." What a great way to eat your greens!

Wash, trim, and thinly slice the greens. Heat the oil in a large nonstick skillet or pot, and add the garlic. Cook it just until it starts to change color—don't brown it. Add the greens and sauté for about 10 minutes, or until tender and all the liquid has evaporated. Add salt and pepper to taste. Set aside to cool.

Make the Piadine dough and roll out as directed in the recipe on page 200. Drain the greens and spread some of them ½-inch thick over one half of each round, leaving a ½-inch edge. Fold the other half over, and seal with a fluted pasta wheel or a fork. Cook as for piadine, 4 or 5 minutes each, turning frequently. Serve hot.

Per dumpling: Calories: 216, Protein: 5 g, Carbohydrate: 31 g, Fat: 7 g

Focaccia (pronounced foh-*kah*-cha) makes a great snack, open-face sandwich bread, or accompaniment to soup or salad. It is the pizza of the Genoa area, but each region has its own special varieties of focacce. The most basic focaccia is smeared with 2 or 3 table-spoons of good extra-vir-gin olive oil and a sprin-kling of salt. To get more elaborate, you can scatter this with pitted Italian olives; fresh herbs, such as whole sage or basil leaves; a little thinly sliced raw garlic; chopped walnuts or hazelnuts; and/or onion, either rings of raw sweet onion or yellow onion sautéed until soft and starting to brown.

Other varieties are topped with tomato slices or a thin layer of Pizza Sauce, p. 203; chopped fresh rosemary, oregano, basil, thyme, or marjoram; for anchovies substitute bits of light soy or chick-pea miso; capers; sliced roasted peppers; or bits of oil-packed, sun-dried tomatoes—always with some extra-virgin olive oil, salt, and freshly ground black pepper.

Focaccia

ITALIAN "HEARTH BREAD"

(soy-free)

Yield: one 11 x 15-inch focaccia (15 servings)

One recipe Pizza Dough, p. 199
Topping(s) of your choice (See left sidebar.)

Preheat the oven to 425°F (400°F for a convection oven). Roll the once-risen pizza dough to fit an 11 x 15-inch cookie sheet (nonstick or lightly oiled). See note below if you are using a baking stone or tiles. Don't make a rim around the edge of the dough, as you would for pizza. Cover the dough and let it set for 20 to 30 minutes, while the oven heats up. Make deep dents in the dough at intervals with your fingertips.

Spread the dough with 2 or 3 tablespoons of extra-virgin olive oil or thinly with Pizza Sauce, p. 203, canned crushed tomatoes, or chopped or sliced fresh plum tomatoes. Sprinkle with salt, freshly ground black pepper, and any other toppings that you are using. (Drizzle the top with olive oil if you used tomato sauce.)

Note: If you want to use baking stones or ceramic tiles to bake your focaccia on, heat them in the oven as it comes up to temperature. If you don't have a baking peel, slide the focaccia onto the tiles from an oiled, well-floured flat cookie sheet (with no lip or rim) or baking parchment over stiff cardboard. Be aware, though, that toppings, sauce, and oil that may drip on the clay may be difficult to remove and may smell up the oven next time you bake.

Bake for 15 minutes, or until the bottom is golden and crispy and the edges are browned. You may need to turn the oven down 25°F and bake 5 to 10 minutes longer. Brush the edges with extra-virgin olive oil. Cut into 2 x 5-inch strips while hot.

Per serving without toppings: Calories: 97, Protein: 3 g, Carbohydrate: 19 g, Fat: 1 g

Focaccie with Fruit:

A very ancient type of focaccia is made by making deep dents in the dough and strewing the top with any type of sweet, fresh grapes. I like to cut them in half or crush them slightly, so that the juice comes out. Sprinkle the top with a handful of unbleached sugar, and bake as directed. This is so indescribably delicious! I love it for breakfast in the fall.

You can do the same thing with other fresh fruits, especially plums, peaches, nectarines, figs, and apricots.

Panettone
ITALIAN SWEET CHRISTMAS BREAD
(can be soy-free)

Yield: 1 loaf (8 servings)

½ cup warm water

2 teaspoons regular baking yeast

¼ teaspoon Spanish saffron

½ cup full-fat soymilk

¼ cup light unbleached sugar

3 tablespoons good-tasting nondairy margarine

Grated zest of 1 orange (organic, if possible)

Grated zest of 1 lemon (organic, if possible)

½ tablespoon anise seed

2 teaspoons vanilla

1 teaspoon pure almond extract

¾ teaspoon salt

2¾ cups unbleached white flour

¼ cup wheat germ

½ cup golden raisins

½ cup chopped dried apricots

Optional: ⅓ cup chopped lightly toasted almonds or pine nuts

Add the yeast and saffron to the warm water in a cup, and let set 5 or 10 minutes until bubbly.

In a small saucepan or a microwave, heat the soymilk until it is just hot, with bubbles around the edges. Add the sugar and margarine

My father fondly recalled the panettone his Aunt Maria made in the brick oven in the central courtyard of his boyhood home in Lima, Peru. Because of his memories, I began making panettone for Christmas many years ago, and my oldest daughter Bethany now continues this tradition.

Panettone is a yeast bread, slightly sweet, flavored with citrus rinds, dried fruit, anise, and almonds. It is usually made rich with butter and eggs, but I now use soymilk (which acts as a dough conditioner to make a light bread) and a little good-tasting nondairy margarine. Saffron gives the golden color of egg yolks.

My great-aunt was probably making pandolce rather than the panettone di Milano which most Italians simply call panettone now. Pandolce is a bit more compact, not as rich as the Milan version, and flavored with orange flower water, fennel, pine nuts, and other spices, with a bay leaf placed on top. The original version was leavened only with an egg—no yeast was used. (See the variation on page 212.)

This recipe includes a bread machine version, which is quite good.

Modern Pandolce or Panettone Genovese

You can omit the almond extract and instead use 4 teaspoons orange flower water (available in many Middle Eastern markets or gourmet stores). Omit the lemon zest. For the dried fruit, use ⅓ cup *each* golden raisins, dried currants, and chopped dried apricots. Use the pine nuts. Omit the anise seed and use ½ teaspoon fennel seeds, crushed, instead. Add ¼ teaspoon ground coriander.

The remaining ingredients and instructions are the same. The loaf is traditionally served with a whole bay leaf resting on top and is cut first by the youngest member of the family.

Italian Easter Bread Ring

This bread is usually made with colored raw eggs baked in the twists of dough. To stay vegan, you can mound candy eggs in colored paper "straw" in the center of the baked ring, polished, colored egg-shaped rocks that are used for decoration or paperweights, or colored egg-shaped candles.

Cut the risen dough in half. Roll each half on a lightly floured board into a 2-foot rope. Twist the two

and stir to dissolve. When the soymilk has cooled down a bit, add it to the yeast and water. Pour this into a large mixing bowl or the bowl of a heavy-duty mixer with a bread hook. Place the anise seed on a square of waxed paper, and fold part of it over to cover the seeds. Crush the seeds with a heavy rolling pin.

Add the citrus zests (colored part only), crushed anise seed, vanilla, almond extract, and salt to the bowl. Stir in the wheat germ and 1 cup of the flour. Beat well for a minute or two, then gradually add the remaining flour. Knead with a dough hook or by hand on a floured surface for 5 to 10 minutes, adding as little flour as you can get away with—oil your hands and the surface, if necessary. Place the dough in a lightly oiled bowl, and turn it over to coat the top. Place the bowl in a large plastic bag or cover with a clean, damp tea towel, and let rise in a warm place until doubled in size, 1 to 1½ hours.

Turn the risen dough out on a lightly floured surface, and pat it out into a flat rectangle. Sprinkle the surface with the dried fruits and optional nuts, if using. Roll up the dough jelly roll style, then fold in the ends. Knead the dough gently by folding and rolling until these ingredients are well-distributed throughout the dough.

Tuck under the edges of the dough to form a ball. Place this on an oiled heavy cookie sheet, pizza pan, or large cake pan with low sides. Cover and let rise in a warm place until doubled in size, about 1 hour.

Preheat the oven to 350°F. With a razor blade or sharp knife, cut a cross in the top of the dough about ½-inch deep. Bake for 30 minutes in the center or upper half of the oven, or just until the loaf is a deep golden brown and sounds hollow when tapped on the bottom. Cool on a rack before slicing.

To make the dough in a food processor

You can make this dough in a food processor, following the directions given with your machine for making bread dough. *Do not* add the dried fruit and nuts to the machine—knead them in by hand after the first rising as instructed in the recipe. Process the dough (knead) for 30 to 60 seconds.

To make the dough or bake the bread in a bread machine

This is the only bread in this chapter that you can successfully bake in a bread baking machine. This recipe was developed so that it doesn't result in an overly fluffy loaf. The bread should be light, but not like "Wonder Bread." If you prefer the mounded shape, you can knead and rise the bread in the machine, then bake as instructed in the recipe.

Place the ingredients in the bread container in the order you usually use for your machine. *Do not* add the dried fruit and nuts at the beginning. If your machine has a sweet bread cycle, it will beep when it's time to add these ingredients. Otherwise, you'll have to add them toward the very end of the kneading cycle, so that they don't get pulverized.

If you are baking the bread in the machine, just let it go through the sweet bread cycle or use the white bread cycle with a regular crust. If your machine has a glass window above the bread, cover it with foil on the outside. This makes a browner top on the bread. Remove the bread from the container immediately to cool on a rack.

To make soy-free: If you can't use soymilk (which helps make a light loaf), substitute 1 cup of commercial low-fat almond milk or other nondairy milk for the soymilk and water, and add 1 tablespoon of instant mashed potato flakes to the dough. The potato flakes are not necessary when you bake the bread in a bread machine.

Per serving: Calories: 273, Protein: 7 g, Carbohydrate: 50 g, Fat: 5 g

ropes of dough together loosely (starting in the middle), and form them into a ring on a lightly oiled baking sheet, tucking the ends together neatly and evenly. Rise and bake as directed for Panettone. Place on a rack to cool.

Make a simple glaze by beating together ½ cup powdered good-tasting vegan "milk" (such as light tofu beverage mix) with ¼ cup Grade A maple syrup and ¼ teaspoon vanilla, pure almond, lemon, or orange extract with a hand blender, beater, or miniprocessor until smooth. Spread this on the bread while it's still warm, and sprinkle the top with colored candy sprinkles, if you like.

If you prefer a powdered sugar glaze, you can powder any unbleached sugar by blending 1 cup with 1 tablespoon cornstarch or other starch in a *dry* blender until powdery. Mix 1 cup powdered sugar with 1½ tablespoons nondairy milk and ½ teaspoon of the desired flavor extract.

XVII
Sweets
DOLCI

"Cakes in fanciful shapes filled with chocolate and crowned with candied fruits; cylinders of golden crust wrapped around chocolate paste blended with vanilla; a pink and green almond loaf embedded with cherries, orange peel and pistachio nuts; wine jellies in the form of saints, shields and flowers. These are the glories of the kitchens of Sicily."

Waverly Root
The Cooking of Italy
(New York: Time-Life
Books, 1968)

A Word About Sugar and Other Sweeteners

You will notice that I call for unbleached sugars and a little bit of Grade A maple syrup or corn syrup as sweeteners in this book. I know that many in the vegetarian and health food movements will disagree with me, but I think that depending upon so-called "natural" sugars is a mistake. Many consumers think they can eat large quantities of dessert foods

You may have heard that Italians never eat dessert, just fruit and nuts or cheese. This may be true in some homes, but in restaurants most diners save room for something from the elegant and extravagant dessert table on display at the entrance. And the pasticcerrias (pastry shops), with their windows crowded with mouth-watering pastries, cookies, and cakes, are busy throughout the day. Gelato bars grow ever more elegant and trendy.

Desserts have a long history in Italy and reflect the seasons and the foods that grow well from one region to the next, as well as the invasions of other cultures in the past—flaky pastries with almonds in Sicily, reminiscent of Middle Eastern desserts; fruit tarts in the north, where orchards of pears, apples, peaches, apricots, and cherries bloom; creamy rice puddings in the central valleys.

This chapter offers but a teasing glimpse of the wonderful variety of Italian desserts, vegan-style. I have devised some delicious vegan dessert staples, which I hope will enable you to convert your favorite family desserts to dairy-free delights—a basic cake, pastry cream, sweet pastry, frothy wine "custard," various creamy toppings, almond "macaroons," biscotti, and a wide variety of frozen desserts. These are not low-fat foods, but they are lower in fat than the traditional recipes and do not contain animal fats. Combined with fresh fruits and consumed in moderate servings, they can be part of a balanced vegan diet.

Baked Stuffed Peaches

PESCHE RIPIENE

(soy-free)

Yield: 4 servings

Try this easy but sumptuous fruit dessert when peaches are in full season—it's a great company dessert.

4 ripe peaches, washed, halved, and pitted

Stuffing:
½ cup fresh bread crumbs
½ cup light unbleached sugar
⅓ cup ground, lightly toasted almonds
2 tablespoons Dutch cocoa
1 tablespoon dry white wine (can be nonalcoholic), marsala, or sherry
½ teaspoon pure almond extract

½ cup dry white wine (can be nonalcoholic)
1½ tablespoons light unbleached sugar
1 tablespoon good-tasting dairy-free margarine

Preheat the oven to 350°F.

Scoop out a little of the peach flesh from the centers of the peach halves. Chop the peach flesh and set aside. Mix the stuffing ingredients together, and add the chopped peach flesh. Fill the peach halves evenly with the stuffing, and place the halves in an oiled baking dish. Pour the wine over the peaches, and sprinkle them with the 1½ tablespoons sugar. Dot the tops with the margarine. Bake 25 minutes. Serve hot.

Note: This recipe can also be used with pear halves.

Per serving: Calories: 307, Protein: 4 g, Carbohydrate: 43 g, Fat: 8 g

made with fruit and grain syrups, but researchers have found that ingesting *any* fruit sweetener, even orange juice, leads to a significant drop in the body's white blood cell count, reducing the effectiveness of the immune system. All sugars, indeed all refined carbohydrates, can effect insulin levels.

For this reason, I believe in saving desserts for special occasions or eating them only once or twice a week. It stands to reason that such a concentrated, refined carbohydrate as sugar, stripped of its natural components, may not be particularly good for us, but I don't believe that you are contributing to good health by eating desserts made with "natural" sugars every day. Boiled down fruit juice, maple sap, or grain syrup are all very concentrated sweeteners, and the origins of them are no more natural than sugar cane (and usually not organic, either).

Sugar is the easiest and most affordable sweetener to work with and is now available unbleached in a variety of forms. Most cane sugar is not vegetarian because it is bleached by filtering through bone ash, and brown sugars may be simply bleached sugar with molasses added, so I use only products that state on the package that they are unbleached, no matter what the color. The most common unbleached sugars are turbinado and granulated sugar cane juice (Sucanat, etc.), but there are other products with different names that also specify they are unbleached. In some recipes, I call for a light unbleached sugar, such as turbinado; in others a brown unbleached sugar, or granulated sugar cane juice.

Grade A maple syrup is used in some recipes where even light unbleached sugar leaves a faint molasses taste (like vanilla gelato), or where a liquid sweetener is preferable. It is expensive, but easily available and still cheaper and sweeter than brown rice syrup.

Let's use some common sense when it comes to sugar and desserts. Sugar and other refined, concentrated sweeteners have been consumed by healthy populations for centuries. It is only when they are *over*-consumed, as they are in the modern North American diet along with so many processed foods, that they become a problem.

Pears Baked in Wine
PERE AL VINO
(soy-free)

Yield: 6 servings

A very simple rendition, but always delicious.

6 ripe, firm pears

2 cups dry red wine, such as a Barolo (can be nonalcoholic)

½ cup light unbleached sugar

6 whole cloves or 1 stick cinnamon

Preheat the oven to 400°F.

Wash the pears, but leave them unpeeled with the stems on. Stand the pears in a large baking dish, and pour the wine over them. Sprinkle with the sugar and cloves, or add the cinnamon stick. Bake for 1 hour, or until the pears are tender.

Lift out the pears and place on a serving dish. Pour the remaining wine into a small pan, and cook it down until it's almost like a syrup, discarding the cloves or cinnamon. Pour it over the pears, and serve hot or cold.

Per serving: Calories: 257, Protein: 1 g, Carbohydrate: 41 g, Fat: 0 g

Chocolate Mousse
SFORMATINI DI CIOCCOLATA
(can be soy-free)

Yield: 8 servings

2 cups soymilk, rice milk, or almond milk

1 cup unbleached sugar

3 tablespoons cornstarch

¼ teaspoon salt

4 ounces dairy-free unsweetened baking chocolate

2 ounces dairy-free semisweet chocolate

¼ cup amaretto, Frangelico (hazelnut) liqueur, orange liqueur, brandy, or rum

1 teaspoon vanilla

Optional: 2 tablespoons good-tasting nondairy margarine

½ cup ground toasted almonds or hazelnuts (filberts)

Chopped toasted almonds or hazelnuts (filberts) or "Amaretti" Crumbs, p. 243, for garnish

Mix the milk, sugar, cornstarch, and salt in a heavy saucepan. Grate the baking chocolate and break the semisweet chocolate into small pieces. Cook the milk mixture over medium-high heat, stirring all the time. When it bubbles and begins to thicken, add the chocolate and continue stirring until the chocolate has melted and the mixture has thickened. Whisk in the liqueur (and optional margarine and nuts, if using).

Microwave Option: Mix in a large microwave-proof bowl the milk, sugar, cornstarch and salt. Add the chocolate, broken into chunks, and microwave for 3 minutes. Whisk and microwave 3 minutes more. Whisk vigorously and add the liqueur and vanilla, and optional margarine and nuts, if using.

Whisk until smooth and pour into 8 custard cups. Place small squares of plastic wrap right on the pudding (touching the surface) and refrigerate several hours, or until firm.

To serve, pull up the plastic wrap and loosen the puddings by immersing for a few seconds in hot water. Invert on a small dessert plate. If you like, sprinkle the top with ground roasted nuts or "Amaretti" Crumbs.

Per serving: Calories: 245, Protein: 3 g, Carbohydrate: 33 g, Fat: 10 g

Chocolate is not used a great deal in Italian cooking—it's more likely to be used as a decoration or in a cake. One delicious exception to that rule is this very rich pudding, which should be reserved for special occasions! It's very easy to make, though. You can use a good-quality unsweetened baking chocolate and a good, eating-quality semisweet chocolate.

Variation: For a lighter, frothier mousse, fold in 1 recipe hot Zabaglione (p. 218, made with more water in place of the wine) while the chocolate mousse mixture is still warm. Pour into wine glasses. This will serve 12 to 14 people.

Lemon Creme

CREMA DI LIMONE

(can be soy-free)

Yield: about 1¾ cups

This simply delicious creme can be used as a pudding or a topping for fruit or cake. You can use low-fat tofu if you're counting calories.

1 (12.3-ounce) box extra-firm *silken* tofu, crumbled
⅓ cup Grade A maple syrup
3 tablespoons fresh lemon juice
1 tablespoon grated lemon zest (preferably organic)

Blend the ingredients well in a blender, until *very* smooth. Chill in a covered container.

To make soy-free, use about 1½ cups Cashew Mascarpone, p. 36, instead of the tofu. Add only ¼ cup maple syrup and 2 tablespoons lemon juice to start with, then taste to see if it needs more.

Per ¼ cup serving: Calories: 68, Protein: 3 g, Carbohydrate: 11 g, Fat: 1 g

Zabaglione

(can be soy-free)

Yield: 6 servings

I didn't think this classic frothy wine custard or dessert sauce could be done without eggs, but this vegan custard is really quite lovely. It works best with a microwave, which causes the mixture to froth up, but I give stove-top instructions as well.

Custard powder is a common item in Canada, Great Britain, Ireland, and Australia. If you can't find it in international gourmet food stores in your area, use an equal amount of cornstarch and add a pinch of Spanish saffron to the water.

1¼ cups water
½ cup marsala or good sherry
6 tablespoons crumbled extra-firm *silken* tofu
6 tablespoons raw cashews
½ cup light unbleached sugar
2 tablespoons plain custard powder
¼ teaspoon salt
1 teaspoon vanilla, or grated orange or lemon zest (organic, if possible)

Notes: You need to use a *total* of 1¾ cups liquid for this recipe, but you can use all water if you are mixing the Zabaglione with a chocolate mousse, or you can use ¾ cup water and 1 cup champagne.

To make soy-free, omit the tofu, use commercial rice or almond milk in place of the water, and increase the cashews to ½ cup.

If you are allergic to corn, use 3 tablespoons white rice flour instead of cornstarch or custard powder.

Blend the liquids in a blender with the tofu, cashews, sugar, custard powder, and salt until it is *very* smooth and frothy with absolutely no graininess. Pour this into a large microwave-proof bowl. Microwave on high for 2 minutes. Whisk and microwave 2 minutes more. Whisk in the vanilla or citrus zest.

Microwave 1 minute to froth it up. Pour into wine glasses. Let it cool slightly, but serve it hot.

To make on top of the stove, whisk the blended mixture in a heavy saucepan over medium-high heat. Whisk it constantly until it is thickened and frothy. Whisk in the vanilla or citrus zest, and pour into wine glasses.

Per serving: Calories: 165, Protein: 3 g, Carbohydrate: 23 g, Fat: 5 g

Tartara Dolce
Make the Zabaglione, using all water for the liquid. Add the grated zest of one whole lemon (preferably organic) at the end, and stir in 1 cup of ground almonds. Serve hot or cold.

Cashew Pastry Creme
CREMA PASTICERRA DI ANACARDI
(soy-free)

Yield: about 2 cups

1½ cups water
5 tablespoons raw cashew pieces
¼ teaspoon salt
½ cup finely ground unbleached sugar (or use ⅔ cup Grade A maple syrup and reduce the water by 2 tablespoons)
1½ tablespoons cornstarch or wheat starch
¼ cup unbleached white flour (Use only 2 tablespoons for a thinner cream.)
1½ teaspoons vanilla extract
1½ teaspoons lemon extract

Make a cashew milk first by blending the water, cashews, and salt

This type of pastry cream (usually thickened with flour and egg yolks and made with dairy cream) is used frequently in Italian desserts. Fortunately, we can use raw cashews to make an extremely rich-tasting creme that contains only about 2 grams of fat per ¼ cup.

To use for Tiramisú, omit the lemon extract and add 2 tablespoons rum or amaretto, or 1 to 2 teaspoons rum extract.

For a dessert sauce, add ¼ cup nondairy milk to each ½ cup of Cashew Pastry Creme.

together in a blender until *very* smooth with absolutely no graininess. Add the remaining ingredients *except* the flavor extracts. Blend until very smooth.

Pour into a heavy-bottomed medium saucepan, and stir constantly over medium-high heat until the mixture is quite thick. Simmer over low heat for 1 minute. Remove from the heat and whisk in the flavoring extracts.

Microwave Option: Pour the blended mixture into a medium microwave-proof bowl or beaker. Microwave on high for 2 minutes. Whisk and microwave 1 minute more. Whisk in the flavoring extracts.

Pour the mixture into a bowl or container, cover with waxed paper or plastic wrap (touching the surface), and refrigerate for up to a week. The mixture should be thoroughly cooled before using.

Per ¼ cup serving: Calories: 97, Protein: 1 g, Carbohydrate: 17 g, Fat: 3 g

Note: To blanch almonds, place whole shelled almonds in their skins in boiling water and boil for about a minute, then drain them and plunge them into cold water. Squeeze each almond between your thumb and forefinger, and it will pop out of the skin. (Be careful that it doesn't shoot across the room!)

Almond Creme
CREMA DI MANDORLE
(soy-free)

Yield: about 1¼ cups

1 cup hot water
½ cup raw blanched almonds (see sidebar above left)
1 to 2 teaspoons Grade A maple syrup
Pinch salt

Almond milk has been used in Europe since medieval times for delicate desserts and sauces. The Arabs brought the use of almonds in cookery to Sicily, and the practice spread to the rest of Italy. Almond milk is still used in desserts in some parts of Italy, particularly in Mantua.

This rich, slightly sweet creme is delicious on desserts or in hot beverages, for those who are allergic to soy, or if the following Sweet Soy Creme isn't rich enough for your purposes. It is higher in fat than the soy creme, however, so use sparingly.

Place all the ingredients in a blender, and process until almost smooth. Strain the creme through fine cheesecloth, squeezing and twisting to get as much liquid out as possible. (The almond pulp can be used as a body or facial scrub.) Store the creme in a tightly covered, sterilized jar in the refrigerator, and shake it before pouring. It only lasts in the refrigerator for 3 or 4 days.

Per 2 tablespoon serving: Calories: 47, Protein: 1 g, Carbohydrate: 2 g, Fat: 4 g

Sweet Soy Creme
CREMA DI SOYA DOLCE

Yield: about ⅞ cup

Thinner Version
¾ cup soymilk, rice milk, or almond milk
¼ cup extra-firm *silken* tofu
2 teaspoons Grade A maple syrup, or to taste
Pinch salt
Optional: ⅛ teaspoon coconut extract (This doesn't make it taste like coconut, but gives the creme a rich flavor.)

Thicker Pouring Version
½ cup soymilk, rice milk, or almond milk
½ cup extra-firm *silken* tofu
4 teaspoons Grade A maple syrup
Pinch salt
Optional: 1 tablespoon neutral cooking oil
¼ teaspoon coconut extract

"Whipped Creme" Version
To the Thicker Pouring Version, add 1 more teaspoon Grade A maple syrup and 2 tablespoons well-cooked short-grain white rice, p. 31.

Combine all the ingredients in a blender, and process until *very* smooth. This can be refrigerated for several days; stir gently before using.

Per 2 tablespoon serving (thinner creme): Calories: 20, Protein: 1 g, Carbohydrate: 2 g, Fat: 1 g

Per 2 tablespoon serving (thicker creme and "whipped" creme): Calories: 28, Protein: 2 g, Carbohydrate: 3 g, Fat: 1 g

This is a very smooth creme for beverages and desserts with a rich flavor and texture that belies its low fat content (which you can reduce even more by using low-fat milk and tofu). You can make a pouring version of two thicknesses or a thicker version that can be used instead of whipped cream.

Sweet Ricotta Creme
CREMA DI RICOTTA DOLCE
(can be soy-free)

Yield: about 1½ cups

Serve this creme over fruit flavored with wine or liqueurs for a simple, sophisticated dessert.

1½ cups Tofu Ricotta, p. 32, or Almond Ricotta, p. 35
¼ cup Grade A maple syrup
1 teaspoon vanilla

Blend the ingredients until *very* smooth. Chill before serving.

Per 2 tablespoon serving: Calories: 57, Protein: 2 g, Carbohydrate: 6 g, Fat: 2 g

Vegan Genoise Cake
TORTA MADDALENA O PASTA GENOVESE VEGAN
(can be soy-free)

Yield: two 8-inch layers (8 servings)

This is the basic layer cake for Italian desserts. It can also take the place of Pan di Spagna or Bocca di Dama (sponge cakes), or even Savoiardi (ladyfingers), when cut into "fingers." I wanted to make a cake that was light and "buttery," but fairly low in fat and easy to make. This one won't disappoint if you use a good-quality dairy-free margarine.

1¾ cups white or whole wheat pastry or cake flour
1 cup light unbleached sugar, finely ground in a dry blender
2 teaspoons baking powder
1 teaspoon baking soda
½ teaspoon salt

¼ cup good-tasting dairy-free margarine
⅔ cup water
½ cup soymilk or rice milk
2 teaspoons vinegar
2 teaspoons vanilla, or 1 teaspoon pure almond or lemon extract

Preheat the oven to 350°F.

Mix the dry ingredients together with a whisk in a large mixing bowl. Add the margarine and water, and beat with an electric mixer for a minute. Add the remaining ingredients, and beat one more minute. Divide equally between two round 8-inch greased and floured cake pans. Bake for 25 minutes, or until the cakes test done. Cool on racks for 5 minutes, then loosen the cakes and remove from the pans to finish cooling.

Per serving: Calories: 235, Protein: 3 g, Carbohydrate: 42 g, Fat: 6 g

Tiramisú

(can be soy-free)

Yield: 6 to 8 servings

1 layer Genoise (half recipe, p. 222), either vanilla, almond, or the chocolate variation (see sidebar, this page)

⅓ cup freshly brewed espresso or espresso made with 1 packet instant espresso powder

3 tablespoons rum, amaretto, or liqueur-flavored Italian syrup (the type found in espresso shops)

1 recipe Cashew Pastry Creme, p. 219, omitting the lemon extract and adding either 2 tablespoons rum or amaretto or 1 to 2 teaspoons rum extract

1 recipe Sweet Soy Creme ("whipped creme" version, p. 221), or the almond variation of Sweet "Ricotta" Creme, p. 222

1 tablespoon Dutch cocoa powder, or 2 tablespoons grated semisweet chocolate

Cut the cake layer in half horizontally. Combine the espresso and rum in a small cup.

In a shallow, flat-bottomed casserole or bowl (preferably clear glass and about 9 inches in diameter), place one half of the cake. Sprinkle with half the espresso-rum mixture. Spread half the pastry creme over the cake, then place the second slice of cake over that. Sprinkle that with the remaining espresso mixture, and

Torta Maddalena al Cioccolato

In the Genoise recipe, substitute ⅓ cup of Dutch cocoa powder for ⅓ cup of the pastry flour. Use vanilla or almond extract.

Tiramisú, a fairly modern invention, means "pick-me-up," and it is currently one of the most popular desserts in both Italy and North America. It can be loosely described as an Italian trifle—cake or ladyfingers layered with custard and liquor and topped with whipped cream. The custard layer is usually a mixture of egg custard and mascarpone cheese, but I have found that Cashew Pastry Creme makes an excellent, rich-tasting alternate.

You can create your own recipe by using different liqueurs and layering fresh fruit with the Creme, if you like.

This should be made several hours or even days before serving—the perfect company dessert!

spread the remaining creme over that. Top with the "whipped creme," and sprinkle with the cocoa. Cover and refrigerate for at least 4 hours; use within 3 days.

Per serving: Calories: 295, Protein: 5 g, Carbohydrate: 49 g, Fat: 7 g

"Diplomatica"

Make the Tiramisú, but replace the Pastry Creme, layer with ½ recipe of Chocolate Mousse, p. 216, mixed with ½ recipe Zabaglione, p. 218, made with all water instead of wine.

Dessert Crepes with Creme Filling
CRESPELLE ALLA CREMA
(can be soy-free)

Yield: 4 servings

Sweet crepes are an excellent choice for a company dessert, because all of the components can be made ahead. These are delicious with strawberries, peaches, or other fresh fruit added to the sauce.

You can make the crepes the day before or in the morning, if you like. They can even be frozen for a week or two, but thaw them thoroughly before using in this recipe.

The sauce can also be made ahead and reheated.

12 Dessert Crepes, p. 106
1 recipe Cashew Pastry Creme, p. 219, well chilled
⅓ cup rum or brandy*
⅓ cup bottled Italian fruit syrup of your choice, Grade A maple syrup, or frozen fruit juice concentrate (such as orange)
Optional: **1 cup of fresh fruit, trimmed and chopped**
1 tablespoon light unbleached sugar

*If you prefer not to use alcohol, you can use any favorite fruit sauce, flavored with citrus zest or almond flavoring.

Make the pastry creme *at least* an hour before you plan to assemble the crepes. It should be chilled when you spread it.

Preheat the oven to 450°F.

Spread each crepe generously with some of the chilled pastry creme, and fold it into quarters. Arrange the crepes slightly overlapping in an attractive shallow, baking dish. Heat the rum or brandy and the syrup together over medium heat, stirring constantly until it bubbles. (Add fruit at this point, if using.) Pour it over the crepes, and sprinkle the sugar over them. Bake the crepes for about 10 minutes, or until the sugar begins to caramelize.

Per serving: Calories: 480, Protein: 12 g, Carbohydrate: 80 g, Fat: 8 g

Italian Sweet Pastry

PASTA FROLLA

(can be soy-free)

Yield: 1 or 2 (9″ to 10″) crusts (12 to 24 servings)

One 9- or 10-inch crust

½ cup minus 1 tablespoon white cake or pastry flour plus ½
cup whole wheat flour,
or ½ cup minus 1 tablespoon whole wheat pastry flour plus
½ cup unbleached white flour

⅜ teaspoon baking powder

⅜ teaspoon salt

2 to 4 tablespoons finely ground unbleached sugar

3 tablespoons nondairy milk mixed with ½ teaspoon lemon
juice

3 tablespoons neutral cooking oil, such as canola or safflower

½ teaspoon pure lemon extract

¼ teaspoon vanilla

Two 9- or 10-inch crusts

⅞ cup white cake or pastry flour plus 1 cup whole wheat flour,
or ⅞ cup whole wheat pastry flour plus 1 cup unbleached
white flour

¾ teaspoon baking powder

¾ teaspoon salt

¼ to ½ cup finely ground unbleached sugar

6 tablespoons nondairy milk mixed with 1 teaspoon lemon
juice

6 tablespoons neutral cooking oil, such as canola or safflower

1 teaspoon pure lemon extract

½ teaspoon vanilla

Italians prefer a rather sweet crust in their pastries, and most recipes for this are rich with butter. I have adapted the Low-Fat Oil Pastry from my second book, *The Almost No-Fat Holiday Cookbook*, and I think the results are wonderful—a light and tender crust with half the fat of ordinary pastry and which utilizes oil rather than hydrogenated fats or butter.

Note: It is important to use half cake or pastry flour.

Mix the dry ingredients in a bowl. In a smaller bowl, whisk the
nondairy milk and lemon juice mixture with the oil and extracts.
Quickly stir the liquid mixture into the dry ingredients, and mix

briefly, forming the pastry into a ball. If it's too dry, add cold water just a few drops at a time until it holds together. Don't overmix or the pastry will be tough.

If made ahead of time, place the dough in a plastic bag and refrigerate it until you're ready to roll it out. (You can do this several hours or even several days ahead of time.) Use the pastry as instructed in the recipe you're making.

To pre-bake an unfilled crust, preheat the oven to 425°F. Roll out the dough to fit a 9- or 10-inch tart or pie pan. (If using a pie pan, just bring the pastry up to the inside top of the pan and flute it to make a shallow shell—not over the edge.) Trim the top edge neatly, then prick the bottom and sides with a fork. Place a square of foil over the dough, and weight down with a layer of dried beans. Bake 6 minutes. Remove the beans and foil, and bake 8 minutes more. Cool the pastry on a rack.

Microwave Option: Use a glass or ceramic pan, prick the pastry all over, and microwave on high for 6 to 7 minutes, or until the pastry is opaque and the bottom is dry. The pastry will not brown.

Note: The recipe for one crust will make 12 small tart shells (cut into 4-inch circles). To bake unfilled shells, prick the bottoms with a fork and bake at 425°F for 8 to 10 minutes.

Per serving: Calories: 72, Protein: 1 g, Carbohydrate: 9 g, Fat: 3 g

Almond Ricotta Tart
TORTA DI RICOTTA DI MANDORLE
(soy-free)

Yield: 12 servings
Italian Sweet Pastry, p. 225, for one 9-inch crust

Filling
½ cup golden raisins soaked in 2 tablespoons marsala, dry sherry, or a nonalcoholic sweet wine for 15 minutes
½ teaspoon agar powder, or 1 tablespoon agar flakes

Sweet ricotta tart is one of the best known Italian desserts. This smooth and creamy version utilizes the Almond Ricotta that I devised for soy-allergic vegans, but it's so delicious that I can't decide whether I like it, or the Tofu Ricotta Tart on page 228 better! Let the tart cool for several hours before serving.

1 cup hot water
½ cup whole blanched almonds
1 cup cold water
4 teaspoons fresh lemon juice
4 tablespoons cornstarch or wheat starch
1 tablespoon neutral cooking oil, such as canola or safflower
½ teaspoon salt
½ cup light unbleached sugar
¼ cup chopped dried cherries, apricots, or cranberries
2 tablespoons toasted pine nuts or chopped toasted almonds
Grated zest of 1 medium orange (preferably organic)

Preheat the oven to 350°F.

Roll out the crust and place it in a 9-inch pie or tart pan; trim or crimp the edge of the crust. Refrigerate while you make the filling.

Pour off any wine that hasn't soaked into the raisins, and mix it with the agar and 1 tablespoon of water. Set aside.

Place the hot water and almonds in the blender, and process until a very smooth "cream" results. Be patient—it cannot be grainy. Add the cold water, lemon juice, cornstarch, oil, and salt. Blend again, then pour the mixture into a medium, heavy-bottomed saucepan, and stir constantly over medium-high heat until it thickens and comes to a boil. Turn the heat down to medium, and cook one minute more, stirring.

Microwave Option: Pour the mixture into a large, microwave-safe bowl or beaker. Microwave on high for 2 minutes. Whisk and microwave 1 or 2 minutes more, or until thickened.

Whisk the sugar into the hot mixture, then add the dissolved agar. Stir in the raisins, other dried fruit, chopped nuts, and orange zest.

Scrape the mixture into the prepared pie crust, and bake for 45 minutes. Cool the tart on a rack for a couple of hours, covered by a clean tea towel, then refrigerate it until it is thoroughly cooled and firm. Cut into small wedges to serve.

Per serving: Calories: 198, Protein: 3 g, Carbohydrate: 27 g, Fat: 8 g

Tofu Ricotta Tart

TORTA DI RICOTTA DI SOYA

Yield: 12 servings

A classic Italian dessert and very simple to make.

Italian Sweet Pastry, p. 225, for one 9-inch crust

Filling

**½ cup golden raisins soaked in 2 tablespoons marsala, dry
    sherry, or nonalcoholic sweet wine for 15 minutes**
1 pound medium-firm tofu, drained and crumbled
6 ounces firm tofu, drained and crumbled
¾ cup light unbleached sugar
2 tablespoons fresh lemon juice
1 tablespoon neutral cooking oil, such as canola or safflower
1 tablespoon cornstarch or wheat starch
1 teaspoon pure vanilla extract
1 teaspoon lemon extract
½ teaspoon agar powder, or 1 tablespoon agar flakes
¼ cup chopped dried cherries, apricots, or cranberries
2 tablespoons lightly toasted pine nuts, or chopped almonds
Grated zest of 1 medium orange (preferably organic)

Preheat the oven to 350°F.

Roll out the crust and place it in a 9-inch pie or tart pan; trim or crimp the edge of the crust. Refrigerate while you make the filling.

Pour off any wine that hasn't soaked into the raisins. Set the excess wine aside.

Place the two kinds of tofu, the sugar, lemon juice, oil, cornstarch, extracts, agar, and excess wine in a food processor or blender. Process until quite smooth. If using a processor, add the orange zest, raisins, other dried fruit, and nuts. Pulse just briefly to distribute them, not chop them. Otherwise, pour the mixture into a bowl, and mix in the fruits and nuts with a spoon.

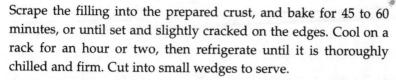

Scrape the filling into the prepared crust, and bake for 45 to 60 minutes, or until set and slightly cracked on the edges. Cool on a rack for an hour or two, then refrigerate until it is thoroughly chilled and firm. Cut into small wedges to serve.

Per serving: Calories: 209, Protein: 5 g, Carbohydrate: 29 g, Fat: 7 g

Apple Tart
CROSTATA DI MELE
(can be soy-free)

Yield: 1 10-inch tart (8 servings)

This delicious tart is very popular during winter months in Italy, as I'm sure it will be in your home.

Italian Sweet Pastry for one 10-inch crust, p. 225
3 large, tart apples
¾ cup thick, lightly sweetened applesauce
Optional: **Pinch of ground cinnamon**
Nondairy milk for brushing

Apricot Glaze:
½ cup apricot preserves (preferably fruit-sweetened)
2 tablespoons fresh lemon juice

Preheat the oven to 350°F.

Roll out the dough to fit a 10-inch tart or pie pan. (If using a pie pan, just bring the pastry up to the inside top of the pan and flute it, to make a shallow shell—not over the edge.) Trim the top edge neatly. Prick the bottom and sides with a fork, and pre-bake the dough for 5 minutes. Cool the pastry on a rack. Leave the oven on.

While the pastry cools, peel, halve, and core the apples, then thinly slice. Mix in the cinnamon, if using, with the applesauce, and spread it over the cooled pastry shell. Arrange the apple slices overlapping in concentric circles. Brush the apples with a little nondairy milk.

Bake about 25 to 30 minutes.

Meanwhile, make an apricot glaze by combining the preserves and lemon juice in a small saucepan and bringing to a boil. Strain it through a fine mesh sieve. While the syrup is still hot, brush the glaze over the apples. Cool before serving. Serve with Zabaglione, p. 218, the "whipped creme" version of Sweet Soy Creme, p. 221, or Sweet Ricotta Creme, p. 222.

Per serving: Calories: 212, Protein: 2 g, Carbohydrate: 38 g, Fat: 5 g

Strawberry Creme Tart
CROSTATA DI FRAGOLE CON CREMA
(can be soy-free)

Yield: one 9-inch tart (8 servings)

Italian Sweet Pastry for one 9-inch crust, p. 225
2 pounds whole small strawberries, or large strawberries, quartered or halved
Optional: **3 tablespoons cherry liqueur or rum**
¼ cup light unbleached sugar (plus a little to sprinkle on top)

Cashew Pastry Creme, p. 219, cooled

Italians are very fond of strawberry desserts, and this is a sumptuous version of strawberry tart. Use sweet, ripe berries.

Don't make this too far ahead of time or it will get soggy and the strawberries will run. Enjoy it the day that it is made.

Wash and trim the strawberries, then mix with the ¼ cup sugar and optional liqueur. Set aside while you make the pastry.

Preheat the oven to 425°F.

Roll out the dough to fit a 9-inch pie or tart pan. (If using a pie pan, flute the edge just below the top of the pan to make a shallow shell.) Trim the edge neatly and prick the dough all over with a fork. Place a square of foil over the dough, and weight down with a layer of dried beans. Bake 6 minutes. Remove the beans and foil, and bake 8 minutes more. Cool the pastry on a rack. (To microwave, see the option on page 226.)

Spread the pastry creme over the bottom of the crust. Arrange the drained strawberries attractively over the creme, and sprinkle with a little sugar. Chill until serving time.

Per serving: Calories: 262, Protein: 3 g, Carbohydrate: 43 g, Fat: 8 g

Lemon Tart
CROSTATA DI LIMONE
(can be soy-free)

Yield: one 10-inch tart (10 servings)

The filling for this tart is very much like a lemon meringue pie, but without the meringue.

Italian Sweet Pastry for one 10-inch crust, p. 225

Filling
1 cup light unbleached sugar
⅔ cup soymilk or rice milk
7 tablespoons hot water with a pinch of saffron soaked in it
6 tablespoons cornstarch or wheat starch
¼ teaspoon salt
½ cup freshly squeezed lemon juice
2 tablespoons grated lemon zest (preferably organic), or 2 teaspoons pure lemon extract
1 to 4 tablespoons good-tasting dairy-free margarine (depending on how rich you want it)

Sweet Soy Creme ("whipped creme" version, p. 221), or Sweet Ricotta Creme, p. 222

Preheat the oven to 425°F.

Roll out the dough to fit a 10-inch pie or tart pan. (If using a pie pan, flute the edge just below the top of the pan to make a shallow shell.) Trim the edge neatly and prick the dough all over with a fork. Place a square of foil over the dough, and weight down with a layer of dried beans. Bake 6 minutes. Remove the beans and foil, and bake 8 minutes more. Cool the pastry on a rack.

Microwave Option: Use a glass or ceramic pie plate or tart pan. Prick the pastry all over with a fork, and microwave on high for 6 to 7 minutes, or until the pastry is opaque and the bottom is dry. The pastry will not brown.

To make the filling, whisk the sugar, nondairy milk, water/saffron mixture, cornstarch, and salt in a medium saucepan with a heavy bottom. Stir over high heat until it thickens and boils. Let it boil one minute, then whisk in the lemon juice, lemon zest or extract, and margarine. (Do not add the lemon juice to the cornstarch mixture until it is fully cooked, or the acid will interfere with the thickening of the starch.) Cool 5 minutes.

Microwave Option: Pour the blended mixture into a medium microwave-proof bowl, and cook on high for 2 minutes. Whisk. Microwave on high 1 or 2 more minutes, or until thick and glistening or translucent. Whisk in the lemon juice, lemon zest or extract, and margarine. Cool 5 minutes.

Pour the lemon mixture into the crust, and smooth it out evenly. Cover the filling with a piece of waxed paper cut to fit. Refrigerate for a couple of hours or until cool and firm.

Just before serving, lift off the waxed paper and decorate with the whipped or ricotta creme.

Per serving: Calories: 233, Protein: 3 g, Carbohydrate: 37 g, Fat: 8 g

Italian Fresh Fruit Tart
CROSTATA DI FRUTTA FRESCA
(can be soy-free)

Yield: one 9- or 10-inch tart (8 servings)

Italian Sweet Pastry for one 10-inch crust, prebaked, p. 225
½ recipe Cashew Pastry Creme, p. 219, chilled
2 to 3 cups prepared fruit (see sidebars at left and right)

This tart can be made with any fresh, ripe berry or fruit. The fruit is placed raw over Cashew Pastry Creme in a baked pastry shell and glazed to shiny perfection with jelly. A perfect ending to any festive meal or a delightful mid-afternoon snack!

Use whole, halved, or sliced berries or grapes (depending on their size), halved, pitted sweet cherries, or peeled, sliced

Glaze:

½ cup apricot or peach jam or preserves

2 tablespoons fresh lemon juice

Spread the cooled baked pie shell with the chilled pastry creme. Arrange the fruit artistically over the creme. Overlap slightly, if necessary, and cover the creme completely.

To make the glaze, bring the jam and lemon juice to a boil in a small saucepan. Strain it through a fine-mesh sieve.

While the glaze is still hot, brush the glaze over the fruit in a thin film. Keep brushing thinly until it is used up. Chill the tart until serving time.

Per serving: Calories: 284, Protein: 3 g, Carbohydrate: 50 g, Fat: 8 g

Vegan Italian Vanilla Ice Cream
GELATO VEGAN ALLA VANIGLIA
(can be soy-free)

Yield: 4 cups

Mixture #1

¾ cup water

½ cup white corn syrup

1 tablespoon vanilla

Mixture #2

1 cup water

¾ cup commercial soymilk, almond milk, or rice milk

½ cup raw cashew pieces

½ cup Grade A maple syrup

1 tablespoon tapioca starch

¼ teaspoon salt

pears, nectarines, peaches, apricots, plums, even kiwis or mangoes. Paint the fruit with the glaze right away to prevent browning, and serve the tart the same day it is made.

Note: You can make individual-sized fruit tarts, if you like.

In this delightful frozen treat, I use a combination of white corn syrup, which has a neutral flavor and discourages ice crystals from forming, and Grade A maple syrup instead of white sugar. I found that the flavor of even the lightest unbleached cane sugars wasn't "clean" enough for this vanilla version, though it's fine in coffee, chocolate, or mocha-flavored gelati. Tapioca starch makes this gelato smooth and custardy without the mouth-feel of a "frozen pudding."

This gelato is not fat-free, but it is lower in fat than so-called premium ice creams. You can use the basic recipe to make up your own favorite flavors of gelati or regular North American-style "nice cream."

Italian "Ice Creams," Sherbets, and Ices

(Gelati, Sorbetti, e Granite)

Homemade frozen desserts tend to get rock-hard in the freezer, because they don't contain chemicals that trap air in the mixture, as commercial ice creams often do. If you add some wine or liqueur to your mixture, they won't freeze as solidly, however (see Sorbetti, page 238). For non-alcoholic frozen desserts, plan ahead before serving them to guests. Place the container in the refrigerator for 45 to 60 minutes, or let set at room temperature for 20 to 30 minutes, to soften a little.

If you have forgotten to take the gelato out to soften, you can soften the whole container in the microwave at 50 percent power for about 2 minutes, checking at 1 minute or 30 second intervals. (For less than a full batch, it will take less time.)

Blend Mixture #1 in a blender, then set aside in a measuring cup.

Blend Mixture #2 in a blender until *very* smooth and frothy. (Make sure that it doesn't feel grainy.) Place this mixture in a heavy-bottomed medium saucepan, and stir over medium-high heat until thickened.

Microwave Option: Place Mixture #2 in a large, microwave-proof bowl, and microwave on high for 2 minutes. Whisk and cook 2 minutes more. Whisk and cook 1 minute more.

Whisk Mixture #1 into cooked Mixture #2. Chill the gelato mixture and then freeze according to directions for your ice cream machine. Scoop into a 1-quart plastic container, cover, and freeze for several hours before serving.

Per ½ cup serving: Calories: 175, Protein: 2 g, Carbohydrate: 32 g, Fat: 5 g

"Ice Cream" Variations

Italian gelati tend to be simple flavors.

Banana (Banane)

Use only 1 teaspoon vanilla. Add 1 cup mashed ripe banana to Mixture #1 when blending.

Marsala "Custard" (Zabaglione)

Omit the vanilla and use ⅓ cup marsala wine (or good sherry) plus water to make ¾ cup in Mixture #1.

Coffee (Caffé o Cappuccino)

You can use any kind of unbleached cane sugar instead of maple syrup, if you wish. Use only 1 teaspoon vanilla and add 2 tablespoons (4 little packets) espresso powder to Mixture #2. If you like, you can also add 1½ tablespoons coffee liqueur to Mixture #1.

Lemon (Limone)

Omit the vanilla and use 1 tablespoon pure lemon extract.

Almond *(Mandorle)*

Use only 1 teaspoon vanilla, and add ½ teaspoon pure almond extract. If you like, add 2 tablespoons amaretto liqueur to Mixture #1. Add ½ cup chopped roasted almonds when the mixture is half-frozen. (You could also add ½ cup dairy-free chocolate chips, if you like.)

Hazelnut or Filbert *(Nocciole)*

Use only 1 teaspoon vanilla, and add ½ cup chopped roasted hazelnuts (filberts) when the mixture is half-frozen. If you like, you can add 2 tablespoons Frangelico (hazelnut liqueur) to Mixture #1.

Walnut *(Noci)*

Use only 1 teaspoon vanilla, and add ½ cup chopped toasted walnuts when the mixture is half-frozen.

Pistachio *(Pistachio)*

Use only 1 teaspoon vanilla, and add ½ cup chopped roasted pistachios when the mixture is half-frozen.

Frutta *(Fruit)*

Use only 1 to 2 teaspoons vanilla. Omit the 1 cup water from Mixture #2. Blend the rest of the ingredients until very smooth, as instructed, then add 3 to 3½ cups (¾ to 1 pound) berries or pitted, peeled, chopped fresh fruit, which have been previously blended smooth in a food processor or blender. To tangy fruits, add 1 tablespoon fresh lemon juice. To more bland fruits, such as cultivated blueberries, use 2 tablespoons lemon juice. Blend together well, then proceed with the recipe. Yield: about 5 cups

You can use any berry, or peaches, mangoes, kiwis—whatever you like or have an abundance of. If you like, add a bit of citrus rind or citrus extract, or an appropriate liqueur (up to 2 tablespoons).

Note: You can use frozen fruit, too, but measure it while frozen, and then let it thaw out before puréeing.

If You Have No Ice Cream Machine

You can still make smooth gelati and sorbetti. Freeze the mixture in flat pans, not too deep, placed inside of plastic bags. When ready to serve, cut the frozen mixture into chunks and run them quickly through your food processor or Champion juicer with the blank in place until creamy. Serve *immediately*, or just keep in the freezer for a very short time before serving. This method can also be used to make hard-frozen churned gelati and sorbetti smooth just before serving.

Vegan Chocolate Ice Cream
GELATO DI CIOCCOLATA VEGAN
(can be soy-free)

Yield: 1 quart

This is so smooth and rich tasting that your guests will not believe it is dairy-free!

4 ounces dairy-free semisweet chocolate, cut into small pieces, or semisweet chocolate chips

Mixture #1
¾ cup water
½ cup corn syrup (any kind)
1 teaspoon vanilla
***Optional*: 1½ tablespoons amaretto, Frangelico, Kahlua, or other coffee, chocolate, or nut liqueur**

Mixture #2
1 cup water
¾ cup commercial soymilk, almond milk, or rice milk
½ cup raw cashew pieces
½ cup unbleached sugar, or Grade A maple syrup
¼ cup Dutch cocoa powder (unsweetened)
1 tablespoon tapioca starch
¼ teaspoon salt
***Optional*: ½ cup chopped toasted nuts and/or ½ cup dairy-free semisweet chocolate chips**

Melt the 4 ounces chocolate in a small pan over barely simmering hot water. Keep melted over the hot water but off the heat.

Combine Mixture #1 in a blender until well mixed, then set aside in a bowl.

Blend Mixture #2 in blender until it is *very* smooth and frothy. (Make sure that it is not grainy at all.) Place this mixture in a heavy-bottomed medium saucepan, and stir over medium-high heat until thickened.

Microwave Option: Place Mixture #2 in a large, microwave-proof bowl, and microwave on high for 2 minutes. Whisk and cook 2 minutes more. Whisk and cook 1 minute more.

Whisk Mixture #1 into cooked Mixture #2, along with the melted chocolate. Chill the gelato mixture and then freeze according to the directions for your ice cream machine. Scoop into a 1-quart plastic container, cover, and freeze for several hours before serving.

Per ½ cup serving: Calories: 253, Protein: 3 g, Carbohydrate: 40 g, Fat: 9 g

Mocha "Ice Cream"
Omit the cocoa powder and add 2 tablespoons (4 little packets) espresso powder. If using a liqueur, use a coffee one.

Chocolate "Ice Cream" Ball
TARTUFO
(can be soy-free)

Yield: 8 balls

¾ cup dairy-free semisweet chocolate, chopped up, or chips
1 recipe Vegan Chocolate Ice Cream, p. 236, made with ½ cup
small chunks of dairy-free semisweet chocolate or mini-chips
added

Grind the ¾ cup chocolate in a dry blender or food processor until almost powdery. Place in a mound on waxed paper.

Scoop the gelato into 8 equal portions, and shape somewhat into balls with your hands or two large spoons.

Roll the balls in the ground chocolate to coat all over. Place slightly apart on a chilled cookie sheet, and freeze until firm, at least one hour. You can store them for up to two weeks, but in that case, cover them well in plastic wrap.

Serve the tartufi on cold dessert plates or glasses. You can garnish them with your favorite sweet "cream" (pp. 219-22), if you like.

Per ball: Calories: 388, Protein: 4 g, Carbohydrate: 54 g, Fat: 17 g

This is a rich chocolate confection found in Roman ice cream bars. It is a perfect ending for a memorable dinner party.

When making tartufo, work quickly, preferably with a friend!

Sometimes the ice cream balls are rolled in ground toasted almonds or hazelnuts (filberts) instead of chocolate.

Sorbetti e Granite

It used to be that gelati and sorbetti referred to the same thing, but now most people think of gelati as a rich ice cream, and sorbetti as a smooth, light fruit ice, almost like a sherbet. Granite are actually crystallized sweetened juices or coffee. I find that these no-fat desserts are so intensely flavored that you don't need to eat much to feel satisfied. Then you aren't tempted to overeat calories, as you are with some other no-fat desserts.

These desserts are descendants of recipes that came originally from China, travelled to India and the Middle East, and then to Sicily with the Arabs.

All of these ices will get very hard in the freezer unless they contain a good proportion of wine or other alcohol, which doesn't freeze, or you can add a bit of kosher (vegetarian) gelatin or agar. Ideally they should be made as needed. If not, they can be cut into chunks and run through a food processor or Champion juicer to become smooth again.

Note: When I call for white wine in a sorbetto, I prefer a dry one, but you can use one with a higher sugar content, such as a Riesling, if you wish.

Pear Sorbet

SORBETTO DI PERE

(soy-free)

Yield: about 3 cups

So simple, but it seems the very essence of the fruit.

4 large, ripe, firm pears
1 cup white wine (can be nonalcoholic), white vermouth, or a
  hard or soft pear cider
⅔ cup light unbleached sugar
2 tablespoons fresh lemon juice
Optional: **1 teaspoon grated lemon zest (preferably organic)**

Note: If you use a nonalcoholic cider or wine, add 1 teaspoon Emes Kosher Gelatin soaked in 1 tablespoon water to the hot mixture, or use ¼ teaspoon powdered agar or 1½ teaspoons agar flakes, soaked in the cider for a few minutes, and then cooked with the pear mixture. This keeps the sorbet from going rock-hard without the alcohol.

Place the wine, sugar, and lemon juice in a stainless steel or enamel saucepan over medium heat.

Peel, quarter, core, and chunk the pears, and add to the pan. Simmer the pears uncovered for 5 to 8 minutes, or until tender. Purée the whole mixture in a blender or food processor until smooth. Chill the mixture, then freeze according to directions for your machine.

Per ½ cup serving: Calories: 173, Protein: 1 g, Carbohydrate: 35 g, Fat: 0 g

Peach Sorbet

SORBETTO DI PESCHE

(soy-free)

Yield: about 4 cups

This makes peach season worth waiting for!

2½ cups fresh ripe peaches (about 6 medium peaches), peeled
  and cut-up,
  or 16 ounces frozen unsweetened peaches, almost thawed

¾ to 1 cup light unbleached sugar

1 cup water

1 cup white wine (can be nonalcoholic), champagne or other
    sparkling wine, white vermouth, or a hard or dry peach cider

3 tablespoons fresh lemon juice

Optional: 1½ teaspoons grated orange zest (organic, preferably)

Note: If you prefer, you can omit the wine and use ½ cup marsala (or good sherry) and ½ cup more water, or ¾ cup water and ¼ cup Amaretto or peach brandy. If you use a nonalcoholic cider or wine, add 1 teaspoon Emes Kosher Gelatin soaked in 1 tablespoon water to the hot mixture, or use ¼ teaspoon powdered agar or 1½ teaspoons agar flakes, soaked in the cider for a few minutes, and then cooked with the peach mixture. This keeps the sorbet from going rock-hard without the alcohol.

Blend the peaches and lemon juice in a blender or food processor until smooth. Dissolve the sugar in the water in a small stainless steel saucepan over high heat, stirring occasionally. Pour this into the blended peaches with the wine and orange zest, if using. Blend briefly and chill. Freeze according to directions for your machine.

Per ½ cup serving: Calories: 117, Protein: 1 g, Carbohydrate: 24 g, Fat: 0 g

Granite should consist of rather coarse crystals. To achieve this, freeze the granita mixture in a shallow pan until it's nearly firm. Stir the ice crystals at the edge of the pan into the center, and scrape the granita crystals into tall dessert glasses.

If you let the granita mixture freeze solid, you can either let it thaw a little until you can scrape the crystals, or you can break it into chunks and run it quickly through the food processor—however this will make it a bit smoother than a real granita.

Strawberry Sorbet
SORBETTO DI FRAGOLE
(soy-free)

Yield: about 4 cups

2 pints fresh strawberries, sliced

1 tablespoon lemon juice

¾ cup light unbleached sugar

¾ cup water

¾ cup fruity white wine, such as Riesling (can be
    nonalcoholic), or a hard or soft cider

Optional: 2 tablespoons orange liqueur

Strawberries are always a favorite Italian fruit.

If you wish, instead of water you can use fresh orange juice or ½ cup water and ¼ cup marsala (or good sherry).

Note: If you use a nonalcoholic cider or wine, add 1 teaspoon Emes Kosher Gelatin soaked in 1 tablespoon water to the hot mixture, or use ¼ teaspoon powdered agar or 1½ teaspoons agar flakes, soaked in the cider for a few minutes, and then cooked with the strawberry mixture. This keeps the sorbet from going rock-hard without the alcohol.

Purée the strawberries and lemon juice in a food processor or blender. Dissolve the sugar in the water in a stainless steel saucepan over high heat, stirring. Combine with the berries and wine. Chill and freeze according to the directions with your machine.

Per ½ cup serving: Calories: 105, Protein: 1 g, Carbohydrate: 22 g, Fat: 0 g

Chocolate Sorbet
SORBETTO DI CIOCCOLATA
(soy-free)

Yield: about 3 cups

This dessert tastes so rich and intense that it's hard to believe that it is a water ice! Only for confirmed chocolate-lovers!

Note: Be sure to use only Dutch cocoa.

2¼ cups water
1 cup unbleached sugar
½ cup unsweetened Dutch cocoa
2 tablespoons coffee, almond, hazelnut, or orange liqueur
(If you don't use alcohol, see note below and omit liqueurs; in that case, you can use some coffee or orange juice in place of some of the water for increased flavor)
Optional: **1 tablespoon grated orange zest (preferably organic)**

Note: If you omit the liqueur, add 1 teaspoon Emes Kosher Gelatin soaked in 1 tablespoon water to the hot mixture, or use ¼ teaspoon powdered agar or 1½ teaspoons agar flakes, soaked in the cider for a few minutes, and then cooked with the chocolate mixture. This keeps the sorbet from going rock-hard without the alcohol.

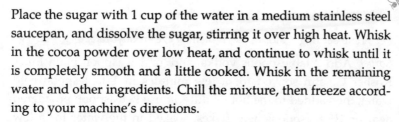

Place the sugar with 1 cup of the water in a medium stainless steel saucepan, and dissolve the sugar, stirring it over high heat. Whisk in the cocoa powder over low heat, and continue to whisk until it is completely smooth and a little cooked. Whisk in the remaining water and other ingredients. Chill the mixture, then freeze according to your machine's directions.

Per ½ cup serving: Calories: 150, Protein: 2 g, Carbohydrate: 33 g, Fat: 1 g

Lemon Granita or Sorbet
GRANITA O SORBETTO DI LIMONE
(soy-free)

Yield: about 4½ cups

3 cups water
1 cup light unbleached sugar
⅔ to 1 cup fresh lemon juice
Finely grated zest from 1 lemon (preferably organic)
2 teaspoons pure lemon extract
Dash salt

Granita: In a medium stainless steel pot, heat 1 cup of the water with the sugar over high heat, stirring until it is dissolved. Add the remaining ingredients and chill. You can freeze this according to your machine's directions, or freeze the granita mixture in a shallow pan until it's nearly firm. Stir the ice crystals at the edge of the pan into the center, and scrape the granita crystals into tall dessert glasses. The crystals are supposed to be rather coarse—not smooth like a sorbet.

If you let the granita mixture freeze solid, you can either let it thaw a little until you can scrape the crystals, or you can break it into chunks and run it quickly through the food processor. This, however, will

Lemon granita is one of the most popular ices in Italy. If you omit the vodka or vegetarian gelatin, it's a granita; if you use the alcohol or gelatin, it stays smooth and is more like a sorbet.

Grapefruit Granita
Omit the lemon juice, lemon zest, and lemon extract. Use 2 cups fresh grapefruit juice in place of 2 cups of the water. Use about 1 tablespoon finely grated grapefruit zest (preferably organic.)

Orange Granita
Omit the lemon juice, lemon zest, and lemon extract. Use 2 cups orange juice in place of 2 cups of the water. Use the finely grated rind of 1 orange (preferably organic). You may like to add 2 to 3 tablespoons fresh lemon juice to the mixture.

Herbal Granita
You might like to try adding some fresh herbs from your garden to a citrus sorbetto or granita. Try 2 tablespoons of fresh chopped mint, lemon balm, or basil, or 1 tablespoon fresh tarragon or rosemary.

make it a bit smoother than a real granita.

Per ½ cup serving: Calories: 86, Protein: 0 g, Carbohydrate: 43 g, Fat: 0 g

Sorbet: Add 2 tablespoons vodka, and/or 1 teaspoon plain Emes Kosher Gelatin soaked for a few minutes in 1 tablespoon cold water, then added to the hot mixture, *or* use ¼ teaspoon powdered agar or 1½ teaspoons agar flakes, soaked in the water for a few minutes, and then cooked with the sugar mixture. This keeps the sorbet from going rock-hard without the alcohol.

Coffee Ice

GRANITA DI CAFFÉ

(can be soy-free)

Yield: about 4 cups

This is a great way to take your afternoon coffee on a hot summer day! Use dark roast coffee, freshly brewed (preferably freshly ground)—it can be Swiss water-decaffeinated. If possible, use organic, "fair trade" coffee.

1 cup water
¾ cup unbleached sugar
2 cups strong coffee or espresso
***Optional*: Piece of cinnamon stick or a strip of orange zest (preferably organic), or 2 tablespoons coffee, chocolate, hazelnut, almond, or orange liqueur, or brandy**
***Optional*: Sweet Soy Creme, p. 221, or Almond Creme, p. 220**

In a small stainless steel saucepan over high heat, dissolve the sugar in the water, stirring often. (If you are using the cinnamon or orange zest, add it to this.) Add the coffee and liquor, if using. Chill.

Freeze the granita mixture in a shallow pan until it's nearly firm. Stir the ice crystals at the edge of the pan into the center, and scrape the granita crystals into tall dessert glasses (Add a little Sweet Soy Creme, or Almond Creme, if you like.). The crystals are supposed to be rather coarse, not smooth like a sorbet.

If you let the granita mixture freeze solid, you can either let it thaw a little until you can scrape the crystals, or you can break it into chunks and run it quickly through the food processor. However, this will make it a bit smoother than a real granita.

Per ½ cup serving: Calories: 69, Protein: 0 g, Carbohydrate: 18 g, Fat: 0 g

"Amaretti" Crumbs

(soy-free)

Yield: 2⅔ cups

1 cup lightly toasted ground almonds
1 cup toasted white or sweet bread crumbs
½ cup Grade A maple syrup
1 teaspoon pure almond extract

Preheat the oven to 300°F.

Mix all of the ingredients together well. Spread the mixture on 2 cookie sheets, and place in the heated oven. Toast the mixture for about 15 minutes or until it has dried out a bit, but is still slightly chewy. Cool the mixture, then freeze in rigid plastic containers.

Per ¼ cup serving: Calories: 122, Protein: 3 g, Carbohydrate: 15 g, Fat: 6 g

Italians use crumbled amaretti cookies (almond macaroons) in many desserts, even in a few savory dishes that date back to the Renaissance. Since macaroons are made with eggs, we can't use packaged cookies for this purpose. I have included a vegan version of amaretti in this chapter, but you can use this easy recipe when you need amaretti crumbs, and do away with the need to have baked amaretti on hand all the time.

Nuts and bread crumbs can be quickly toasted in your microwave, if you like. One cup of bread crumbs or 1 cup chopped nuts takes about 2 to 3 minutes in the microwave on high. Otherwise, toast them in a heavy, dry skillet over medium heat, stirring often, until they are a pale golden color. You can grind them easily and quickly in a small electric spice or coffee grinder, or mini-chopper.

Vegan Almond "Macaroons"
AMARETTI VEGAN
(soy-free)

Yield: 36 macaroons

These are sure to become a favorite vegan cookie.

½ cup water
2 tablespoons powdered egg replacer
2 cups unbleached sugar, finely ground in a dry blender
1 tablespoon pure almond extract
2¼ cups fresh white or sweet bread crumbs, or rice bread
  crumbs
1 cup ground lightly toasted almonds (see page 243)

Preheat the oven to 325°F. Lightly oil 2 cookie sheets or spray with nonstick cooking spray.

In a medium-sized, deep bowl, beat the water and the egg replacer with an electric beater until it is like softly mounded beaten egg whites. (This may take 5 to 7 minutes.) Beat in the sugar and the almond extract.

With a rubber spatula, fold in the bread crumbs and the toasted almonds.

Roll tablespoonfuls of the mixture into balls with wet hands, and place on the prepared cookie sheets, leaving some space in between the cookies. Bake for 15 minutes. Let them cool a bit to firm up, then loosen them gently with a metal spatula, and place them on racks to cool thoroughly.

Per macaroon: Calories: 88, Protein: 2 g, Carbohydrate: 16 g, Fat: 1 g

Hazelnut Macaroons (Bruti ma Buoni)

These cookies are literally called "ugly, but good!" Use toasted hazelnuts or filberts instead of the almonds. Use Frangelico (hazelnut liqueur) or Italian hazelnut syrup (for flavoring special coffees) instead of almond extract and add 1 teaspoon vanilla. You can add 2 tablespoons cocoa powder, if you like.

Almond Biscotti
BISCOTTI DI PRATO
(soy-free)

Yield: about 40

1½ cups whole wheat pastry flour
1½ cups unbleached flour
1 tablespoon baking powder
½ teaspoon salt
1½ cups unbleached sugar
¾ cup smooth unsweetened applesauce
1 to 3 tablespoons cooking oil
1 teaspoon vanilla
1 teaspoon pure almond extract
1½ cups almonds, toasted and chopped, or use half almonds
    and half hazelnuts (filberts)

Preheat the oven to 325°F. Lightly oil 2 cookie sheets. Use double-layer or shiny ones, if you have them. If yours are very black, line them with foil.

In a large bowl, whisk together the flours, baking powder, and salt. In a medium bowl, whisk together the sugar, applesauce, oil, and extracts. Stir the sugar mixture into the flour mixture, add the nuts, and finish mixing with your hands.

With floured hands, shape the dough into two 3-inch wide "logs," about ¾ inch thick, with the ends squared off. Place these on the cookie sheets. Bake the "logs" for 25 minutes. Remove the pans and reduce the oven heat to 300°F.

Cool the "logs" on a rack for 15 minutes. Cut the "logs" carefully with a sharp knife straight across into ½-inch wide slices. Place the slices cut-side-down on the cookie sheets. (You can remove the foil, if using.) Bake 5 to 10 minutes, or until just golden on the bottom. Turn the slices over and cook 5 to 10 minutes more, or until golden on the bottom. Cool on racks, then store airtight for up to two

These Italian, twice-baked cookies are delicious dunked in wine, as is traditional, or in coffee, tea, or even hot cocoa!

Biscotti were originally made with a yeasted dough and they are supposed to be *hard* so that they don't fall apart when dunked. Authentic versions do not call for any butter, just eggs. Some modern versions contain so much butter that they resemble pound cake slices!

I have substituted unsweetened smooth applesauce for the eggs, and added a little oil to make up for the fat of egg yolks. One tablespoon oil makes a fairly hard biscuit; 2 to 3 tablespoons makes one that can be bitten into easily undunked.

I'm giving you a few suggestions for variations, but feel free to improvise. If you prefer to cut out all or some of the nuts, you can substitute chopped dried fruit.

weeks (or freeze).

Per biscotti: Calories: 94, Protein: 5 g, Carbohydrate: 15 g, Fat: 3 g

Lemon Biscotti

Omit the vanilla and almond extracts, and use 2 teaspoons pure lemon extract. You may add the grated rind of a lemon (preferably organic), as well, if you wish. This is good with walnuts.

Cornmeal Biscotti

Use ½ cup whole wheat pastry flour and 1 cup corn flour or finely ground cornmeal, along with the unbleached flour.

Chocolate Biscotti

Instead of the two flours, use 2 cups unbleached flour and 1 cup unsweetened Dutch cocoa. If you wish, add 1 packet (½ tablespoon) espresso powder. This is good with hazelnuts (filberts).

Mocha Biscotti

Omit ¼ cup of the whole wheat pastry flour and use ¼ cup unsweetened cocoa powder. Add 1 packet (½ tablespoon) espresso powder. This is good with almonds.

Espresso Biscotti

Add 4 packets (2 tablespoons) espresso powder. If you like, add 2 tablespoons coffee liqueur.

Anise Biscotti

Omit the vanilla and add 1 tablespoon ground anise seeds.

Biscotti Di Fruitti

Use 2 teaspoons lemon extract in place of the vanilla and almond. Add ½ cup *each* diced pitted prunes, figs, and sultana raisins, and 1 teaspoon ground nutmeg. You can also add 1 tablespoon grated orange zest (preferably organic) and ½ cup chopped toasted nuts.

Vegan, Organic, and Dealcoholized Wines

Wine is indispensable to Italian cooking, but it is not widely known that most traditional clarifying (fining) agents in the wine-making process are of animal origins—egg white, blood, gelatin, etc. Fortunately, many winemakers are using clay or bentonite instead. Unfortunately, it is difficult to get hard information on who uses what. The Vegetarian Resource Group (see sidebar at right) is currently compiling a list of wineries in North America that do not use animal products for clarification of wines. They were, at the time this book was written, only able to give me one winery that they were sure of:

Frey Vineyards
1400 Tomki Rd.
Redwood Valley, CA 95470
800-760-3739

I suggest that you contact the makers of your favorite wines personally and ask what they used as a fining agent. Contact the Vegetarian Resource Group if you know of other vegan wines on the market in North America. You can also write to the Vegetarian Society of UK for a list of vegetarian European wines. The Vegan Society of UK can also provide you with a list. (See the sidebar at right for both their addresses and web sites.) Some of these wines may be available from North American wine merchants.

Organic wines are becoming more widely available in American natural food stores, as well as wine stores. For more information on this, see the article "Make Mine Wine" in the December 1996 issue of *Vegetarian Times* magazine.

Dealcoholized wines are made the same way as regular wines, then most of the alcohol is removed. Because of increasing demand, these wines are improving every year, and there are several that are very good to drink and cook with. I recommend the following dealcoholized wines:

Ariel Johannesburg Reisling
Ariel Blanc
Ariel White Zinfandel
Ariet Merlot

Ariel Prospero (sparkling)
Sutters Home Fré (sparkling)
Prive Peach

For more information on vegetarian and vegan wines, contact

Vegetarian Resource Group
P.O. Box 1463
Baltimore, MD 21203
410-366-8343
www.vrg.org
vrg@vrg.org

Vegetarian Society of UK
Parkdale, Dunham Rd.
Alternsham, Cheshire,
WA14 4QG, UK
www.vegsoc.org

Vegan Society of UK
P.O. Box 121
Crewe, Cheshire
CW1 4SD, UK
+44 1424 427393 (phone)
+44 1424 717064 (fax)
www.vegansociety.com
info@vegansociety.com

Mail Order Sources

Most large North American cities have at least several good Italian food stores, but if you live in an out-of-the-way place, you might need to use the services of one of these mail order importers. Health food stores often have a selection of olives, olive oil, chickpeas and white beans, and flavor extracts. Chick-pea flour and basmati rice can be found in Middle Eastern stores; chick-pea flour (called besan) is available in East Indian stores.

Marmite, the best tasting yeast extract on the market (which I use in many of my meat substitute recipes) is easy to find in any Canadian supermarket or health food store. You may have to go to an import store to find it in the U.S. See the listings below for Italian food companies that also carry Marmite.

Italian and Mediterranean Foods

Cardullo's Gourmet Shop (carries Marmite)
6 Brattle Street
Cambridge, MA 02138

Dean and Delucca Retail and Mail Order Dept.
560 Broadway
New York, NY 10012
800-221-7714, ext. 223 or 270

G. B. Ratto & Co. (carries Marmite)
821 Washington Street
Oakland, CA 94607
outside of California: 800-325-3483
in California: 800-228-3515

Zabar's Mail Order Catalog
2245 Broadway
New York, NY 10024
800-221-3347
212-787-2003

Hard-to-Find Vegetarian Ingredients:

Allergy Resource
195 Huntington Beach Dr.
Colorado Springs, CO 80921
719-488-3630
unusual flours and pasta

ABC Vegetarian Foods
Call their toll-free number for the location nearest you.
800-765-6955
meat analogs, agar, kosher gelatin

Bickford Flavors
19007 St. Clair Ave.
Cleveland, OH 44117
800-282-8322
top-quality nonalcoholic flavor extracts

The Mail Order Catalog
P.O Box 180
Summertown, TN 38483
800-695-2241, 931-964-2241
www.healthy-eating.com, catalog@usit.net
gluten powder, textured soy protein products, soy products,
nutritional yeast

In Canada:
Choices Market
2627 West 16th Ave.
Vancouver, B.C., V6K 3C2
604-736-0009 (phone)
604-736-0011 (fax)
natural foods, soyfoods, allergy products, ethnic foods, spices, organic
foods, vegan products. No catalog, but will take phone or fax orders and
ship COD to anywhere in Canada. Volume discounts; friendly service

Sources for Soymage Parmesan Cheese Alternative

You can find this delicious vegan Parmesan alternative in small 4-ounce shakers in most health food stores, but if you use it as much as I do, you'll probably want to take advantage of the substantial savings you get by buying it in bulk. (A case contains four 5-pound bags.) It freezes well or you could order it through your co-op or food buying group and share a case with several people.

To find a distributor or health food store which carries this product in your area, contact:

Galaxy/Soyco Foods
800-441-9419, ext. 322.

In western Canada, the distributor is:

Sunrise Soya Foods
765 Powell St.
Vancouver, B.C., V6A 1H5
604-254-8888

In eastern Canada contact:

Timbuktu
Markham, Ontario
905-477-7755

Koyo Foods
Montreal, Quebec
514-744-1299

Dairy-Free Margarines and Spreads

Spring Tree Corporation
P.O. Box 1160
Brattleboro, VT 05302
802-254-8784 (phone)
802-254-8648 (fax)
springtr@sover.net
Manufacturer of Canoleo 100% Canola Oil Margarine. Contact for information on where you can obtain this product in your area. All ingredients, including vitamins and flavorings, are plant-based.

Spectrum Naturals, Inc.
Petaluma, CA 94952
800-995-2705
www.spectrumnaturals.com
Makers of dairy-free nonhydrogenated margarine-style spreads: Only Olive Spread and Essential Omega Spread (contains soy oil)

INDEX